Nikkeiren and Japanese Capitalism

```
I0129515
```

This book provides a comprehensive history of Nikkeiren – the Japan Federation of Employers' Associations – from its formation in 1948 to its merger with Keidanren in 2002. Nikkeiren's role within Japanese capitalism is explored, both in its early days as a union-busting organ of class power and in its later mode, where it more often resorted to manipulation and mystification.

Using the different periods of postwar Japanese capitalism as a context, the author carefully traces the history of Nikkeiren. Up until 1960 the federation led Japanese employers in the campaign to win back 'the right to manage', which had been lost in the chaotic aftermath of Japan's defeat in the Second World War. Nikkeiren achieved this by forging solidarity between employers in order to win a succession of bitterly fought labour disputes where the objective was not merely to defeat but to annihilate militant unions. Subsequently, Nikkeiren switched its emphasis to manipulation of the workforce and to a mutually advantageous trade-off with the leaders of increasingly enterprise-orientated unions. The federation also put a great amount of effort into generating a mystifying ideology.

Largely based on Japanese sources, this is the first comprehensive study of Nikkeiren to appear in English. In addition to providing a detailed empirical account of Nikkeiren's organization and activity, this book throws light on the nature and function of class power, the inherent tendency of unions to collaborate with capitalist institutions and the limitations of capitalism as a mode of production. As a result, Crump suggests that coercive class power, manipulation and mystification are not confined to Japan, but are inevitable features of capitalism everywhere.

John Crump was formerly Professor of Japanese Studies at the University of Stirling and Director of the Scottish Centre for Japanese Studies. He is now Senior Editor of *Japan Forum*.

Sheffield Centre for Japanese Studies/RoutledgeCurzon Series
Series Editor: Glenn D. Hook
Professor of Japanese Studies, University of Sheffield

This series, published by RoutledgeCurzon in association with the Centre for Japanese Studies at the University of Sheffield, both makes available original research on a wide range of subjects dealing with Japan and provides introductory overviews of key topics in Japanese Studies.

The Internationalization of Japan
Edited by Glenn D. Hook and Michael Weiner

Race and Migration in Imperial Japan
Michael Weiner

Japan and the Pacific Free Trade Area
Pekka Korhonen

Greater China and Japan
Prospects for an economic partnership?
Robert Taylor

The Steel Industry in Japan
A comparison with the UK
Hasegawa Harukiyo

Race, Resistance and the Ainu of Japan
Richard Siddle

Japan's Minorities
The illusion of homogeneity
Edited by Michael Weiner

Japanese Business Management
Restructuring for low growth and globalization
Edited by Hasegawa Harukiyo and Glenn D. Hook

Japan and Asia Pacific Integration
Pacific romances 1968–1996
Pekka Korhonen

Japan and North Korea
Christopher W. Hughes

Japan's Contested Constitution
Documents and analysis
Glenn D. Hook and Gavan McCormack

Japan's International Relations
Politics, economics and security
Glenn D. Hook, Julie Gilson, Christopher Hughes and Hugo Dobson

Japanese Education Reform
Nakasone's legacy
Christopher P. Hood

The Political Economy of Japanese Globalisation
Glenn D. Hook and Hasegawa Harukiyo

Japan and Okinawa
Structure and subjectivity
Edited by Glenn D. Hook and Richard Siddle

Japan and Britain in the Contemporary World
Responses to common issues
Edited by Hugo Dobson and Glenn D. Hook

Japan and United Nations Peacekeeping
New pressures, new responses
Hugo Dobson

Japanese Capitalism and Modernity in a Global Era
Re-fabricating lifetime employment relations
Peter C.D. Matanle

Nikkeiren and Japanese Capitalism
John Crump

Nikkeiren and Japanese Capitalism

John Crump

Routledge
Taylor & Francis Group

LONDON AND NEW YORK

First published 2003
by RoutledgeCurzon

This edition published 2013 by Routledge
2 Park Square, Milton Park, Abingdon, Oxfordshire OX14 4RN

Simultaneously published in the USA and Canada
by Routledge
711 Third Avenue, New York, NY 10017

Routledge is an imprint of the Taylor and Francis Group, an informa business

First issued in paperback 2015

© 2003 John Crump

Typeset in Sabon by The Running Head Limited, Cambridge

British Library Cataloguing in Publication Data
A catalogue record for this book is available from the British Library

Library of Congress Cataloging in Publication Data
Crump, John Derek, 1944–
    Nikkeiren and Japanese capitalism / John Crump.
    p. cm.—(Sheffield Centre for Japanese Studies/Routledge series)
    Includes bibliographical references and index.
    1. Nihon Keieisha Dantai Renmei—History. 2. Employers'
associations—Japan—History. 3. Capitalism—Japan—History.
    II. Series.
    HD6948.J3C78 2003
    338'.006'052—dc21
    I. Title.
    2003005293

ISBN 978-0-415-30572-3 (hbk)
ISBN 978-1-138-97721-1 (pbk)

This book is dedicated to Midorikawa Taeko,
for her comradeship

Contents

Acknowledgements

I was able to undertake the research in Japan on which this book is based thanks to a fellowship from the Japan Foundation. During the six months I spent in Japan in 2001 I was a visiting research fellow at Hitotsubashi University in Tokyo, where Watanabe Osamu, Katō Tetsurō and Kikuchi Nobuteru all helped to make my stay more productive. After I returned from Japan, a fellowship from the Leverhulme Trust released me from wage labour for a further six months during 2001–2. My productivity was boosted thanks to the Leverhulme fellowship which enabled me to write the bulk of this book while mercifully free of the usual academic treadmill.

Author's note

Japanese names are given in the customary East Asian form, i.e. family name followed by personal name. Long vowels in Japanese words are indicated by macrons (e.g. ō).

1 The nature of Japanese capitalism
Perceptions and reality

Interpretations

Japanese capitalism first started to impress Western commentators in large numbers in the high growth era of the 1960s. For a generation, droves of Western commentators attempted to analyse the reasons for Japanese capitalism's success (this, of course, meant success measured against capitalist criteria) and draw lessons for the countries of North America and western Europe. At the risk of simplification, one can say that the vast majority of their interpretations of Japanese capitalism fitted into five main categories, which I shall identify as the culturalist, bureaucratic guidance, supermanagement, labour harmony and free ride approaches. These categories were not necessarily mutually exclusive, since it was not uncommon for a single commentator to have feet planted in different camps. Nevertheless, for the purpose of analysis, these categories will be examined separately here.

The culturalist approach argued that there are aspects of Japan's culture that lend themselves to the successful operation of a capitalist economy. These aspects stand in sharp contrast to the predominant values of Anglo-American capitalism, symbolized by Adam Smith's famous analogy of the 'invisible hand'. Smith argued in *An Inquiry into the Nature and Causes of the Wealth of Nations* that in a capitalist economy everybody thinks only of their own interest yet that, out of this universal pursuit of self-interest, society benefits since the most efficient use of resources is supposedly achieved (Smith 1880). Morishima Michio (a Japanese who was a long-term resident in Great Britain) and Ronald Dore can be taken as representative of the culturalist approach, since both argued that Japanese capitalism generated its own form of efficiency, not by relying on the invisible hand of incessant profit maximization, but by utilizing supposedly Confucian traits that are inherent features of Japanese culture.

Morishima saw Japanese-style Confucianism as very different from the original Confucianism found in China (Morishima 1982). As a Japanese follower of Max Weber, Morishima believed, like Weber before him, that Confucianism in China had acted as a barrier to capitalist development (Weber 1968). The new twist that Morishima gave to this Weberian doctrine lay in his assertion that, by reinterpreting the fundamentals of Confucianism, the Japanese version of the same philosophy was able to fulfil a role that was analogous to the Protestant ethic. Morishima's argument was that, like the Protestant ethic in western Europe, Confucianism had served to facilitate the spirit of capitalism in Japan. By placing loyalty at the heart of Japanese-style Confucianism, a different national ethos from that found in China had been synthesized in Japan. This was why, in Morishima's eyes, Japan had 'succeeded' (the inverted commas were Morishima's) while China had stagnated, at least from the standpoint of his 1982 comparative study.

Economic actors in a Japanese-style capitalist economy were said by Dore to exhibit characteristics such as a preference for mutually supportive, long-term relationships rather than impersonally focusing on the best deal that could be clinched at any particular moment. The short-term costs of forgoing the keenest prices at any particular juncture were more than compensated for in Japanese eyes by the long-term advantages of stable supply relations. Whereas Smith expected his economic actors to be motivated entirely by 'their own interest' and 'self-love', Dore invoked 'trust' and 'goodwill' as key factors in doing business in Japan (Dore 1987 and 1988). Japanese capitalists would not walk away simply because the price was wrong, but would show forbearance while suppliers got their act together, in the expectation that they too would be recipients of similar favours when the boot was on the other foot. Not only did mutually supportive, long-term relationships thereby provide a kind of insurance against business difficulties, but they also furnished the opportunity to think strategically over an extended period.

The bureaucratic guidance approach attributed the success of Japanese capitalism to far-sighted officials in government agencies, such as the former Ministry of International Trade and Industry (MITI), who allegedly applied a deft touch to the macro-economic tiller. Chalmers Johnson's *MITI and the Japanese Miracle* was the most famous contribution to this genre. MITI's bureaucrats were portrayed by Johnson as a dedicated élite of economic nationalists who were committed to the goals of the developmental state long after Japanese capitalism had left behind the stage of a developing economy. Johnson traced the growth of industrial policy over the half century 1925–75 and analysed the contribution to it of a single government ministry as it passed through successive metamorphoses from the prewar Ministry of Commerce and Industry, to the wartime Ministry of Munitions, to the reconstituted Ministry of Commerce and Industry and then the Ministry of International Trade and Industry in the postwar era. Essentially, the argument was that the same zeal and flair which ensured that shells got into the barrels of the Imperial Japanese Army's artillery were later utilized so that Japan could win the economic battles of the postwar era. In contrast to the inefficiencies of the type of centralized planning practised in the former USSR, which was said to be deformed by ideological fixations, it was claimed that Japan's economic planners had optimally combined the plan and the market. Instead of intrusive intervention into the micro-economy at the level of industrial enterprises, which typified the USSR's centralized planning, Japan's planners supposedly applied only a light, macro touch. Their self-appointed task was to nudge otherwise independent companies, which primarily responded to market stimuli, towards industries in which Japanese capital was anticipated to enjoy a competitive advantage and away from industries where it was becoming more difficult for Japanese companies to compete. Thanks to the long-range vision of its economic bureaucrats, Japanese capitalism was claimed by MITI itself to function as a plan-oriented market economy system (Johnson 1982).

Johnson's seminal work stimulated a rash of subsequent research, much of it projecting a broadly similar image of Japan as a country where spectacularly successful economic development was orchestrated by an industrial policy that flouted conventional Anglo-American wisdom on how capitalism should be administered. The editors of a volume arising from one such research project typically claimed that competitive advantage in the world markets derived from government policy rather than other factors, with the Japanese variety of capitalism performing so strongly precisely because its government's policy was exceptionally dynamic and developmental (Tyson and Zysman 1989). Others, like Daniel Okimoto, attempted to distance themselves from Johnson's model by arguing that Japanese capitalism occupied the middle ground between market forces and economic intervention by the state. According to Okimoto, one reason for the supposed effectiveness of Japanese industrial policy was that, even when agencies like MITI intervened in the economy, the methods employed conformed to the market rather than jarred against commercial priorities (Okimoto 1989). Even in this attenuated form, the bureaucratic guidance approach located the roots of Japanese capitalism's strong performance to a significant extent in the skilful handling of the macro-economy by government officials.

The supermanagement approach believed that the success of Japanese capitalism primarily derived from the gains in productivity achieved on the shopfloor by the application of 'just in time' and similar organizational devices. Such devices included the continuous improvement of production (*kaizen*), teamwork, multiskilling, job rotation, quality control circles and the expectation that learning should be an integral part of work. These and a host of other micro-economic techniques employed in Japanese enterprises were designed to make production more integrated, flexible, lean and, of course, profitable. Largely ignoring the inefficiencies of Japanese agriculture and the service sector, those favouring this approach took the operational techniques of giant companies at the forefront of manufacturing as representative of Japanese capitalism as a whole. Their focus was on industries such as steel, motor cars, machine tools, electronics and other high-tech sectors. Hence two exponents of this approach, Martin Kenney and Richard Florida, coined the term 'fujitsuism' (after the electronics company Fujitsu) as a descriptive label for this supposedly new system of production (Kenney and Florida 1988). Their purpose in so doing was to elevate Fujitsu to the same model role that Ford had fulfilled within the American brand of mass production, known as Fordism. Fujitsuism was said to have transcended Fordism in various respects, such as encouraging flexible rather than repetitive labour practices and putting a premium on workers' intelligence and knowledge rather than deskilling the workforce. In later work, Kenney and Florida favoured the term 'innovation-mediated production' over fujitsuism, so as to reinforce their contention that this was not a specifically Japanese phenomenon, but rather a sea change within global capitalism that just happened to have been pioneered in Japan (Kenney and Florida 1993).

In their earlier work Kenney and Florida fudged one key issue which brought down criticism about their ears (Kato and Steven 1993). In contending that the social organization of production in Japan was post-Fordist, it was not clear whether they were identifying fujitsuism as a superefficient variety of capitalism or as a new social system which had empowered the employees of large Japanese corporations. Stung by their critics, they denied in later work that they were either romantic or naïve and conceded that the worker was even more intensely exploited than before under the new methods of organizing work (Kenney and Florida 1993). Nevertheless there were many who shared the same supermanagement approach who had no such misgivings. The authors of a book issuing from a Massachusetts Institute of Technology research project on the future of the motor car, which cost $5 million and extended over five years, believed that the 'lean production' emanating from Japan would usher in a new age where the world would be a much better place than previously (Womack *et al.* 1990).

The labour harmony approach asserted that Japanese capitalism benefited from the cooperation between management and labour that had become the norm in postwar Japan. Historically, it was the distinctive pattern of labour relations that was the first aspect of the Japanese economy to attract significant Western interest, even though Japan was still not held up as a model worthy of Western emulation at that early stage. As early as the 1950s, James Abegglen pointed to the allegedly harmonious nature of labour–management relations in Japan, interpreting them as quasi-familial and imprinted with conventions inherited from earlier social arrangements. He claimed that labour harmony delivered advantages both to the workers and to the company. Workers were said to enjoy long-term security of employment and substantial benefits, in exchange for which they demonstrated unwavering loyalty to the company and identified with its aims (Abegglen 1959).

Abegglen noted three distinguishing features of Japanese labour relations: so-called lifetime employment, the seniority wages system and enterprise unionism. While these practices were principally examined in this early work as curiosities from the standpoint of Anglo-American capitalism, by the 1970s commentators were associating them with the perceived success of Japanese capitalism. Not only was this so in Abegglen's own later work (Abegglen 1973) but two influential OECD studies presented these practices as connected to the strong performance of the Japanese economy (OECD 1973 and 1977). 'Lifetime employment' signified that workers would be recruited straight from school or university and would then remain in the same company's employ until retirement. Over the intervening years these workers would virtually be guaranteed not to be made redundant. The 'seniority wages system' referred to regular salary progression in proportion to length of service with the company, in contrast to wages being a function of individual skill or output. 'Enterprise unionism' described a situation where a single union organized the entire workforce in an enterprise up to the middle-management level, resulting in a marked tendency for employees to identify with the company's interests and a correspondingly weak identification with other workers beyond the confines of the enterprise. The labour harmony approach took this lifetime employment/seniority wages/enterprise unionism package and frequently presented it as though it constituted Japanese labour relations *in toto*. This was despite the fact that the package applied only to male workers on the permanent payroll of large companies (30 per cent of the entire workforce at most) and did not approximate to the conditions that the majority of employees experienced in Japan.

Not surprisingly, the free ride approach was mainly articulated by American commentators, since Japanese capitalism's 'free ride' was said to be primarily at the expense of the USA. The argument was that Japanese capitalism had benefited disproportionally from open American markets, while employing various means to protect its own industries from American competition. Critics of Japanese trading policy, such as Edward Lincoln, deplored the long-standing trade imbalance with the USA and attributed it to unfair practices, which were said to include infringing patents, industrial espionage, visible and invisible barriers to Japan's own markets and the setting of artificially low prices as a ploy to capture market share. Despite its global success, Japan was said to have retained an insular outlook, which was manifested in a deep-rooted hostility to importing manufactured goods from other countries. Like other late industrializing countries, Japan had practised import substitution as a means of developing its own industries and catching up with more advanced states, but the argument ran that this strategy had been maintained long after any justification for it had disappeared (Lincoln 1990).

The free ride approach was often equated with 'Japan bashing' because its exponents frequently advocated applying pressure to Japan so as to force it to accept greater quantities of imports from the USA. Yet, however much American commentators might have complained about Japanese 'unfairness' and urged that retaliatory measures should be adopted, ultimately Japan's strategic importance to the USA's military capability outweighed the economic pain inflicted on American companies. Hence, despite the perennial complaints about the allegedly advantageous terms of trade enjoyed by

Japanese capitalism, strategic considerations meant that the scope for American retaliation against Japan was limited. One response to this conundrum by those utilizing the free ride approach was to incorporate expenditure on armed forces into their explanation of Japanese capitalism's success. In addition to the American market generating enormous profits for Japanese exporting industries, the free ride was said to be equally relevant to the cut-price cost at which the Japanese state obtained defence. Owing to the military alliance with the USA, the Japanese state was able to restrict military expenditure to an unusually low percentage of gross domestic product (GDP), which conversely left an unusually high percentage of GDP available for capital accumulation. Investment rates in Japanese industries were contrasted to those of Western rivals and this train of argument was used to explain the speed and scale of Japanese capitalism's rise within a few decades from military defeat to become the second most powerful economy in the world. (The military free ride argument is succinctly, although in this case critically, stated in Hook 1996: 58ff.) Against this backdrop, some commentators advocated partially correcting the supposed free ride enjoyed by Japanese capitalism by means of Japan shouldering a sizeable proportion of the cost of the American military presence in Asia and similar measures (Prestowitz 1988).

This review of the major Western interpretations of successful Japanese capitalism has a historically dated ring to it now because of the subsequent downturn in Japan's economic performance. From the 1990s the Japanese economy came to be no longer associated with success. Instead, Japan acquired the image of the sick man of world capitalism. Japanese capitalism's problems in the 1990s and subsequently, like its earlier success, require explanation and it is ironic that many of the factors previously cited to explain the strong performance of the Japanese economy have since been advanced as reasons for its relative decline. Whereas Japanese management methods were one of the staples of Western business education in the 1980s and into the 1990s, as the latter decade progressed so the competitiveness of Japanese capitalism was increasingly written off by the gurus of business administration. By the turn of the century, Michael Porter was pointing to bureaucratic guidance as one of Japanese capitalism's failings, not a source of its previous success. The fruits of supermanagement (called 'operational effectiveness' by Porter) were not denied, but were nevertheless downplayed as an inadequate substitute for competitive strategy. Similarly, while the benefits of labour harmony were recognized, Porter viewed the labour market in Japan as too inflexible and praised atypical Japanese companies whose wages structure favoured performance rather than seniority. Regarding the free ride approach, Porter took the view that restraining imports and blocking foreign investment into Japan had damaged Japanese capitalism. As an apostle of free trade, he insisted that having unproductive sectors of the economy shielded by protectionist barriers was a luxury that Japanese capitalism could ill afford, because it deprived it of the stimulus of competition.

As for the culturalist approach, underpinning all Porter's arguments was a fervent devotion to the competitive, profit-maximizing values of Anglo-American capitalism which left little room for culturally based variations. If Japanese culture had any role to play within this context, it was at most as a condiment to an essentially Anglo-American capitalist brew (Porter *et al.* 2000).

Critique

This book is a study of Nikkeiren (*Nihon Keieisha Dantai Renmei* or the Japan Federation of Managers' Organizations) from its formation in 1948 up to its merger with Keidanren (*Keizai Dantai Rengōkai* or the Federation of Economic Organizations) in 2002. Although the book was conceived in the period when Japanese capitalism was still riding high, the research was undertaken in the period when the problems besetting Japanese capitalism became ever more severe. Throughout both periods I found myself profoundly out of step with the prevailing interpretations of Japanese capitalism. My initial motivation for engaging with the subject was simply to inject a degree of balance into the accounts of Japanese economic success. Not only did the various explanations of Japanese economic success strike me as inadequate, but also I was offended by the way in which most skated over the costs involved in, and the pain inflicted by, 'success'. All too often, the available accounts of successful Japanese capitalism projected a Walt Disney image where all was light and bright because their focus was on economic growth which barely faltered, per capita income which moved ever upward, unemployment which was defined in such a way as virtually to eliminate it and so on. It was never my intention to counter this Walt Disney imagery with a rival, horror movie depiction of capitalism in Japan, but I did want to tell the other side of the story and thereby show that there were costs as well as benefits. Similarly, the prescriptions for curing Japan of its current economic ills mostly address abstractions, such as the 'economy', 'growth' or 'competitiveness', but do not dwell on the medicine's side effects, namely pain, insecurity and anxiety for working men and women. Here, too, there is another side of the matter which, in the interests of balance, should not be swept under the carpet.

Capitalism in Japan, as elsewhere, is a socio-economic system that has accomplished major achievements. It has vastly expanded the pool of wealth, it has revolutionized methods of production and it has swept aside former barriers to economic activity. At the level of flesh and blood individuals, it has provided masses of people with previously unattainable standards of consumption, seen their life expectancy increase by several decades and equipped them with education and knowledge which were once the preserve of privileged minorities. It is true that there is also a negative side to capitalism's achievements. For example, during the capitalist era death and destruction in military conflicts, environmental damage and economic turmoil have been on a scale previously unimaginable. Nevertheless, these negative factors do not nullify the major advances achieved under capitalism. Equipped with a time machine, few in modern Japan would choose to get off in the Heian era (794–1185) or the Edo era (1600–1867) in preference to present-day capitalism.

However, the alternatives to capitalism are not only represented by the archaic systems of bygone ages. It could well be argued that the productive techniques and resources that have been developed under capitalism have opened up possibilities for the realization of alternative social arrangements that could deliver both a better quality of life and greater social and economic security to people at large. Indeed, such alternative possibilities should be particularly visible from the vantage point of a country such as Japan. In terms of geography and population, Japan is minuscule. Its geographical size represents 0.25 per cent of the world's surface area and its population just over 2 per cent of the people in the world. Yet, despite being so poorly endowed with land and population (not to mention natural resources), Japan was estimated to account for 7.3 per cent of world production in 2001, even in the midst of its worst recession for 50 years when much of its industrial capacity was not being used for want of profitable outlets (CIA 2003). Bearing these contrasting figures in mind, it is clear that, whatever might be the economic problems that currently beset Japan, they clearly do not include a lack of the productive resources to provide its population with the goods and services they require for quality of life and social and economic security. Of course, to state the situation in that way is misleading, because Japan is not and could not be a self-sufficient or isolated economic unit. Although it is convenient to use the expression 'Japanese capitalism' to describe social and economic conditions within this corner of the globe, another of the changes brought about by capitalism has been to turn the world into one global economy. This means that any alternative to capitalism would have to be equally global too, so it would be more accurate to say that the productive resources located in the poorly endowed corner of the globe called Japan illustrate that there are no technical impediments to the world as a whole equipping itself with the means to satisfy the needs of all people.

Although those of us who argue in this fashion are often made to feel like the small boy who pointed out that the emperor was not wearing any clothes, this vision of possible alternative social arrangements is well within the understanding of the working population. Indeed, left to think things out for themselves, they could scarcely avoid coming to such conclusions. Since they are the ones who devise and operate the productive resources, they are equally the ones who are best placed to grasp the potential locked up in the means of production, but dammed by capitalism's requirement to produce only for profit and not directly for the satisfaction of human needs. Within society, they are the ones best placed to see the gap between how we live and how we might live. As additional spurs to thinking beyond the boundaries of the present system, they are also the ones who are overworked and whose consumption is limited to the second rate during capitalism's boom periods, while their skills are devalued and their lives disrupted when capitalism periodically goes bust.

How is it, then, that working men and women in Japan as elsewhere do not more often grasp the irrationality of capitalism's social arrangements and the straitjacket it imposes on production? The answer which this study comes up with is that built into capitalism are features which virtually all the approaches examined earlier gloss over: namely, coercion, manipulation and mystification. In other words, powerful groups with an interest in seeing the present system continue are organized to suppress those who question capitalism's priorities, to deflect working men's and women's energies into harmless directions and to fix heads so that they harbour only acceptable thoughts. Many will react to this contention with disbelief. How could this be so in these liberal democratic times, they will object, and above all in Japan where it is well known that class analysis does not work? Government surveys regularly show that 90 per cent of the population thinks of itself as located in the middle-income bracket, which is surely proof that, for practical purposes, classes no longer exist (Naikakufu 1999). My response is 'read on'. In the pages that follow is an account of how and why Nikkeiren was formed, its activity during the various stages that Japanese capitalism has passed through, its policy objectives and so forth. Not all readers will come to the same conclusions about capitalism as those set forth in Chapter 9 of this book, but I defy anybody to argue that the following account of Nikkeiren does not provide ample evidence of coercion, manipulation and mystification.

Nikkeiren

The question arises why choose Nikkeiren to exemplify the nature of Japanese capitalism and the techniques of coercion, manipulation and mystification used to maintain it? It is true that Nikkeiren has not been by any means the only capitalist pressure group in Japan. Other candidates have existed, such as Keidanren or *Keizai Dōyūkai* (literally Economic Comrades' Association, although its official English title is Japan Association of Corporate Executives). Alternatively, one might have opted for the Liberal Democratic Party which has been the principal party of government throughout most of Japan's postwar history. Then again, there are commercial companies, the largest of which in particular expend considerable resources on dragooning their workforces and probing into their behaviour and thoughts. This list of controlling agencies could be extended much further without even shifting gear into the realm of outright organs of the state, which in their turn extend from the apparatus of repression, starting with the police, to the purveyors of ideology, such as the schools. As this brief excursion across the terrain of capitalist power shows, the mechanisms of control are intimidatingly multi-layered and Nikkeiren has been only one cog in a large and complex machine.

Nevertheless, Nikkeiren selected itself for the purpose of this study for a number of reasons. First, from its formation it assigned to itself the role of handling what its publications habitually referred to as the *rōdō mondai* ('the labour problem' or 'the labour question'; alternatively one could pluralize these, since Japanese does not distinguish between singular and plural). Owing to this orientation, there is a prima facie case for seeing Nikkeiren as an organization dedicated to prosecuting the class struggle from the bosses' side. Second, Nikkeiren's constituent groups consisted of a warp of regional business associations that extended across the length and breadth of Japan and a woof of industrial associations that ranged across the entire Japanese economy. This scale of organization makes it legitimate to view Nikkeiren as a body that sought to devise labour policy for Japanese capital as a whole. Third, Nikkeiren frequently fulfilled a vanguard role *vis-à-vis* the general run of employers, particularly in its early years when it led the assault on militant unions. Its behaviour on such occasions was particularly unambiguous and worthy of attention. Fourth, since Nikkeiren was not engaged in productive operations, it was freed from the need to make compromises of the type that are often forced on commercial companies in the interests of keeping production going. This enabled Nikkeiren to act as a particularly strident articulator of capitalist interests in undiluted form.

Another reason for choosing to focus on Nikkeiren is that no full-scale study of it has appeared in any language for many years. Kitagawa Takayoshi's *Nikkeiren: Nihon no shihai kikō* (Nikkeiren: Japan's ruling mechanisms) dates from as long ago as 1968 and there is no equivalent in English. Nikkeiren does, of course, crop up in more recent studies of Japan's political economy or industrial relations (see Watanabe 1990 and Gordon 1998 as examples of these two categories in Japanese and English respectively) but their authors' purposes lie elsewhere than in a systematic and thorough account of this organization. There is thus a gap in the existing literature that needs to be filled in order to demonstrate the extent to which coercion, manipulation and mystification have been part of the fabric of postwar Japanese capitalism. While not dealing with Nikkeiren, Sheldon Garon's *Molding Japanese Minds: the state in everyday life* (1997) is a recent addition to the literature that has added to our knowledge of the subtle ways in which oppression can work. By using a model of 'social management', Garon showed that the history of modern Japan is not only the story of how a powerful state has dominated society, but also how favoured social groups, often of a 'progressive' or 'liberal' hue, have repeatedly been co-opted into this process in order to mobilize the population and lead people towards the goals targeted by officialdom. One can concur with this without losing sight of the fact that much domination nevertheless conformed to an unambiguous, top-down, no-nonsense model. Nikkeiren was not an organization renowned for its subtlety and at times was far more openly coercive than even the direct organs of state power. Defeat in the Second World War undermined the authority of the state for a while and inhibited the readiness of bodies like the police to throw about their weight. In the sphere of labour, Nikkeiren stepped into the breach with alacrity.

Summary

The chapters which follow are mostly an empirical study of Nikkeiren's organization and activity during its more than 50 years' history. This account is arranged into chapters so as to convey the distinct periods that Japanese capitalism passed through and Nikkeiren's various adaptations so as to meet the different challenges that occurred.

Chapter 2 looks at the situation which confronted Japanese employers in 1945 and considers the prewar legacy which they inherited. This review of the past is important because, despite the vastly changed conditions brought about by military defeat and the Occupation, there was a considerable degree of continuity between the prewar and postwar eras, both ideologically and in terms of some of the leading figures involved.

Chapter 3 is concerned with the initial attempts of Japanese employers to reorganize after the war in the face of hostility from the Occupation authorities. Wishing to see unions emerge as a counterweight to Japan's ruling circles, which had recently gone to war with the USA, the Occupation authorities deliberately blocked the formation of an employers' federation dedicated to confronting labour, such as Nikkeiren.

Chapter 4 deals with the setting up of Nikkeiren in 1948, following a shift in policy by the Occupation authorities, and the tumultuous years up to 1960 during which the employers' priority was to teach the workers who was boss. In part, this was achieved by a succession of major labour disputes, including those involving the Tōhō Film Company (1948), the Electric Power Companies (1952), the Nissan Motor Company (1953), the Ōmi Silk Thread Company (1954) and the Mitsui Miike Coal Mines (1959–60) which are covered in this chapter.

Chapter 5 examines the high-speed growth era between 1961 and 1973 and brings out the changes in Nikkeiren's strategy that flowed from this.

Chapter 6 engages with the period 1974–80, during which Japanese capitalism was rocked by the so-called oil shock. Nikkeiren's principal concern in this period was to rein in wages in the face of rampant inflation.

Chapter 7 focuses on the decade from 1981 to 1991. Japanese capitalism performed relatively strongly when compared to its principal rivals during this period but, although this was reflected in a high level of self-satisfaction on Nikkeiren's part, it did not translate into any detectable generosity *vis-à-vis* labour.

Chapter 8 brings us to Japan's economic problems from 1992. Nikkeiren perceived that it was only at labour's expense that Japanese capitalism could extricate itself from its difficulties and lobbied hard for changes to

'Japanese-style management'. Ironically, however, Nikkeiren was not immune to change itself. The fact that it merged with Keidanren in 2002 was itself indicative of the changing face of Japanese capitalism.

Although the bulk of this book is an empirical study of Nikkeiren, as summarized above, it has provided the opportunity to address a number of questions that are fundamental to grasping the nature and operation of capitalism in general and its Japanese variety specifically. These issues include the nature of social classes, the role of labour unions and so on. Since these questions apply equally as much to other capitalist economies as to Japan, they enable parallels to be drawn and comparisons to be made in Chapter 12. Hopefully, this will be the point at which non-Japanese readers will be encouraged to reflect on the extent to which they too are pinned down by means of coercion, manipulation and mystification.

2 Japan's bosses in 1945
Knocked down but not knocked out

The postwar situation

At the end of the war in 1945, Japan's employers were in an unusually difficult situation. Various factors combined to put them on the defensive and to
undermine their morale. Foremost among these was that their state had
been militarily defeated and lay prostrate at the feet of the USA. The American Occupation authorities were deeply hostile to the existing Japanese
establishment and were determined that Japan would never again pose a
threat to the USA's interests. To this end, the Occupation authorities
embarked on a wide-ranging programme of reforms which are sometimes
summarized under the headings demilitarization, democratization and deindustrialization.

'Demilitarization' involved demobilizing the armed forces and dismantling the war machine, in which Japanese capital had played a full and
profitable part. 'Democratization' took the form of establishing the structure of a liberal democratic state, with the National Assembly and Cabinet
government as the key institutions, the Emperor reduced to a symbol, the
franchise extended to women and fundamental liberties (such as freedom of
speech, press and assembly) enshrined in the new constitution. Other aspects
of so-called democratization were the decentralization of the police force,
the disbanding of the political police, the abolition of the Ministry of the
Interior and the overhauling of the previously highly militarized and centralized education system. 'Deindustrialization' encompassed dismembering the
industrial and financial conglomerates (known as *zaibatsu*) which had been
at the heart of the war economy, dissolving the wartime administrative
bodies which had regulated industry and drawing up plans to ship entire
factories overseas as reparation for Japanese military aggression. A purge of
prominent individuals who had played important roles in prosecuting the
war effort was also instituted and this netted more than 1,500 industrialists
and financiers, starting in early 1947 (Nikkeiren 1981: 57).

Forced change of this order had a shattering effect on employers' morale.
Comfortable certainties, such as the prerogatives of authority and seniority,
evaporated as the power structure which had bolstered them collapsed. In

addition, most businesses were in tatters. Loss of Japan's colonial territories and the destruction of shipping meant that overseas supplies of raw materials dried up and markets disappeared. Much production had been tailored to supplying the military and, when the war suddenly ended, so too did the demand for the goods many companies were geared up to produce. As for the domestic consumer economy, quite apart from its wartime disruption, much of it ceased to function along normal commercial lines following Japan's surrender. Barter, foraging and the black market took over as millions of destitute and hungry people scrabbled for food and the other necessities of life wherever they could find them. This was not a setting in which normal production for profit could flourish and many companies ceased operations and dismissed their workers. Faced with this, and desperate to generate some form of income in order to survive, workers not infrequently took over factories and started up production themselves. Hence 'production control' was the main form of labour dispute in the immediate aftermath of the war, with 118 cases recorded in the first half of 1946 alone (Nikkeiren 1981: 89).

It has been said that 'the end of the war brought change of historical proportions to all sections of Japanese society, but the influence exerted on the Japanese labour movement was more profound than any other' (Nikkeiren 1958: 7). Whether this is strictly accurate is open to question, since there were massive impacts on other sectors too, but these words certainly capture how the upheaval in established procedures felt to employers caught up in the whirlwind of change. There was a flood of labour legislation which started with the Labour Union Law that was promulgated on 22 December 1945 and came into effect on 1 March 1946. Other landmarks were the Labour Relations Adjustment Law (1946) and the Labour Standards Law (1947). Such legislation was enacted at the insistence of the Occupation authorities and their encouragement was equally crucial in stimulating the formation of unions, which the Americans saw as useful counterweights to the established wielders of power in Japanese society. The resulting growth in the union movement was phenomenal. From a base of 509 unions and a total membership of 380,000 when the Labour Union Law was enacted in December 1945, the movement expanded to 12,007 unions and 3.68 million members in June 1946 and to 17,265 unions and 4.85 million members in December 1946 (Sōhyō 1964: 27). Further growth continued after that.

Theodore Cohen, who headed the Labour Division of the Supreme Commander of Allied Powers (SCAP) in Tokyo, had some revealing comments on which of these developments Japanese employers found the most intolerable:

> For big businessmen from the prewar period, previously secure in their niche at the top of Japanese society and accustomed to directing their employees as they saw fit, it was difficult to adjust to the new

atmosphere. Many of them found defeat at the hands of foreigners easier to accept than equal status with their workers. From time to time we received reports that the 'old guard,' fulminating privately at their meetings, had threatened to smash unions and, as before, to call in the police to suppress 'radicals.' Had such attitudes prevailed, the whole new labor relations system might have been destroyed.

(Cohen 1987: 203)

Faced with such attitudes, the Occupation authorities did not pretend to be even-handed, believing that it was necessary to check the employers' power if unions were to have the opportunity to establish themselves. Workers seized the opportunities to assert themselves and, emboldened as much by their desperate economic situation as by the temporary disarray of the bosses, put forward demands which went far beyond improved wages and conditions to take in issues such as how production should be organized. As Nikkeiren put it in later years, 'it was a very tough period when managers were at a loss regarding what to do and had lost their confidence' (Nikkeiren 1981: 88).

Nevertheless, despite all the unaccustomed pressures acting on them, one should not lose sight of the fact that Japanese employers remained the bosses, with much of their capital still intact. Indeed, war had been very good business for many companies, which often emerged from the conflict with vastly expanded assets, despite the wartime destruction. To take the Mitsui, Mitsubishi, Sumitomo and Yasuda conglomerates as examples, they came out of the war with between them estimated assets of ¥3 billion, which dwarfed the ¥875 million they had collectively been worth in 1930 (Cohen 1973: 101). Whatever the temporary difficulties the employers encountered in the early stages of the Occupation (including the breaking up of the conglomerates into their constituent parts) they remained in control of the most significant means of production within society and thus continued to occupy an inherently powerful position in the social order. Even though the American Occupation authorities were determined to take the employers down a peg or two, as a capitalist state itself, the USA had no intention of overturning property rights. Conversely, while it suited the USA to side with the unions for a while, Japanese workers remained propertyless and hence vulnerable to any change of policy by the Occupation authorities or to a counter-offensive by the capitalist class. In other words, the fundamental contours of capitalist power remained unchanged in Japan and ultimately reflected the standing of different classes in relation to the means of production.

The prewar legacy

As Japanese employers struggled to acclimatize to the postwar situation, they brought with them organizational skills and ideological outlooks which

they had acquired in the prewar and wartime years. As Nikkeiren acknowledged, it would have been far more difficult to organize employers'
federations after the war had there not been equivalent organizations in the
prewar era (Nikkeiren 1981: 25–6). Nikkeiren recognized the large degree
of continuity with its predecessors when it described Zensanren (*Zenkoku
Sangyō Dantai Rengōkai* or the All-Japan Federation of Industrial Organizations) as 'the prewar Nikkeiren' (Nikkeiren 1981: 4). It is also significant
that, from its formation in 1948, Nikkeiren's headquarters were located in
the Japan Industry Club's (*Nihon Kōgyō Kurabu*) building in central Tokyo.
The Industry Club is an employers' organization which was formed towards
the end of the First World War and has maintained a shadowy existence
down to the present day. The following account of the organizational and
ideological influences from the prewar era that acted on Nikkeiren in its
early days will therefore focus on the Industry Club and Zensanren, with
other employers' organizations dealt with only in so far as is necessary to
provide context.

   The first employers' organizations to appear in Japan were the Chambers
of Commerce that were formed in imitation of their Western equivalents at
an early stage of the development of Japanese capitalism. A Tokyo Chamber
of Commerce was organized in 1878 and by 1892 a nationwide federation
of such Chambers existed. Relations with the government were occasionally
tense as the Chambers of Commerce, which had originally been organized
under the patronage of the authorities, came to assert their independence in
the early years of the twentieth century as the wealth and confidence of
those they represented grew. In 1927 they were renamed Chambers of Commerce and Industry, which again reflected changes within Japanese capitalism. Numerically speaking, it was small and medium-sized enterprises that
comprised the bulk of the membership and whose interests the Chambers
have mainly represented over the years.

   The Industry Club was a very different type of employers' organization
to the Chambers of Commerce. It was formed on 10 March 1917, at a time
when Japanese industry was booming thanks to the stimulus provided by
the First World War. Although an ally of the Anglo-American side in that
war, Japan was far removed from the main arena of conflict and benefited
from the fact that its military allies (but commercial rivals) were locked in a
debilitating struggle in Europe. Having the field largely to themselves
during the war, the exports of Japanese companies increasingly penetrated
Asian markets, so that their value in 1918 was three times the 1913 figure
(Allen 1972: 98). Industry expanded rapidly to meet the opportunity presented by the war and the total number of factories in Japan in 1918 was
up by 42 per cent compared to 1913 (Crump 1983: 152). Economic
advance spurred industrialists to organize themselves so as to promote their
interests more effectively and the result of this initiative was the Industry
Club. From the start, it was very much the mouthpiece of big industry, with
Dan Takuma of the Mitsui conglomerate as its first Managing Director

(*rijichō*) and Toyokawa Ryōhei of the Mitsubishi conglomerate as Chairman (*kaichō*). Indeed, the industrial bias of the Industry Club would eventually lead financial capitalists to lobby for the creation of a federation that was more representative of all branches of the economy (Nihon Kōgyō Kurabu 1972: 102–4). This resulted in the formation on 1 August 1922 of the Economic League of Japan (*Nihon Keizai Renmeikai*) which functioned as a spokesman for the interests of big business generally.

On the face of it, the Industry Club's objectives were innocuous enough. The prospectus issued in 1917, when the Industry Club was set up, read in part:

> Our intention in the current situation is to organize a corporate body for the public good with the objectives of strengthening links between industrialists and striving to develop business. As the means of achieving these objectives, we principally have in mind investigation into various problems relating to industry, striving to perfect our knowledge of industry and making efforts to propagate that knowledge. In addition to these tasks, we also desire: to promote research and invention to the best of our ability; to construct a meeting place for the Club; to seek the mutual friendship of Club members and the exchange of knowledge; to organize various meetings; to offer hospitality to foreign guests; and to facilitate investigation and research into business for the benefit of each individual member.
>
> (Nihon Kōgyō Kurabu 1972: 28)

There was not a great deal that anyone could object to here, yet beneath the surface there was an unstated agenda that reflected the Industry Club's keen interest in keeping the workers in their place. As industry had expanded during the First World War, so the working class had grown proportionally. In line with the increase in the number of factories, the number of factory workers in 1918 was 54 per cent up on 1913 and the number of labour disputes had increased more than eightfold over the same period (Crump 1983: 154, 160). It was as a result of these developments that, soon after its formation, the Industry Club's Council decided on 21 December 1918 to establish a committee for investigating labour problems. As one Industry Club (and subsequently Nikkeiren) official later described the organization:

> From its founding, it took an extremely passionate interest in labour problems. It habitually formulated opinions from the standpoint of the industrialists regarding how to change or block the enactment of labour legislation and wielded omnidirectional political power so as to realize its wishes. Without doubt, it was the leading centre of power in industrial circles.
>
> (Morita 1958: 64)

One can best convey the Industry Club's approach to the problem represented by labour by contrasting it with the line taken by another organization, known as the Cooperation Society *(Kyōchōkai)*. The Cooperation Society was formed on 22 December 1919 against the background of the rising incidence of labour disputes to which reference was made above. Alarmed by this tendency, the Ministry of the Interior had first established a board of enquiry into relief work in June 1918 and then in December 1918 asked it to investigate 'means for harmonizing capital and labour'. The board of enquiry reported back in February 1919 and recommended setting up a supposedly private body whose aim would be to foster cooperation and harmony between capital and labour. It is worth noting that the same report also took a relatively relaxed attitude towards the emergence of labour unions, recommending that this be allowed to proceed as a natural development (Nihon Kōgyō Kurabu 1972: 125). After several months of preparatory work, the Cooperation Society was launched, with ¥2 million provided by the government and ¥4 million from business sources (including ¥1 million each from the Mitsui and Mitsubishi conglomerates) (Morita 1958: 58 and Young 1921: 50).

The Industry Club was sufficiently positive about this new body to participate in the preparatory work leading to its formation, but ultimately it was disappointed in the character of the Cooperation Society. Although the Cooperation Society stressed the need for cooperation between capital and labour, in the Industry Club's eyes this was a flawed approach because it was tantamount to admitting that there were two sides of industry in the first place. Likewise, when the Cooperation Society recognized the workers' right of association, it grated against the Industry Club's belief that workers had no need to organize against the fatherly figure of the employer. From the Industry Club's standpoint, the Cooperation Society was overly influenced by Western intellectual fads, such as the German school of social policy. Against this, the Industry Club counterposed 'the time-honoured, beautiful customs of our country', whereby 'harmonious cooperation between labour and capital and the beauty of the two becoming one' were allegedly brought about (Nihon Kōgyō Kurabu 1972: 130). From this perspective, the Industry Club regarded the Cooperation Society as having failed to realize its potential because it had abandoned, for newfangled Western ideas, the 'patriarchalism and paternalism which could be said to be Japanese characteristics' (Nikkeiren 1981: 8).

What one sees here in this juxtaposition of the Industry Club and the Cooperation Society is ambivalence within the capitalist class about how best to handle labour, with the Industry Club occupying a position at the opposite pole to those elements who favoured reaching an accommodation with the unions as the best means of pacifying the workforce (for more on this, see Marshall 1967, Large 1981, Garon 1984, Gordon 1991 and others). Although the earliest attempts to organize unions had been thwarted by enacting a draconian Public Peace Police Law in 1900, by the end of the First

World War unions had achieved a *de facto* status where they were still subjected to a good deal of oppression but were no longer driven out of existence. Elements then emerged within the state bureaucracy and among the employers who favoured regularizing the unions' activity by introducing appropriate legislation.

The first noteworthy initiative came on 18–19 August 1925 when the Ministry of the Interior's Social Bureau held a consultative conference to discuss a proposed Labour Union Bill. The Industry Club was represented at this conference, as were employers' federations representing mining and textile interests, and it led the opposition to the draft bill on the grounds that it was 'biased towards providing an amazing degree of protection for unions' (Morita 1958: 125). Soon after the conference, the Industry Club called an emergency meeting of its Council on 29 August 1925 and this appointed a study group to prepare a report. A hostile report duly appeared on 15 September 1925 and the upshot of the Industry Club's campaign was that, when the bill was presented to the National Assembly on 9 February 1926, 'it had become a fairly conservative item, compared to the Social Bureau's original draft' (Morita 1958: 128). Nevertheless, even in its emasculated form, the Industry Club continued to campaign against it. Eventually the bill died when it ran out of time in the committee stage in the Lower House. The following year, the bill was brought to the National Assembly again in February 1927, but the outcome was the same.

Battle was joined again in August 1929, when a Social Policy Deliberative Council was set up to consider the question once more. In his *History of the Development of Japanese Managers' Organizations*, Morita Yoshio describes the Industry Club's renewed struggle in heroic terms, because he claims that this time the partisans of a Labour Union Bill were in the stronger position. Again, the Industry Club issued on 3 December 1929 a hostile report on the new bill, the significance of which was supposedly 'epoch-making' in that it formulated a range of arguments against union legislation. These included opposition to class-struggle socialism (which the Industry Club chose to identify with labour unions), to the unthinking adoption of foreign practices (which were said to be designed to meet very different circumstances to those found in Japan) and to neglecting groups of workers who favoured cooperation between labour and management (so-called company unions) by giving protection only to combative unions (Morita 1958: 170). Whatever the merits of these arguments, they proceeded from an underlying frame of mind which it is probably best to allow the Industry Club to express in its own words, since it was a very influential attitude at the time and had a perceptible influence even in postwar years. As the Industry Club's official *50 Years' History* puts it:

> The Japan Industry Club's opposition movement against the enactment of the Labour Union Bill proceeded from the basis that, as already has been mentioned, in Japan a spirit of mutual affection and cooperation

existed, as if the enterprise were a single family, which was different from the western European concept of profit-and-loss confrontation where the contract reigns supreme. Furthermore, since conditions at that time were so much tending towards struggling for socialist revolution, we probably feared that, if labour unions were authorized under such conditions, we would slide into a situation where it would be impossible to maintain the free economic system. One can say that it was for these reasons that we opposed the enactment of the Labour Union Bill to the bitter end.

(Nihon Kōgyō Kurabu 1972: 187)

As before, a lengthy campaign against the bill ensued, with the Industry Club in the thick of it. As happened previously, the bill was modified in the course of this campaign, but the changes did not mollify the Industry Club. Support for the bill certainly was stronger this time round, as became clear when it was passed by the Lower House of the National Assembly on 17 March 1931. However, the House of Peers represented a formidable hurdle and the bill failed when time ran out in committee stage and the National Assembly was dissolved on 27 March 1931. Despite the bill ultimately failing, it had been a close enough call to induce its opponents to launch a new organization, Zensanren ('the prewar Nikkeiren,' as was mentioned earlier). Zensanren grew out of a meeting attended by representatives of 175 business organizations from throughout Japan which was held at the Tokyo Chamber of Commerce and Industry on 27 February 1931. This was at the peak of the campaign against the Labour Union Bill and the meeting passed unanimously two resolutions – one hostile to the bill and the other agreeing to establish Zensanren. Hence it is no exaggeration to say that it was the campaign against legally recognizing unions which gave birth to Zensanren (Morita 1958: 182–7).

Zensanren was formally launched on 6 May 1931 and remained in existence until 21 May 1942, when it dissolved in the face of government pressure for all industrial organizations to merge into the wartime Sanpō (*Dai Nippon Sangyō Hōkoku Kai* or the Great Japan Industrial Patriotic Association). By the latter date, many employers were also playing a full part in the 'Control Associations', which were state organs for running the war economy. For example, Uemura Kōgorō and Ishikawa Ichirō, both of whom were later prominent in the postwar employers' federations, were leaders of the Coal Industry Control Association and the Chemical Engineering Control Association respectively during the war (Nihon Kōgyō Kurabu 1972: 343–4). Ironically, in view of its express purpose, Zensanren's founding virtually coincided with the end of any realistic prospect of introducing a Labour Union Bill in prewar Japan. The Manchurian Incident erupted in September 1931 and from then on society was increasingly militarized and labour was ever more severely repressed. Far from unions achieving legal recognition, they were driven out of existence as the 1930s progressed and replaced by Sanpō's twin, the Great Japan Labour Patriotic Association (*Dai Nippon Rōdō Hōkoku Kai*). Instead of Zensanren being deprived of its *raison d'être*, however, it hitched itself to this train of events and adapted the language of its pronouncements to the ever more strident nationalism that was the hallmark of the era. Zensanren's research into labour problems and activity to further the employers' cause were increasingly given a gloss of supposedly high-minded, patriotic endeavour with never a thought apparently for self-interest or profits. The explanation of why the organization was dissolving itself that was offered in 1942 by Zensanren's Standing Committee (*jōnin iinkai*) captures the tone nicely:

> Zensanren was formed with the objective of establishing labour–management relations based on the unique industrial spirit of this country. This was in 1931 as an outcome of the question of the Labour Union Bill. The Western way of thinking which accepted as natural the confrontation between labour and capital, and likewise the class struggle, was at that time flooding society. Owing to this, and the tendency for all manner of social policies also to be discussed and then drafted under such influences, our further objective was to correct these mistakes. Now, however, the trend of the times has changed completely and the essence of Japan's industrial spirit has been affirmed at home and abroad. It has reached the point where the industrial patriotic movement, which takes as its programme the enterprise as a family being a form of occupational public service, has unfolded as national policy. Furthermore, we have been able to cooperate with the government in instituting the various labour protection laws and regulations. In these ways, Zensanren's mission has been completely accomplished.
> (Morita 1958: 300–1)

What characterized both the Industry Club and Zensanren was the way in which they extolled the wonders of 'the unique labour relations found in the industry of our country, based on labour and capital existing as one flesh' (Morita 1958: 305) at the same time as they disseminated via their organizational networks best practice for bringing about the domination of labour by capital. As a practical means for achieving these twin objectives, both organizations favoured setting up company unions (that is the workforce organized into a so-called union by the company). It has already been mentioned that one of the Industry Club's specific arguments against the proposed union legislation in the 1920s and 1930s was that the treatment of combative unions was too generous, compared to the lack of support for company unions. As for Zensanren, Maeda Hajime of its Industrial Peace Policy Investigation Committee (and an employer in the coal steamer business in Hokkaidō) gave a speech on 17 March 1934 in which he angrily denounced the government for being 'full of zeal to protect and assist labour unions, but it is lukewarm about assisting the development of company

unions and it is outrageous that it is apt to treat the latter like stepchildren'
(Nikkeiren 1981: 10). Maeda represented a direct link between Zensanren
and Nikkeiren, becoming one of the postwar federation's chief executives
(Nikkeiren 1958: 24).

It was thanks to the influence of people like Maeda that Nikkeiren drew
a parallel between the prewar 'company unions' and the 'enterprise unions'
of the postwar era, arguing that:

> The postwar enterprise unions certainly did not appear from out of the
> blue. In other words, one can point to the prewar 'company unions' (or
> 'employees' groups') as their prototypes, although before the war the
> government was reluctant to recognize them legally. By way of contrast,
> after the war establishing regulations to deal with so-called unfair labour
> practices . . . proceeded from the premise that unions were guaranteed
> the right to organize. However, what should be noted is that, with the
> [support of] the labour leaders included, in the vast majority of cases it
> was the organization of enterprise unions that went ahead at a fast rate.
> The reason for this can be said to be that people could not help respect-
> ing their special character, which was imbued with 'Japaneseness'.
>
> (Nikkeiren 1981: 11)

These remarks usefully complement those of other Nikkeiren veterans, such
as Yuasa Yūichi. Yuasa was President of Yuasa Batteries and at one time was
Chairman of Kansai Managers' Association (one of the regional bodies of
which Nikkeiren was composed). Looking back to the prewar and wartime
periods, he recalled:

> We had all been involved, in our various ways, in Sanpō [Industrial
> Patriotic Association] type of activity. We had worked to create truly
> Japanese-style unions, within which workers and bosses were like one.
> In our place too we had been twenty years in building what we called
> the *shayūkai* [Friends of the Company Association] but that contra-
> vened Occupation policy and had to go.
>
> (Nikkeiren 1981: 709)

Taken together, these quotations convey both the continuities and discon-
tinuities between the prewar and postwar periods. Old-style company
unions were swept away by the Occupation, but on the employers' side
the ways of thinking that had accompanied them were frequently not re-
linquished. In the prewar era, the type of employers who were attracted to
the Industry Club and Zensanren had seen company unions as, on the one
hand, the means for maintaining tight labour discipline and, on the other, a
prop for the image of the company as one happy family. For precisely the
reverse reasons, they were intensely wary of unions that were organized by
workers independently of the company and as a challenge to the company.

After the war, unions of the latter type became part of the given social fabric and yet, as will become clearer in later chapters, there were factors at work which induced the vast majority of such unions sooner or later to conform to an enterprise union structure and outlook. Nikkeiren was very much following in its antecedents' footsteps, both when it fought implacably against independently spirited and combative unions and when it cooperated with compliant enterprise unions.

In addition to Maeda and Yuasa, Zen Keinosuke was another employers' activist who spanned the prewar and postwar periods. Zen joined the Industry Club as its Manager (*shuji*) in December 1926 and went on to take a leading role in opposing the Labour Union Bill. He toured most of Japan during 1930, addressing innumerable anti-Labour Union Bill meetings and attempting to rally the employers' opposition to the proposed legislation. When Zensanren was organized, Zen became its Managing Director (*jōmu riji*) at the same time as he continued to hold an equivalent position (*jōnin riji*) in the Industry Club. Zen played such a pivotal part in Zensanren that people reportedly made a pun out of the names, asking whether it was a case of 'Mr Zen's Zensanren or Zensanren's Mr Zen?' (Nihon Kōgyō Kurabu 1972: 192).

After the war, Zen was involved in early unsuccessful attempts to form a Nikkeiren-style organization (see Chapter 3) and was Director-General of the Economic Stabilization Board in Yoshida Shigeru's government in 1946. In the latter role, he requested SCAP's permission to ban strikes in crucial industries, such as coal mining, electric power and food distribution. SCAP refused to allow this and at this juncture Zen made a poor impression on its officials as an unreconstructed antagonist of the labour movement. For example, the head of SCAP's Labour Division, Theodore Cohen, regarded Zen as 'bellicose' and 'bullet-headed' and criticized his 'headstrong stubbornness' (Cohen 1987: 271, 311). In keeping with this assessment, Zen was purged by the American Occupation authorities in 1947 and had to give up his leading position in the Industry Club. Nevertheless, this did not mean that the link with prewar days that he represented was severed for good. By 1950 the USA's priorities had changed to such an extent that a 'red purge' was instituted to eliminate left-wingers from positions of influence (see Chapter 4). Shortly before his death in November 1951, Zen was appointed as an advisor to Nikkeiren (as also were Uemura Kōgorō and Ishikawa Ichirō, who were mentioned earlier) which symbolized the extent to which by that stage the ideas he personified were back in fashion (Nikkeiren 1981: 260).

Morita Yoshio was another person whose career trajectory indicated the connections between the prewar and postwar employers' organizations that were dedicated to opposing the labour movement. He was employed by the research section of the Industry Club from 1921 and rose to become its head. When Zensanren was formed, he became head of its Secretariat and, after the demise of this federation, was head of the Labour Council Office of the Central Headquarters of Sanpō. In the postwar years, he was first on the staff of the Kantō Managers' Association and later became a director of Nikkeiren. In the foreword to his book, *History of the Development of Japanese Managers' Organizations* (1958), Morita referred to both Zensanren and Nikkeiren. Regarding the former, he wrote that he would be delighted if the book could serve 'as a humble monument to "Zensanren", about which I have the most profound memories of my entire life'. As for Nikkeiren:

> At a time when Nikkeiren, which was newly started after the war, is approaching the tenth anniversary of its founding, nothing will give me more satisfaction than if this book, in however limited a fashion, can convey the significance of the preceding history of managers' organizations in our country.
>
> (Morita 1958: 6)

As an old Zensanren hand, Morita's self-appointed role as a bridge between the prewar and postwar militant employers' federations is well expressed here.

On the face of it, there was a world of difference between the situation in which employers found themselves after 1945 and what it had been in the prewar and wartime periods. In the early years after the war, employers felt themselves to be in a much more hostile and uncertain environment than previously. Yet to focus only on the changes that affected employers, and to overlook the substantial undercurrent of continuity that was part of the total picture, would be misleading. The employers' continued possession of the means of production provided them with formidable means to sit out temporary difficulties. In addition, as this chapter has demonstrated, there was much in their fund of experience and their ideological armoury that would prove serviceable in the unfolding postwar situation. By taking into account the considerable number of individuals who played roles in employers' organizations both before and after the war, we can see that the changes brought about by military defeat and the Occupation were less far reaching than first impressions suggest.

3 We're all workers now

Ideological and organizational defence (1945–7)

First attempts at organization

When the existing apparatus for controlling industry was dismantled during the early days of the Occupation, it created a power vacuum which new organizations rapidly sought to colonize. Even before Sanpō was dissolved on 30 September 1945, a Joint Committee of Economic Organizations on Economic Policy (*Keizai Dantai Rengō Keizai Taisaku Iinkai*) was established on 18 September (Nikkeiren 1981: 1). Within the framework provided by the Joint Committee, there were already moves by mid-February 1946 to set up an employers' organization specializing in labour problems, similar to the prewar Zensanren. One of the instigators of this initiative was Adachi Tadashi who was Director of Ōji Paper Manufacturing Company and a protégé of Fujiwara Ginjirō, a former head of both Zensanren and Ōji Paper (Keizai Dōyūkai 1956: 17). Matsumoto Kenjirō, the Chairman of the Joint Committee, organized a roundtable discussion on labour problems at the Industry Club in central Tokyo on 22 February 1946 and among those who participated were several employers whom we have already encountered and/or who would later become key players in Nikkeiren. For example, Adachi Tadashi took part, along with Ishikawa Ichirō (Chemical Engineering Control Association), Uemura Kōgorō (Coal Industry Control Association), Maeda Hajime (Hokkaidō Coal Steamers), Zen Keinosuke (formerly of Zensanren), Noda Nobuō (Mitsubishi Heavy Industries), Moroi Kan'ichi (Chichibu Cement) and others. Out of the roundtable discussion a decision emerged to form a central organization of employers and a small committee was appointed so as to prepare a detailed plan. This committee was comprised of Adachi Tadashi, Maeda Hajime, Zen Keinosuke, Moroi Kan'ichi and Nakata Kenji (Morita 1958: 331).

By 4 March 1946 a plan had been devised to set up a Japan Federation of *Employers'* Organizations (*Nihon Shiyōsha Dantai Rengōkai*) but this name was subsequently modified to Japan Federation of *Managers'* Organizations (*Nihon Keieisha Dantai Rengōkai*). According to Morita Yoshio, the expression 'managers' organizations' (*keieisha dantai*) was coined by Zen Keinosuke and it found favour with the others because it was felt to be more in keeping with the times and with the spirit of 'industrial democracy' than the terms used in the past, which included 'industrial organizations' (*sangyō dantai*), 'enterprise owners' organizations' (*jigyō nushi dantai*) and 'employers' organizations' (*shiyōsha dantai*) (Morita 1958: 331–2). This way of thinking was evidently widely accepted, because 'managers' organizations' passed into general use and was, of course, incorporated into Nikkeiren's formal name (the Japan Federation of Managers' Organizations or *Nihon Keieisha Dantai Renmei*) when it was launched in 1948. The ideological repackaging that was at work here is well conveyed by Nikkeiren's comments on Zen's brainchild more than 30 years later:

> In this book, the postwar neologism 'managers' organizations' [*keieisha dantai*] is invested with the meaning of employers' organizations or economic organizations which deal with labour problems . . . it reflects the new position of enterprise owners [*jigyō nushi*] which accompanied the introduction of industrial democracy and modern labour relations that were entirely different from before the war. The prewar capitalist, who had the power, as lord and master, to do what he wanted with his enterprise, disappeared after the war due to the separation of capital from management. In addition, there was, of course, the change of era to people's capitalism. As a result, we could say that the one who represents the enterprise came to be the manager [*keieisha*].
>
> (Nikkeiren 1981: 22–3)

Whatever one thinks of this line of reasoning, the main point to grasp is that, however anodyne the nomenclature, at this stage of the Occupation the authorities were not prepared to tolerate a bosses' organization of the type envisaged at the roundtable discussion on 22 February 1946. As soon as the Occupation authorities got wind of the moves that were afoot, they signalled that, whatever it was called, the proposed federation would not be allowed on the grounds that 'if a central organization of employers is formed at a time when a national organization of labour unions has still not been established, there is a danger that the development of the unions will be obstructed' (Nikkeiren 1981: 190). The American authorities were fully prepared to back up this ruling with strong-arm techniques of dissuasion when they judged that such methods were necessary. The situation changed as the Cold War intensified, but the Nikkeiren activist Shikanai Nobutaka recalled in later years that, when it suited the American authorities, 'the oppression directed at us was full of extreme hostility'. Shikanai gave as an example the organization that operated out of a building in central Tokyo in a fashion that prefigured the CIA. According to Shikanai, its functions were to investigate and 'brainwash' those whom the American authorities considered undesirables:

> I was called in there, wasn't I? Up till about 12 o'clock at night, for three days or so, they brainwashed me, with me more or less under

arrest. You're an agent of conservatism and reaction, they would say. Setting up Nikkeiren is a disgrace, they'd say.

(Nikkeiren 1981: 707)

The Kantō Managers' Association

In the realm of employers' organizations specializing in labour problems, the most the American authorities were prepared to tolerate were regional associations or similar groups within particular industries. Among these, the most powerful was the Kantō Managers' Association (*Kantō Keieisha Kyōkai*) which was founded at a meeting held at the Industry Club on 17 June 1946 and whose organization covered the Kantō region in the vicinity of Tokyo. Its Chairman and Vice-Chairman were Adachi Tadashi and Moroi Kan'ichi respectively, both of whom had been at the core of the aborted Japan Federation of Managers' Organizations a few months earlier. Another indication of the Kantō Managers' Association's significance was that the employers who backed it provided it with a massive annual budget of ¥2 million (Morita 1958: 334). It used these funds to fulfil unofficially the administrative and networking roles which the banned Japan Federation of Managers' Organizations had been prevented from undertaking. Nevertheless, despite being provided with ample resources, the Kantō Managers' Association had to act circumspectly and took care to project an image of a research-oriented body whose remit was merely to circulate its findings to member organizations and to make available to the public its ideas for solving both labour and social problems. In the speech that he delivered at the founding meeting on 17 June 1946, Adachi Tadashi stressed that the members of the Kantō Managers' Association were reasonable-minded reformers:

> Labour disputes break out all the time and in all parts of the country due to insecurity in the workers' lives. This imposes ever increasing difficulties on rebuilding our country's economy. If one leaves this to sort itself out, as likely as not extremist elements will take advantage of the situation. It really is an unbearably worrying state of affairs which could truly invite an uncontrollable disaster and where hope for the realization of genuine industrial democracy could completely disappear.
>
> As for us, we shall get on with the business of managing in line with our various responsibilities, observing the spirit of the Labour Union Law and acting hand in hand with the healthy unions as we do so. In addition to readily accepting the reasonable demands made by those in the position of employees, we shall reflect deeply as managers on certain past practices. At this juncture, what should be reformed should be reformed decisively. We also believe that, at the same time, the employees' side too should take responsibility and cooperate in reconstruction.

(Morita 1958: 336)

Furthermore, Adachi emphasized that the Kantō Managers' Association had no political affiliations and that it would steer clear of direct involvement in either labour negotiations or labour disputes (Morita 1958: 337).

With its scope for decisive action as circumscribed as this, the Kantō Managers' Association was not in a position to occupy the power vacuum that existed on the employers' side. Neither was the Japan Chamber of Commerce and Industry (*Nihon Shōkō Kaigisho*) which was established on 20 November 1946 and whose constituency was skewed towards small and medium-sized enterprises. Looking elsewhere, the Joint Committee appeared to have the potential to become a powerful player and this was enhanced when it was reconstituted as Keidanren (*Keizai Dantai Rengōkai* or the Federation of Economic Organizations) on 16 August 1946. As a widely based umbrella organization that embraced the full range of industries and the major companies at the heart of Japanese capitalism, Keidanren was well equipped to act as a forum and mouthpiece for business opinion. However, it was constrained by four conditions which the Occupation authorities laid down as the terms for permitting its formation. The most important of these conditions was that Keidanren should not be a centralized organization equipped with powers of control that would enable it to impose its will on its members. In addition, Keidanren was required to act democratically, not to appoint any purged individuals to official positions and not to serve the interests of the conglomerates (Keidanren 1978: 8). It was in this set of circumstances, deliberately engineered by the Occupation authorities, that the most influential employers' organization during 1946–7 became the Economic Comrades' Association (*Keizai Dōyūkai*).

This chapter will therefore focus on the Comrades' Association and the aspirations for reforming capitalism which it championed for a while until the strategic priorities of American occupiers and Japanese employers alike shifted sufficiently to allow Nikkeiren to come to the fore.

The Comrades' Association

The Comrades' Association was launched on 30 April 1946 and, unlike other national employers' organizations, it was not an amalgam of constituent groups but of individual members. The Comrades' Association claimed that this enabled its members often to look at problems from the perspective of 'capital as a whole' and not to be overly influenced by the interests of particular enterprises or industries. Be that as it may, it rapidly became a favourite of the Occupation authorities. Theodore Cohen, the head of SCAP's Labour Division, rated the employers organized in its ranks very highly:

> Fortunately, however, there were also younger and more flexible business leaders. Under the leadership of Moroi Kanichi, President of Chichibu Cement Company, they organized their own group, the *Keizai*

Dōyū-kai, or Economic Comrades Association . . . They too visited the Labor Division from time to time in order to obtain data and advice from our Labor Relations Branch. They made quite an impression on [Anthony] Constantino, the branch chief, for he had been a CIO organizer and wished that his American businessmen adversaries had been as wise and reasonable as their Japanese counterparts.

(Cohen 1987: 203)

Mention of Moroi Kan'ichi in this context is striking because earlier we noted his involvement in the attempt to set up a very different type of employers' body, the Japan Federation of Managers' Organizations, which was unacceptable to the American authorities at the time (early 1946). Shortly thereafter Moroi became the first Chairman (*gichō*) of the Comrades' Association and two years later was appointed Director (*daihyō jōnin riji*) of Nikkeiren. It is tempting to attribute this chameleon-like adaptability to mere opportunism, but maybe there was more to it than that.

Moroi was by no means unique in performing these somersaults. With the benefit of hindsight, it is disconcerting to find some of those who went on to make a reputation as the hard men of Nikkeiren actively participating in the softly, softly approach of the Comrades' Association earlier on. Nikkeiren's later Chairman (*kaichō*) Sakurada Takeshi is a case in point and so, too, is Shikanai Nobutaka whom the American authorities roughed up when he was wearing a different hat. At one level, there no doubt was an element of opportunism in the fast footwork which employers of this ilk displayed. In other words, at different stages they played the various cards that were available to them on a table that was tilted first one way and then the other by the Occupation authorities. However, this explanation probably falls short of the whole story. Those who took the initiative to set up the Comrades' Association were comparatively young by employers' standards. Most were in their forties and even Moroi Kan'ichi, who became chairman by virtue of being the oldest among them, had only just turned 50 (Keizai Dōyūkai 1976: 17). Not only were they comparatively young, and consequently unset in their ways, but they were also inexperienced in the practice of labour–management collaboration. As a country which had habitually employed authoritarian methods of running industry, Japan had been defeated by nation-states which professed to practise more inclusive styles of management, with a role allocated to the unions. Faced with mushrooming union movements and an occupying power that was demanding a change in management culture, not a few employers were willing to relaunch Japanese capitalism in partnership with the unions and under different ideological colours. In retrospect, we know that this did not work and that the experiment was soon abandoned. Nevertheless, it was an important trend while it lasted and there is no reason to believe that employers who embraced the ideology of labourism, albeit temporarily, were necessarily dissembling. As a system of wage labour and capital accumulation, capitalism is open to various organizational arrangements, including those advocated by the Comrades' Association in this period. Hence there was nothing inherently contradictory about capitalists flirting with labourist ideology for a time. Only when it proved ineffective as the means for disciplining wage labour and consolidating profits did they turn elsewhere.

In the period immediately after its formation, the Comrades' Association was at pains to distance itself from the established image of capitalism and loudly proclaimed the need for reform. In doing so, it was responding to the popular mood within Japan at the time, which was extremely negative towards conventional capitalism. The Comrades' Association favoured overhauling capitalism to such an extent that 'reformed capitalism' (*shūsei shihonshugi*) was said to be its 'other name' (Keizai Dōyūkai 1956: 3). Speakers at its founding meeting on 30 April 1946 purposely dissociated themselves from the government and from the financial establishment. Instead, they reached out to the unions as potential partners for running capitalism, providing they could shake off their impetuosity and behave responsibly. Thus Fujii Heigo declared in his address to the meeting:

> Not only the government, but among the financial establishment [*zaikai*] too, the leaders attempt to preserve intact old-style capitalism while putting up a façade of formal democratization. Furthermore, it is deplorable that they are not equipped with feelings that are in accordance with the way of doing things in this new age of the industrial economy. At this juncture, only the union movement has risen to the challenge. It looks as though it is from within this movement that the motive force for constructing a new Japan is sprouting. However, even here there is much that is impulsive. So, from now on, it could be considered that there are many points where more care needs to be taken in order to advance in the right direction.
>
> (Keizai Dōyūkai 1956: 21–2)

The choice of words at this inaugural meeting was highly symbolic. Speakers like Fujii Heigo did not identify themselves as employers, but rather as 'we middle-ranking economic actors' (*wareware chūken keizaijin*) (Keizai Dōyūkai 1956: 22). This was in line with the Comrades' Association's contention that capitalists were as redundant as old-style capitalism itself. The argument ran that the healthy elements within the economy were management and labour who shared a common interest in boosting production and rebuilding the country (Keizai Dōyūkai 1976: 4).

There are numerous instances from this period which illustrate the extent to which many employers temporarily espoused labourist ideology. Soon after its formation, the Comrades' Association had created a Committee for the Study of Labour Problems, whose Chairman was Noda Nobuō, one of the employers who had participated in the roundtable discussion on labour problems on 22 February 1946. Noda's committee looked into the issue of 'production control' which typically arose when workers in dispute took over production in defiance of companies that had suspended operations. In July 1946 this committee reached the remarkable conclusion for a group of employers that 'looked at from the standpoint of the current special circumstances, it is not entirely appropriate to reject completely production control' (Keizai Dōyūkai 1956: 35). In reaching this conclusion, Noda's committee recognized that there were some companies that were little interested in restarting postwar production or in implementing management reform.

While there was sufficient opposition from within the Comrades' Association to deter its Executive Council from endorsing the committee's findings (Ōtake 1987: 369) the Executive Council itself adopted some noteworthy positions on occasions. For example, on 19 October 1946 the Executive Council met in emergency session to discuss the widespread labour unrest that was then sweeping the country and its deliberations resulted in the adoption of a position paper entitled *A View on the Recent Labour Disputes*. At this point in time, the Executive Council of the Comrades' Association counted among its members several who would before long become prominent officials of Nikkeiren, such as Moroi Kan'ichi, Sakurada Takeshi and Shikanai Nobutaka. Despite this composition of the Executive Council, the strategy encapsulated in the position paper was to concede that the economic initiative lay with the 'labouring masses', but to attempt to extract some advantage from this concession by classifying those who managed enterprises as a constituent element of these 'labouring masses'. Hence it was stated in *A View on the Recent Labour Disputes* that:

> The duty of economic reconstruction rests on the shoulders of the labouring masses. However, achieving this can be expected only if it is done by 'labourers in the broad sense' which includes the ranks of enterprise management. It does not mean only workers in the class sense.
>
> (Keizai Dōyūkai 1976: 31)

Managerial councils

'Economic democratization' was a recurrent buzz-word of the period and one of the concrete forms that this might take was considered to be managerial councils (*keiei kyōgikai*). The basic idea was that an enterprise's management would be in the hands of a council comprised of representatives of the capitalist owners, the operational managers and the labour union. Councils of a type had already been formed in many enterprises, but they primarily functioned as fora for discussing labour issues. Extending their responsibilities to management decisions was considered to be a way of defusing labour unrest, since labour's representatives, in the shape of union officials, would become part of the policymaking process. It was with such considerations in mind that the government and the Central Labour

Relations Commission (which had come into existence on 1 March 1946 when the Labour Union Law came into force) flirted with the notion of managerial councils for a while (Endō 1989: 151ff.). Not surprisingly, the concept also evoked a response from within the Comrades' Association.

Once again, it was the Committee for the Study of Labour Problems, under Noda Nobuō's chairmanship, which led the way. On 9 October 1946 it issued a report, entitled *An Opinion on Unemployment Counter-measures*, which countenanced a role for managerial councils. The report argued that agreement between management and labour within the frame-work of the managerial council should form the basis for decisions on enterprise rationalization, including laying off workers. Not surprisingly, such proposals unnerved some of the employers in the ranks of the Comrades' Association. While *An Opinion on Unemployment Countermeasures* expressed the majority's standpoint within the Committee for the Study of Labour Problems, the Executive Council was conscious of the divisions that existed within the Comrades' Association as a whole and deferred the matter (permanently as it turned out) without taking a vote on the committee's report (Keizai Dōyūkai 1956: 41–5).

Despite this inconclusive outcome, the idea of managerial councils continued to enjoy strong support from within the Comrades' Association. Ōtsuka Banjō, who was Chairman of the Comrades' Association's Study Group on Economic Democratization during 1947, was another enthusiastic proponent of managerial councils and they featured prominently in the final report which his study group completed on 1 July 1947 and presented to the Executive Council the following month. Owing to its radical proposals, this report created a considerable stir when it was published in pamphlet form in November 1947 under the title *Draft Plan for the Democratization of the Enterprise: a plan for reformed capitalism*. It is important to note that the status of this document remained that of a committee report, rather than one endorsed by the Executive Council in the name of the entire membership of the Comrades' Association. This was because, once again, the Executive Council considered the report's recommendations to have outstripped the bulk of the membership's commitment to managerial councils (Keizai Dōyūkai 1976: 35–7). While this might have been true, the readiness of many employers to concede fundamental reforms in the way in which capitalism operated, in the interests of consolidating the system as a whole, should not be overlooked. During 1946–7 it was the Comrades' Association which, despite certain reservations, acted as a mouthpiece for the many reform-minded employers.

The Economic Reconstruction Council

The Comrades' Association was also receptive to the proposal to organize an Economic Reconstruction Council (*Keizai Fukkō Kaigi*). This was an idea that originated within the unions and evoked interest in employers' circles during the latter half of 1946. Preliminary discussions were held, in which Sakurada Takeshi, Shikanai Nobutaka, Fujii Heigo, Noda Nobuō and Ōtsuka Banjō among others represented the Comrades' Association. Sakurada Takeshi went on to become one of the Vice-Chairmen of the Economic Reconstruction Council and Fujii Heigo, Moroi Kan'ichi and Noda Nobuō were among those appointed to its Central Standing Committee (Keizai Dōyūkai 1956: 62–9). The objective was to establish common ground on which unions and employers' organizations could stand so as to rebuild the economy. To this end, managerial councils were once again a feature of the 'Declaration' drawn up by the Preparatory Committee of the Economic Reconstruction Council (Keizai Dōyūkai 1976: 35). Sōdōmei (*Nihon Rōdō Kumiai Sōdōmei* or the Japan General Confederation of Labour Unions) and the Comrades' Association took the lead in organizing the Economic Reconstruction Council on the union and employers' sides respectively. They were joined by numerous organizations, including Sanbetsu (*Zen Nihon Sangyō Betsu Rōdō Kumiai Kaigi* or the All-Japan Council of Industrial Labour Unions) on the union side and the Kantō Managers' Association and Kansai Managers' Association on the employers' side.

The Economic Reconstruction Council held its inaugural conference in Tokyo on 6 February 1947 and, in addition to this general meeting, similar conferences were organized to discuss the situation in various industries. Although the council survived until 28 April 1948, by which time Nikkeiren was already in existence, ultimately it achieved very little owing to an inability to reach a consensus. The employers' organizations attributed this failure to obstruction by Sanbetsu, the union federation that was strongly influenced by the Communist Party. In later years, the Comrades' Association referred to Sanbetsu as a 'cancer' within the Economic Reconstruction Council (Keizai Dōyūkai 1976: 35) and Nikkeiren argued that it was rivalry between Sanbetsu and Sōdōmei and political infighting that led to the failure of this experiment in union–employer cooperation (Nikkeiren 1958: 9). Certainly, Sanbetsu had its own agenda, which was tied to the political ambitions of the Communist Party, and there was no love lost between Sōdōmei and Sanbetsu, which were bitter rivals in the struggle for control of the union movement.

Sōdōmei consisted of 1,699 unions with about 850,000 members (22 per cent of the unionized workforce) when it was founded on 1 August 1946. This compared to Sanbetsu's 21 industrial federations with about 1,630,000 members (43 per cent of the unionized workforce) at its formation on 19 August 1946 (Kawanishi 1992: 135). Sōdōmei was all for reconstituting the Economic Reconstruction Council in a manner that excluded Sanbetsu and hence made consensus easier to achieve (Ōtake 1987: 377). However, the Comrades' Association was unenthusiastic because such an arrangement would not have placated the workforce in enterprises organized by Sanbetsu, thereby failing to deliver to the required extent the principal objective of 'reformed capitalism'.

Turning point

Whatever the reason for the Economic Reconstruction Council's lack of success, its failure to live up to the employers' expectations marked a turning point in attitudes. Many employers had pinned their hopes on the Economic Reconstruction Council bringing about a situation where the unions guaranteed industrial peace in exchange for their participation in managing enterprises. As 1947 progressed and this trade-off failed to materialize, so more and more employers were inclined to reconsider their strategy. This turnaround was most noticeable in the Comrades' Association's case because it had been the principal standard bearer of 'reformed capitalism'. In its official *30 Years' History*, the Comrades' Association frankly assessed the change of orientation that it underwent in 1947–8. From 1948 it still advocated what it termed 'cooperation with workers who are equipped with understanding', but it admitted that it abandoned making further approaches to 'labour', by which it meant the unions (Keizai Dōyūkai 1976: 5). The unions had failed to deliver what reform-minded employers expected of them and hence the *Draft Plan for the Democratization of the Enterprise* and similar schemes to incorporate them into the management structure never got beyond the drawing board. The Comrades' Association admitted that, by 1948, Nikkeiren's line had become the new orthodoxy among employers. The labourist ideology that 'we're all workers now' was abandoned in favour of hard-nosed confrontation if needs be. As the *30 Years' History* put it: 'so it came about that the Comrades' Association adopted the approach of tackling the situation realistically. It pursued the policy of "management" itself rebuilding the economy' (Keizai Dōyūkai 1976: 5).

This change of attitude by the employers was made a great deal easier by the shifting priorities of the Occupation authorities. Up until early 1947 the Occupation authorities' principal bogeymen were militarism, right-wing politicians and employers whose companies had profited from the war against the USA. In line with these perceptions, even the Communist Party was looked upon as a useful ally. Hence it was the American authorities who overruled the Japanese government and ordered that the Communist Party's leaders be released from prison in October 1945. By the beginning of 1947 the political landscape within Japan was being reshaped as the international Cold War impinged on the Occupation. What brought matters to a head was a general strike which the public service unions, under the umbrella of the All-Government and Municipal Workers' Joint Struggle Committee, planned to hold on 1 February 1947. Interpreting this as a challenge to the Japanese government by unions manipulated by the Communist Party, on 31 January General Douglas MacArthur ordered the general strike to be called off, using his authority as Supreme Commander of Allied Powers. Almost universally, this incident was interpreted as *the* watershed in Occupation policy. As Nikkeiren later assessed it:

What decisively gave the impression, both inside and outside Japan, of a turning point in Occupation policy was the banning of the so-called 2.1 [1 February] strike. The resurgence of the managers' will to get their act together again, accurately speaking, postdates this event.

(Nikkeiren 1981: 165)

Despite the Occupation authorities adopting a far less indulgent attitude towards the unions after the scuttled general strike, they did not immediately signal a green light for the formation of an employers' organization dedicated to handling labour problems. At most, the signal changed from red to amber, allowing a transitional body, the Federation of Managers' Organizations (*Keieisha Dantai Rengōkai*), to be established on 19 May 1947. Although this functioned as a linking mechanism between the various provincial employers' organizations and those specific to a particular industry, it still held back from acting as a dynamic, centralized body capable of taking decisive action to deal with labour. The Kantō Managers' Association was the driving force behind the formation of the Federation of Managers' Organizations, as it also was behind the Managers' Organizations' Liaison Council (*Keieisha Dantai Renraku Kaigi*) which held a succession of conferences in the latter half of 1947 (Nikkeiren 1981: 191). Nevertheless, even with the Kantō Managers' Association applying the spur, progress was slow because employers remained uncertain how far they could go and had to feel their way at each step, trying to guess what the reaction of the Occupation authorities would be. The following recollection conveys just how finely balanced the situation was throughout 1947:

When the Federation of Managers' Organizations was established as a liaison body, GHQ [the General Headquarters of the Occupation authorities] did not publicly oppose it due to the change of circumstances, but, even so, it certainly was not supportive. From February 1947, the change in Occupation policy gradually progressed, but GHQ remained wary of employers' organizations antagonizing the unions too much. Accordingly, the Federation of Managers' Organizations too continued to face obstacles.

(Nikkeiren 1981: 191)

Only with the arrival of 1948 was the signal switched unambiguously to green by the Occupation authorities. Fortuitously, this coincided with many employers having abandoned the labourist ideology of 'we're all workers now' owing to the failure of the Economic Reconstruction Council to defuse labour unrest. Even the Comrades' Association had concluded by this stage that it was time to take off the gloves, while those who went on to establish Nikkeiren in April 1948 were already reaching for their knuckle-dusters. The era of 'fighting Nikkeiren' was about to begin.

4 Counter-attack

Teaching the workers who is boss (1948–60)

The years 1948 to 1960 were packed with momentous changes. At the start of this period, Japan was still an occupied country afflicted by economic chaos, mass unemployment and political instability. The Korean War (1950–3) gave the first major boost to Japan's economy as the USA's armed forces placed orders with Japanese companies to furnish them with equipment and supplies needed to prosecute the military campaign. During the course of the Korean War, Japan signed a peace treaty with the USA and its allies in 1951 (although not with the USSR and its allies) which was a preliminary step towards ending the Occupation and the recovery of formal independence in 1952. In the political sphere, the so-called '1955 system' gelled in that year and set the mould of politics until well into the 1990s. Under the 1955 system, the conservative Liberal Democratic Party formed the government without interruption, thereby forging a triangle of enduring and profitable links between politicians, bureaucrats and employers.

The ceasefire in Korea on 27 July 1953 snuffed out the economic stimulus that the war had provided and brought about a temporary downturn in the Japanese economy. However, by late 1954 Japan's economy started to pick up as Japanese companies resumed exports to overseas markets from which they had been excluded since 1945. By the mid-1950s Japanese companies were making strenuous efforts to raise productivity so as to be more competitive internationally. Not only did this involve more intensive working practices, but there was also a drive to re-equip, often with machines from abroad. Importing capital goods for this purpose caused Japan's balance of payments to deteriorate at the end of 1956. The government sought to correct this by raising interest rates in 1957 which had a negative effect on economic growth (Nikkeiren 1958: 18). Despite this setback, by the end of the 1950s the era of high economic growth had arrived, with the annual rate of increase of GNP in double figures in 1959 and 1960 (Allen 1972: 245).

The cumulative effect of all these changes was that, in some ways, Japan in 1960 was unrecognizable as the country it had been in 1948. Nevertheless, the constant thread running through this entire period was the employers' determination to win back 'the right to manage', which they felt had been taken from them in the chaotic years immediately after 1945. Nikkeiren was at the centre of the sustained efforts to regain the employers' initiative on the factory floor and re-establish managerial authority. Needless to say, attaining these goals was an essential precondition for raising productivity and achieving high economic growth. Nikkeiren was pre-eminent as the standard bearer of 'the right to manage' and it was its developing organization and activity throughout the period from 1948 to 1960 which gave these years a common identity, despite the momentous economic and political changes that occurred. Since asserting 'the right to manage' necessarily meant confronting militant unions, it was during these years that the reputation of 'fighting Nikkeiren' took root.

This chapter will examine how Nikkeiren was established and the goals which it set for itself. Its regional and industrial structures will be described and information provided on some of those who played key roles in its leadership. The various types of activity in which it engaged (ranging from advisor in labour disputes, to lobbying group, to publishing house) will be analysed, as will some of the issues that it championed during this period (ranging from changes in the law, to reforming education, to raising productivity). Later in the chapter, accounts will be given of five representative labour disputes in which Nikkeiren became involved: Tōhō Film (1948), Electric Power (1952), Nissan Motor (1953), Ōmi Silk Thread (1954) and Mitsui Miike Coal Mines (1959–60). Several other labour disputes will be mentioned at relevant points in the chapter and attention will be paid to the positions that Nikkeiren adopted in relation to the 'red purge' and *shuntō* (the spring-season wages struggle). The intention is that, out of this wide-ranging account, a comprehensive picture will emerge of Nikkeiren's multi-faceted activity and the extent to which it left its mark on the period 1948–60.

Formation

Nikkeiren's founding meeting was held at the Industry Club building in central Tokyo on 12 April 1948. The meeting was attended by 210 employers from a wide range of industries and among the guests who were invited was the head of SCAP's Labour Division. His presence was a signal that the Occupation authorities by now approved of the formation of an employers' federation specializing in labour relations. According to Morita Yoshio, the gist of the address delivered to the meeting by the head of SCAP's Labour Division was that 'firmly correct managers will benefit the workers too and good workers will inevitably emerge under good managers' (Morita 1958: 342). With this endorsement to boost their confidence, the meeting adopted a founding declaration which is revealing regarding Nikkeiren's ambitions. Since this was a document of historical significance, it is worth translating in full:

The key to the rebuilding of Japan's economy lies in planning to secure industrial peace and enhance productivity. To bring this about, in addition to, on the one hand, achieving the healthy and autonomous development of labour unions, on the other, we must strive to realize sound management where managers, acting together, protect their capital and encourage its growth. In this way, labour and capital must mutually respect management rights and labour's rights and in all areas of work without exception must commit themselves to the salvation of the country.

Looking back, since the end of the war, managers have fallen into a condition of being somewhat dazed and at a loss in the midst of the tumultuous course of events taken by the development of the labour movement and the change and confusion in economic circles. Truly, it unhappily has to be said with great sorrow that on the road to rebuilding our economy there have been unsatisfactory aspects of the way in which normal management rights, which are inherent in the position of manager, have been exercised. This is a fact which cannot be denied. While it can be said that these type of managerial shortcomings are due to all manner of circumstances, as far as the majority are concerned, they are due to the fact that, because we have lacked the strength of solidarity, we have been completely unprepared in the fields of theory, data and policy.

At this point in time a tense situation is evident throughout the world in the fields of politics, economics and foreign relations. Amidst the labour unrest that prevails, the basis for economic recovery should be established with the focus on the introduction of foreign capital. Standing at this crucial juncture, we managers shall unify our wills, pool our troubles, and gather together in an effort to reorganize and strengthen the Federation of Managers' Organizations [*Keieisha Dantai Rengō-kai*]. Under the banner of the *Nihon Keieisha Dantai Renmei* [Nikkeiren] we shall concentrate all our strength. By mobilizing our knowledge and experience, and by cultivating our enthusiasm and our courage, we shall establish management rights. We shall devote our determined effort to securing industrial peace and rebuilding Japan's economy.

'Managers, be strong in a right-minded fashion!'

(Morita 1958: 342–3)

Two basic propositions which are embedded in this founding declaration are worth emphasizing. First, there was an acceptance of unions. It is evident that those who launched Nikkeiren had no intention of reverting to the standpoint of prewar organizations like Zensanren and dismantling the legal framework within which the unions now operated. Nikkeiren's founders were realists who recognized that the reforms introduced by the Occupation authorities were here to stay, even if they hoped over time to

nibble away at some of them. Hence unions were now accepted as permanent fixtures. So, rather than seeking to remove them altogether, the priority
was to achieve their 'healthy and autonomous development'. 'Healthy' was
clearly a subjective evaluation and in practice meant whatever caused no
trouble to the employers. As for 'autonomous', this signified that unions
should be free from external influences exerted by organizations such as the
Communist Party.

Second, there was the need for employers to secure the right to manage.
While the declaration alluded to the difficult environment in which employers had been operating since 1945, ultimately it attributed the loss of
managerial authority to their own deficiencies. By pointing to shortcomings
in the fields of 'theory, data and policy', Nikkeiren was implicitly recognizing that its own roles had to include research and policy formation.
However, galvanizing employers into the frame of mind where they could
recapture the right to manage would obviously involve much more than
quiet, backroom activity such as research and policy deliberation. By setting
its sights on the right to manage, Nikkeiren was in effect announcing its
intention to take the lead and propel the general mass of employers towards
that goal. Nikkeiren was thereby assigning to itself a vanguard role which
would be both exhortatory and organizational. It would exhort employers
to be strong, determined and courageous, while building an organization
which could provide the benefits of solidarity and pooled resources when
companies became embroiled in disputes. Ironically, by assuming this vanguard role, Nikkeiren became in some senses the mirror image of the
Communist Party which it vilified.

Also permeating the founding declaration was an acute awareness of the
favourable situation created by the Cold War. Nikkeiren grasped that the
USA's preoccupation with countering any advance by the USSR and its supporters meant that the Occupation authorities would not obstruct a
counter-attack by Japan's employers 'at this point in time [when] a tense situation is evident throughout the world'. This might have been a factor in
encouraging Nikkeiren to adopt the slogan 'Managers, be strong in a right-
minded fashion!', which was undoubtedly provocative by the standards of
the time. It was one of Nikkeiren's directors, Maeda Hajime, who devised
this 'catchphrase', as Nikkeiren called it. Not everyone in Nikkeiren's
leadership agreed that the time was ripe to risk such outspokenness.
Maeda's fellow director, Shikanai Nobutaka, was worried about what the
reactions might be, but in the event 'Managers, be strong in a right-minded
fashion!' was enthusiastically received and captured the mood of Nikkeiren's founder members (Nikkeiren 1981: 201).

The founding meeting also adopted statutes, whose second article
explained Nikkeiren's purpose in predictably innocuous fashion: 'Striving
for improved communication and cooperation between managers' organizations, this federation's objective will be primarily to promote the healthy
development of labour–management relations' (Nikkeiren 1981: 194).

The next article then identified the means by which this end was to be achieved:

a   Mutual communication and cooperation between managers' organizations
b   Strengthening the organization and operation of managers' organizations
c   Investigation and study of labour problems experienced in common by managers' organizations
d   Communication with related bodies
e   Issuing of proposals and opinions on matters connected with labour problems
f   Other matters necessary for achieving this federation's objective.

(Nikkeiren 1981: 194)

While Nikkeiren's roles as a research centre and a lobbying body were clear from clauses (c) and (e) respectively, there was no hint of the aggressive intervention in labour disputes in which it was repeatedly to engage in order euphemistically 'to promote the healthy development of labour–management relations'. Article 18 stipulated that Nikkeiren would hold an annual conference every April and such other extraordinary general meetings as were deemed necessary by the Executive Council (Nikkeiren 1981: 197).

Organization

It was mentioned in Chapter 1 that Nikkeiren's organization consisted of a warp of regional business associations and a woof of industrial associations. This organizational structure was inherited from Nikkeiren's immediate predecessor, the Federation of Managers' Organizations, and maintained subsequently because it proved to be an effective method of linking the centre with the grassroots. At the time of Nikkeiren's formation there were pre-existing managers' associations (*keieisha kyōkai*) in areas such as Kantō, Kansai, Chūbu, Tōhoku, Hokkaidō and Kyūshū, which were incorporated into Nikkeiren as regional 'blocs' (Morita 1958: 343ff.). These were soon joined by other blocs in Chūgoku, Shikoku and Hokuriku to give a full geographical coverage of Japan, although the Hokuriku bloc proved to be too weak to maintain an independent existence and its constituent organizations later transferred to adjacent blocs. Within each bloc there would typically be prefectural managers' associations, so that Nikkeiren's reach soon extended down to the grassroots level in all 44 prefectures (the 42 *ken* plus Kyōto-*fu* and Hokkaidō). This left Tokyo and Ōsaka, which were the responsibility of the Kantō Managers' Association and the Kansai Managers' Association respectively, since these two blocs had their headquarters in these major cities. In this fashion, employers in every corner of Japan were brought into Nikkeiren's nationwide organizational structure (Nikkeiren 1950: appendix).

Meshing into the regional business associations described above, there were 15 industrial associations when Nikkeiren was founded. The industries represented were iron and steel, coal mining, other mining, light metals, electric cable manufacturing, communications, rolling stock, automobiles, chemical engineering, ammonium sulphate, paper and pulp, cement, cotton spinning, construction and electricity (Nikkeiren 1981: 199). In the same way that the regional organization was expanded and strengthened during the period under consideration in this chapter, so too was Nikkeiren's network of industrial associations. By 1950 the number of industrial associations had more than doubled to 31. The additional industries which had by then been brought into Nikkeiren's fold were private railways, man-made fibres, woollen spinning, rubber, silk, oil, industrial machinery, department stores, refrigeration, shipping, life insurance, shipbuilding, accident insurance, heavy electrical machinery, city banks and transport (Nikkeiren 1950: appendix). By the time of its tenth anniversary in 1958, a further 12 industrial associations had been added: regional banks, telegraphs and telephones, hemp spinning, phosphatic fertilizer, private broadcasting, national railways, port transport, mutual banks, the Tobacco and Salt Public Corporation, securities, soy sauce and fisheries (Nikkeiren 1958: appendix). This development more than compensated for the loss of refrigeration and brought the total number of industrial associations belonging to Nikkeiren up to 42.

Nikkeiren's mix of regional associations and industrial associations worked in the proverbial belt and braces fashion. Employers in a typical company would be members both of their prefectural managers' association and of the industrial association specific to their line of business. Membership of the prefectural managers' association would provide useful business contacts in their area, reduce any sense of isolation they might feel and facilitate Nikkeiren's efforts to raise employers' consciousness by means of local meetings and other activities. Membership of the industrial association was particularly vital when a company became involved in a labour dispute. If Nikkeiren judged that the company was engaged in a fight on behalf of the industry as a whole, it would use its good offices to encourage material support from normally rival companies and prevail on them not to take advantage of a competitor's business difficulties, but to act in accordance with their collective interest as employers. Interestingly enough, making due allowance for the different class interests they represented, Nikkeiren's structure of a warp of regional associations and a woof of industrial associations mirrored the syndicalist form of organization practised by the labour movement in Spain and elsewhere. The syndicalist 'dual form of organization', as it was known, was comprised of regional federations along one axis and industry-based federations along the other (Bookchin 1977: 132ff.). By way of contrast, as the period under consideration here progressed, the

Japanese labour movement was increasingly forced into the mould of the enterprise union. One result of this increasing reliance on the enterprise union was that Japanese labour did not benefit from the reinforcing effect that derives from the 'dual form of organization' and hence was at a disadvantage when compared to Nikkeiren.

In addition to Nikkeiren's regional and industrial networks described above, there was also the central organization which was built up in its headquarters in Tokyo. The day-to-day running of headquarters' business was initially overseen by three directors (*senmu riji*). From 1950 this number was reduced to two (Nikkeiren 1981: 259–60). Underneath them was another director who acted as office head (*jōnin riji/jimu kyokuchō*) and beneath him various sections were developed, each headed by a section chief (*buchō*). By 1958 there were 10 of these sections, whose fields of competence were identified as general affairs, research, social security, labour administration, labour economy, education, labour consultation, legal affairs, international affairs and public relations. In most cases their responsibilities are clear from these titles, but it might be useful to clarify the demarcations between labour administration, labour economy and labour consultation. The Labour Administration Section took general responsibility for union matters and labour disputes, in addition to which it monitored wages, allowances and pensions. The Labour Economy Section focused on productivity, enterprise management, employment and other aspects of labour, against the background of economic trends both within Japan and internationally. The Labour Consultation Section provided a discussion service and related support for employers who needed help and advice in handling their workforce (Nikkeiren 1958: 263).

Separate from the sections, which were staffed by full-time officials, was Nikkeiren's system of committees. These were comprised of representative employers and were the fora within which Nikkeiren's policy was deliberated and its strategy formulated. In Nikkeiren's early days, as many as 15 special committees were established, each charged with a discrete policy area, but in 1960 this was reduced to the more manageable number of 10, whose responsibilities were designated respectively as general affairs, education, public relations, employment, social security, labour legislation, labour economy, labour management, wages, and small and medium-sized enterprises. In all, more than 400 members sat on these special committees and, in Nikkeiren's own words, functioned as 'the driving force for policy formation, planning and activity' (Nikkeiren 1963: 10). Supplementing the special committees, a policy committee existed to deal with any emergencies and extraordinary committees were appointed whenever necessary to study specific issues that arose and make appropriate policy recommendations. For example, in addition to its Special Committee on Labour Legislation, Nikkeiren set up an Extraordinary Committee in July 1959 to engage in in-depth investigation into the workings of the Labour Relations Law at a time when this was under review by the government (Nikkeiren 1963: 10).

Individuals

However well constructed Nikkeiren's organization might have been, it could only be as effective as the individuals who occupied the key posts. Some of these men were, relatively speaking, veterans whose attitudes had been formed in prewar employers' organizations, such as the Industry Club and Zensanren. Others became prominent only after the war and were forced to learn fast when the Comrades' Association's labourist ideology failed to deliver industrial peace. Whatever the differences in their backgrounds, what these Nikkeiren leaders shared was a pugnacious determination to give the unions a bloody nose and thereby alter the balance of power within the enterprises. The cases of several individuals who held leading positions in Nikkeiren's organization during the period from 1948 to 1960 will be examined here, albeit briefly, in order to illustrate these points.

Maeda Hajime was a director of the Coal Mining Federation who had been active in Zensanren before the war and had established a reputation within its ranks as an ardent defender of company unions, as opposed to independent labour unions. When Nikkeiren was formed in 1948, he became one of its directors (*senmu riji*) and remained in that post right through the period under consideration here. True to his prewar form, Maeda took a hard line when confronting the unions in the various labour disputes in which Nikkeiren became embroiled. In October 1952 Nikkeiren's extraordinary general meeting was held in the midst of a protracted campaign of strikes and power cuts conducted by the electricity workers. In a report on the current labour situation, which Maeda delivered to the extraordinary general meeting on 16 October, he denounced the electricity workers as a pampered 'labour aristocracy' (Nikkeiren 1981: 264). A year later, with reference to a major labour dispute at the Nissan Motor Company, Maeda claimed disarmingly that the employers 'certainly do not like conflict and do not lightly go on the offensive. However, in order to secure healthy management, it is just that, summoning up our wisdom, composure and courage, we pushed on down the correct path that we should take as managers' (Nikkeiren 1981: 287). Such turns of phrase were clearly intended to convey how moderate and 'modern' Japanese employers had become in the postwar era, but Maeda's ingrained antagonism towards unions was more accurately revealed in the report on the labour situation that he made to the October 1959 extraordinary general meeting. In his report, Maeda claimed triumphantly that the era since 1945, when it was the unions which supposedly had made the running, was now over. According to him, the next 15 years were to be the managers' era (Nikkeiren 1963: 9).

Shikanai Nobutaka was a director of Nihon Denshi Kōgyō (Japan Electronics Industries) who worked alongside Maeda Hajime as one of Nikkeiren's regular directors (*senmu riji*) during its early years. While this was his official post in the organization, unofficially he was one of its principal troubleshooters who was frequently despatched to serve on the front line when the class war erupted. In the previously mentioned electric power dispute in 1952, for example, Shikanai served as a representative of the employers' side. Although his role was supposed to be that of an expert on wages and related questions, in later years he admitted with refreshing candour that in 1952 he was still woefully ill-informed in comparison to his union counterparts. Since at that stage he 'knew nothing at all about what labour problems consisted of', he was initially completely out of his depth and only managed to keep up his end of the negotiations by working madly into the small hours to mug up the necessary information. Shikanai's verdict on the electricity workers' dispute was: 'in that sense, we learnt a hell of a lot from the electric power business, didn't we? The managers' side was completely bereft of theoretical weapons as far as wages were concerned' (Nikkeiren 1981: 728).

From such unpromising beginnings, Shikanai accumulated vast experience over the years, derived from his close involvement in innumerable disputes. While other Nikkeiren officials noticed that it was often those companies which had experienced major disputes that went on to flourish commercially, it was Shikanai in particular who perceived that it was not the strike experience itself that was crucial, but the way in which the dispute was concluded. In an aphorism which became synonymous with Shikanai, he argued that 'when it comes to a fire, it's the first five minutes that count. When it comes to a dispute, it's the last five minutes' (Nikkeiren 1981: 749). In other words, employers had to fight to the bitter end and avoid the temptation to compromise prematurely simply in order to resume production as soon as possible. Their aim should be to destroy combative unions rather than merely defeat them, so *how* a dispute was brought to an end was the most important consideration. In that sense, it was 'the last five minutes' that provided the opportunity to annihilate the enemy.

Sakurada Takeshi was President of Nisshin Spinning and another uncompromising militant at the heart of Nikkeiren. When Nikkeiren was founded in 1948, he was Deputy Chairman of its network of regional associations and the following year he became a general manager (*sōriji*) of Nikkeiren itself. Subsequently, he rose through the leadership to become Nikkeiren's first Chairman (*kaichō*) when that position was created in the 1970s. Sakurada was a hard-nosed and straight-talking individual who tended to express himself a good deal more forthrightly than many employers. For example, it was politically astute for Nikkeiren to pass a resolution at its fourth annual conference in 1951 thanking General MacArthur for his good work as Supreme Commander of Allied Powers and, in line with this, a Tōshiba executive called Kawahara Ryōzaburō made some appreciative, retrospective remarks on one occasion about the role of the Occupation authorities in intervening in strikes to pacify the situation. Sakurada's retort was very much in character:

That's what you say but, if GHQ hadn't made that Labour Union Law in such haste, things wouldn't have been like that anyway. It was nothing more than them making the mess and then having to clear it up. If they had left it to us, things would have gone a lot smoother.

(Nikkeiren 1981: 724)

It does not take much imagination to surmise the reasons why labour relations 'would have gone a lot smoother' if the Occupation authorities had 'left it' to Sakurada and his colleagues from the beginning. As we shall see in due course, he was one of the Nikkeiren activists who threw themselves with gusto into the Tōhō Film dispute as soon as Nikkeiren was established. So too was Shikanai Nobutaka, who had his own reasons for disliking the Americans. As he put it, 'GHQ came out with all sorts of tremendously flowery expressions, like running things democratically between labour and management, but you couldn't trust them' (Nikkeiren 1981: 707).

Even from these short descriptions of a handful of individuals, certain characteristics of Nikkeiren's leaders emerge. Capitalists they might have been, but there were no idle and effete dividend drawers among them. Nikkeiren's organization worked because at its centre were committed and energetic leaders who dedicated themselves resolutely to an unrelenting process of struggle and the attrition of union power. Most had a pronounced streak of ruthlessness, were not prone to self-doubt and did not flinch from confrontation. Through their work, they acquired organizational and propagandistic skills which they used to orchestrate activity, win support, boost flagging campaigns and generally provide determined leadership. If these characteristics call to mind the attributes commonly identified with Bolshevism and its leaders, the association is reinforced by a shared anti-Americanism. One could do worse than think of Nikkeiren as pro-capitalist Bolsheviks who shared many of the authoritarian assumptions, belligerent attitudes and manipulative practices of their Communist Party opponents. The difference was that Nikkeiren's leaders were resolved to consolidate the power and privileges of the existing ruling class, whereas the Communist Party sought to supplant them and become the dominant and privileged class itself. Obviously, this was a major difference, but since neither party questioned the need for inequalities in the ways in which power was concentrated and privileges were distributed, both sides had much in common, although they would never admit it.

Activity

Nikkeiren was a highly active organization and was determined that its presence would make a difference to the status quo within both the enterprises and society generally. For the purposes of analysis, at least six types of activity in which it engaged can be identified, although in practice there was often a considerable overlap between these various endeavours. First, it acted as an advisor in labour disputes and as a consultant regarding labour relations. Second, it actively promoted the class struggle, both by raising the employers' consciousness via its vanguardist role and building solidarity on issues of common interest to some or all employers. Third, it was a research organization, collecting and processing in easily assimilable form data that was useful for employers and identifying trends within the economy in general and wage labour in particular. Fourth, it fulfilled a management training function, running many types of courses, but especially those that would make the management of labour more effective. Fifth, it was a lobbying body, seeking to influence the authorities' formulation and implementation of policy. Sixth, it was a publishing house, issuing a constant stream of publications, mostly to provide information and education for employers, but with the subsidiary purpose of influencing the general public. Each of these different types of activity will be examined in turn, but Nikkeiren's roles as advisor in labour disputes and promoter of the class struggle will be considered only in outline here, because they can be demonstrated more effectively later in the chapter when we look at a number of concrete cases.

Advisor/consultant

No sooner was Nikkeiren formed than it became fully involved in labour disputes, offering advice and support to companies as they confronted their workforce. Tōhō Film is a prime example because its dispute flared up when the company announced staff cutbacks on 8 April 1948, just four days before Nikkeiren's founding meeting. In the course of establishing itself, Nikkeiren urged employers to be strong and to reassert their 'right to manage', so it was acutely aware that its credibility was on the line in a dispute like that at Tōhō Film where the company was attempting to behave in the recommended fashion. As Nikkeiren put it in later years:

> Herein lies the reason why the outcome of this dispute was bound also to call into question the value of Nikkeiren's existence at a time when it had just been established. Hence, it was natural that Nikkeiren too mustered all its strength to set up a support system.
>
> (Nikkeiren 1981: 221)

The Chairman of Tōhō Film, Mabuchi Takeo, had much the same recollection when he recalled the dispute 30 years later:

> Nikkeiren's slogan at that time was . . . 'be strong in a right-minded fashion!' So at Tōhō, for the very first time, it had to ask itself, 'shall we support them?' In short, it decided to do whatever it took to support strong managers. It was like Nikkeiren's opening match being Tōhō, in fact.
>
> (Nikkeiren 1981: 721)

If Tōhō was the opening match, Nikkeiren certainly fielded a strong team which included Sakurada Takeshi, Shikanai Nobutaka, Imazato Hiroki and other top leaders. There was a council of war at Yawata Steel's company dormitory, where Nikkeiren's options *vis-à-vis* the Tōhō dispute were discussed. Mabuchi Takeo describes the outcome in terms of, 'so we said, let's do it!' (Nikkeiren 1981: 721).

In 1952, four years after the Tōhō dispute, the equally bitterly fought electric power dispute occurred. The involvement in this dispute of Nikkeiren leaders such as Shikanai Nobutaka has already been touched on. The reason why Nikkeiren was so prominently involved in this dispute was that the electric power companies felt themselves to be completely out of their depth, confronted as they were by a well organized union employing effective tactics and presenting persuasive arguments to justify its wage demands. As a result, it was Nikkeiren which, behind the scenes, was formulating strategy and pulling strings on behalf of the employers. In the words of Sakurada Takeshi:

> As Mr Shikanai just said, the employers at the electric power companies didn't know a thing. So, because they left it up to the Central Labour Relations Commission or Nikkeiren, we were called to the Industry Club for consultation on any number of occasions.
>
> (Nikkeiren 1981: 730–1)

Nikkeiren was supposed to be neither a direct participant in labour disputes nor directly involved in negotiations. However, when it judged the stakes to be sufficiently high, it could interpret these guidelines very flexibly. The electric power and also the coal mining disputes of 1952 were cases in point because Nikkeiren regarded them as crucial, both for its own credibility and for the well-being of Japanese capitalism. On the one hand, the electricity workers and coal miners were both led by powerful industrial unions, whose example was followed by other sections of the labour movement, so it was vital to resist them strongly in Nikkeiren's estimation. On the other hand, electricity and coal were used so widely as sources of energy that the effects of wage settlements in these industries would be felt throughout the economy. It was these considerations that Nikkeiren was referring to when it wrote that 'accordingly, one could say that the 1952 Electric Power/Coal Miners' strikes . . . formed an opportunity for an unavoidable confrontation between Sōhyō [*Nihon Rōdō Kumiai Sōhyōgikai* or the General Council of Labour Unions in Japan] and Nikkeiren' (Nikkeiren 1981: 262).

Apart from Nikkeiren's intervention in labour disputes, there was the less conspicuous but none the less important consultation service it provided to employers on personnel matters. As we have seen, this service was provided by the Labour Consultation Section (later renamed the Cooperation Section) at Nikkeiren's headquarters in Tokyo. Its full-time staff built up wide expertise on the whole range of personnel issues and this was available to employers whenever the need arose. It was evidently a frequently used service, since Nikkeiren reported in its review of the years 1958–63 that the number of cases handled had grown to over 3,000 per year. Consultation took a variety of forms, from the simplest, where an employer might telephone or write a letter, to the despatch of Nikkeiren staff to a trouble spot. If Nikkeiren's own staff could not provide ready answers to employers' queries, it retained lawyers who could be consulted on questions of labour law (Nikkeiren 1963: 8).

Class struggle

Nikkeiren regarded one of its chief roles as acting as a spur to the general mass of employers by pushing their ideas in the right direction. This was the purpose behind the first national conference it held on 9 September 1948 which was attended by some 450 employers from all over Japan. As well as calling for the promotion of 'healthy' labour relations and the reform of labour law, the conference adopted the slogan 'Managers, take the lead in rebuilding the economy!' Taken out of its historical context, this slogan might seem unremarkable, but against the background of widespread demoralization among employers and their loss of confidence in the years immediately after the war, it had the significance of a call to arms. Nikkeiren's own account of what it aimed to achieve at this and subsequent conferences is worth quoting:

> Looked at in the light of the negative attitude of managers up till then, truly it felt like a different world. This activity of raising managers' consciousness was afterwards pursued in the regions too. Managers' conferences were held in Hokkaidō, Kansai, Chūgoku, Tōhoku and all the other regions as well.
>
> (Nikkeiren 1958: 10)

In its periodization of its early history, Nikkeiren defined the first period as extending from its founding in April 1948 up to its extraordinary general meeting in September 1949 and the second period as following on from this and lasting until the outbreak of the Korean War in June 1950. It labelled these periods respectively 'the period of establishing the right to manage' and 'the period of self-strengthening of management' (Nikkeiren 1958: 9–12). Both periods involved Nikkeiren working hard to raise employers' morale and infuse them with a sense of collective purpose and latent strength. Reinvigorating the employing class in this fashion was achieved partly by educational and agitational methods, showing the bosses where their interests lay and goading them into asserting themselves, but even more so through actual activity. Successful action fed off itself, inducing other employers to follow suit and causing the goals to be redefined ever more ambitiously. Once again, these points can be demonstrated by reference to the dispute at Tōhō Film. On 10 May 1948 Nikkeiren issued a declaration entitled *An Opinion on Securing Management Rights*. Using the ongoing dispute at Tōhō Film, Nikkeiren argued that it provided a striking example of the overwhelming need to secure management rights. It declared that 'we have reached the point of firmly resolving that there is no other way than for managers, in self-protection, to exercise the right to manage, which they possess inherently, and speedily to try to establish an independent organization of their affairs' (Nikkeiren 1958: 9). Stirring stuff though this was to employers who had been forced onto the defensive for several years, it was eventual victory at Tōhō (after 195 days of struggle) that was more decisive in persuading the mass of employers to follow the lead set by Nikkeiren.

Nikkeiren's vanguard role did not disappear even when increasingly 'the right to manage' was secured and the employers rebuilt their strength as the 1950s progressed. Rather, it was a question of Nikkeiren continuing to give a lead to employers collectively, but the issues on which it did so changing over time. Thus in January 1954 Nikkeiren announced 'three principles for wages'. These were, first, that it would not recognize price rises as a reason for raising wages; second, that it would not recognize wage rises that over-stepped the limits set by a company's financial performance; and, third, that it would not recognize wage rises that were unaccompanied by increased labour productivity (Nikkeiren 1981: 377). These principles were further refined in a document on *Current Wages Policy and Wages Problems*, which Nikkeiren published on 18 January 1957. Here it differentiated between large companies and smaller companies, but the basis of both sets of guidelines was uncompromising: wage rises should be held below productivity increases (Nikkeiren 1981: 384–5). A particularly striking example of the implementation of Nikkeiren's wages strategy came in Autumn 1957 when (using the standard jargon) the three big steel companies gave a 'zero reply' to the steelworkers' 'base up' demands. This meant that they rejected the demands for an increase in the pay baseline, so that the steelworkers would receive only increments linked to grade progression. Unsurprisingly, Nikkeiren commended the steel companies' hard line, arguing that they needed to channel their available capital into investing in more up-to-date facilities and portraying the steelworkers as already among the highest paid employees in Japan. The steelworkers launched a wave of strikes during October and November 1957, but were unable to dent the steel companies' resolve and Nikkeiren was gratified when the coal mining companies followed suit with their own 'zero response'. Following a prolonged strike (from 21 March to 18 June 1958) the coal miners did secure a meagre wage rise of ¥770, but more relevant to this discussion was the ability of Tanrō (*Nihon Tankō Rōdō Kumiai Rengōkai* or the Japan Federation of Coal Miners' Unions) to detect Nikkeiren's orchestrating role behind the scenes: 'the reply proffered by all the companies on 6 March [1958] comes based on the policy of freezing the wages of steelworkers and mineworkers, which is Nikkeiren's line' (Nikkeiren 1981: 389).

Another facet of Nikkeiren's promotion of the class struggle was the effort it put into forging solidarity among employers when their collective interests were at stake. This was seen as especially important when companies were involved in labour disputes. Hence, on 27 July 1949, Nikkeiren adopted an *Agreement on Mutual Aid between Managers at Times of Dispute*. The electricity workers' dispute in 1952 provided evidence of how this agreement worked in practice, with Nikkeiren coordinating resistance to the electricity workers' campaign on a class-wide scale, beyond the confines of the electric power industry. At Nikkeiren's extraordinary general meeting on 16 October 1952, a resolution was passed to the effect that 'we cannot turn a blind eye and let the power cut strike take its own course. As managers, let us take hard-hitting measures' (Nikkeiren 1981: 267). Following this, Nikkeiren made arrangements for electricians from other industries to be drafted into the electric power companies when required, so as to scab on striking electricity workers and thereby minimize power cuts. The almost universal use of electricity throughout the economy made Nikkeiren's efforts in 1952 a particularly notable case of employers sinking their sectional and competitive inclinations in the face of a common threat. Nikkeiren boasted that achieving this level of solidarity 'was not unconnected with the fact that the managers of all the electric power companies and Nikkeiren especially felt strongly with their entire beings the necessity of this' (Nikkeiren 1981: 269).

Research

Research was important for Nikkeiren because so many of its other forms of activity were dependent on sound information and the presentation of factually informed arguments. Research was undertaken both by the headquarters staff and by Nikkeiren's different types of committees. When the term 'research' is used, it should be appreciated that this was not academic research (although sympathetic academics were frequently co-opted onto Nikkeiren's committees and study groups, both for their expertise and for the aura of respectability they could provide). Nikkeiren was not motivated by the disinterested pursuit of truth, but by advancing the interests of employers. Hence the research in which it engaged was very much of the applied variety. It focused on issues that were of pressing concern to employers and sought solutions that would benefit the same social stratum. During the years which concern us here, its principal research themes included labour relations, wages and similar questions.

At Nikkeiren's extraordinary general meeting in September 1953, one of the main items discussed was the need for 'frank and modest self-control and self-discipline by managers and how to realize a situation of cooperation between management and labour based on these qualities' (Nikkeiren 1958: 15). The two decisions that arose from this discussion took the form of *Our View on How to Deal with the Stage Now Facing Us* and *A Proposal for Research into Cooperative Labour–Management Relations*. Following this, a Committee for Investigating Cooperative Labour–Management Relations was set up, but Nikkeiren's own description of the outcome of the research initiated by the 1953 extraordinary general meeting is evidence of the extent to which its direction was influenced by the investigators' interests as employers: 'it transpired that much weight was attached to such projects as the study of means to raise labour productivity, investigative research into enterprise rationalization and research investigations aimed at establishing a situation of labour–management cooperation' (Nikkeiren 1958: 15–16). Indeed, the pursuit of productivity gains and the ambition to raise competitiveness through rationalization and automation were constant preoccupations of employers throughout the 1950s and beyond, so it was inevitable that the consequences of these developments for labour relations should be a focus of Nikkeiren's research.

When Japan started to emerge in autumn 1954 from the economic downturn brought about by the end of the Korean War in July 1953, workers in the most dynamic industries were able to push for higher wages. This had the effect of widening wage differentials between different sectors of the economy, which Nikkeiren described as 'a life and death issue for our country' because of the general upward pressure that was exerted on wage rates (Nikkeiren 1958: 16). Alarmed by this tendency, in July 1955 Nikkeiren's Industrial Economy Study Group embarked on research into its various ramifications. The study group split into six sub-committees, which investigated wage differentials, productivity, management analysis, national income, small and medium-sized enterprises and economic policy respectively. University professors were co-opted and in all about 90 individuals were involved in more than 40 meetings. The outcome of their combined efforts was the publication in August 1956 of *The Theory and Corroborative Study of Wage Differentials*, which Nikkeiren called 'epoch-making research' (Nikkeiren 1958: 16). A more accurate assessment would have been that, however meticulously this research was conducted, there was no room for doubt that its purpose was to control wages, not their value-free investigation.

As alternatives to these examples of research on labour relations and wages, one could equally well examine other research subjects to which Nikkeiren devoted attention during the years 1948–60, such as labour's position within the wider economy, labour law and social security. What such an examination would reveal is that, even though the details of the research on each subject would have been different, there was a predictable degree of sameness in the conclusions reached. Whatever the subject, Nikkeiren's research was pre-programmed so as to deliver conclusions that were advantageous to the employing class.

Management training

At its inception, Nikkeiren was aware that labour relations were a two-edged sword. On the one hand, employers needed to be prepared to confront the unions and fight aggressively when necessary, but they also needed to develop routine practices for dealing with their workforce in a non-confrontational fashion outside of periods of open conflict. In other words, Nikkeiren recognized at an early stage the need for skilled personnel managers who were trained in the techniques of achieving the company's goals in ways that would minimize discontent among the workforce. With this in mind, as early as 17 November 1949, Nikkeiren organized the first national conference of personnel managers. Well over 200 attended and listened to presentations on labour management, wages, enterprise reorganization and other topical issues. The following year, the need for management training and the development of what was called 'scientific management' was recognized at Nikkeiren's annual conference in April. This gave rise over the next few months to a succession of lectures and seminars on management in general and personnel management in particular. Nikkeiren also published a position paper entitled *A View on the New Personnel Management* on 9 May 1950 (Nikkeiren 1958:11–12).

One noteworthy initiative that Nikkeiren took was to sponsor short extra-mural courses on practical business management in Tokyo at Waseda University's Department of Commerce over the period 1953–7. These courses were attended by about 700 people during the five years that they ran. Subsequently, from July 1958, Nikkeiren ran this programme independently as a 'Course for Nurturing Management Executives', which became an annual event. This programme aimed to implant both general management skills and specialist knowledge on personnel management. Although originally intended for managers in large companies, it was recognized that there was a corresponding need in small and medium-sized enterprises. Hence, from February 1959 an equivalent course was instituted, targeted at managers outside the major companies (Nikkeiren 1958: 17; 1963: 8; 1981: 36, 442). In addition to these long-standing courses, Nikkeiren provided at various junctures more specialist training on topics that were of current concern to employers. For example, in August 1959 it started lectures on retirement pensions, in response to widespread interest in this subject within enterprises, and in June 1960 it ran a course on the implementation of job specific pay. From September 1960 it also commenced short residential courses targeted at the heads of small and medium-sized companies (Nikkeiren 1963: 11–12).

As can be seen from the foregoing short review of this aspect of its activity, Nikkeiren put much effort throughout the years 1948–60 into providing management training. Whatever success it had in this direction, management training could be described as a labour of Sisyphus. To stick with the metaphor of labour relations as a two-edged sword, the cutting edge of confrontation became increasingly superfluous as the years passed and the most militant unions were defeated. This meant that the reverse edge of routine practices became all the more important, leading to the need to equip ever more managers with the tricks of the personnel officer's trade. This was underscored when a number of labour disputes occurred unexpectedly in 1960 in hospitals, banks and other locations which were not normally associated with confrontational labour relations. Nikkeiren's comment on this turn of events captured nicely the Sisyphean nature of its management training mission: 'these [events] could also be considered a warning regarding generally backward labour management and showed the necessity for managers to be better educated' (Nikkeiren 1963: 9).

Lobbying

Nikkeiren was a vigorous lobbying body, issuing a stream of written opinions (*ikensho*), proposals (*kengi*), requests (*yōbō*), views (*kenkai*), representations (*mōshiire*), statements (*seimeisho*) and the like. The fine distinctions between these various vehicles for making known its ideas need not concern us here and we can refer to them all as 'lobbying instruments'. Nikkeiren's lobbying activity was particularly intense during its early years. For example, during 1948–55 Nikkeiren published 143 lobbying instruments, which was more than in any other period of eight years in its entire history. From this initial peak, the intensity of lobbying relatively declined during the remainder of the period that concerns us here (39 instruments over the five years 1956–60) but was far from negligible even so.

Looking at the issues which Nikkeiren's lobbying instruments addressed, naturally enough these covered a very wide range of matters that were of concern to employers. For comparative purposes, it is useful to group them thematically so as to be able to analyse quantitatively which issues attracted the bulk of Nikkeiren's attention, even though the exercise is somewhat imprecise owing to the difficulty of allocating every lobbying instrument to an appropriate category. The most frequent group of issues addressed by Nikkeiren's lobbying instruments during the period 1948–60 was insurance (health insurance, life insurance, unemployment insurance, social insurance, old-age insurance, etc.) which accounted for 26 out of the total of 182 (14.3 per cent). This was followed by wages problems (21 lobbying instruments or 11.5 per cent), tax issues (19 lobbying instruments or 10.4 per cent), labour legislation (17 lobbying instruments or 9.3 per cent), labour disputes (16 lobbying instruments or 8.8 per cent) and so on. To put the above categories into perspective, health and safety issues accounted for just six lobbying instruments (3.3 per cent).

Of course, quantitative data do not tell the whole story. The fact that over a period of 13 years there was only one lobbying instrument devoted to production control (*An Opinion on Production Control*, issued on 16 June 1948) does not signify that Nikkeiren was relatively unconcerned about this matter. What it does indicate is that the authorities reacted at an early stage after Nikkeiren's formation, and in a determined fashion, to enforce property rights and crack down hard on this form of struggle, so that there was no need for Nikkeiren to keep lobbying on this issue. By way of contrast, insurance and tax were examples of ongoing issues which could never be disposed of because they were not susceptible to a final solution in the same way that production control was. Insurance and tax represented unavoidable burdens on the employers, either directly or indirectly via the upward pressures exerted on wages, and therefore the perennial concern of Nikkeiren was to find ways to minimize these burdens by cutting payments, reducing benefits, shifting responsibility and using other devices. Another distinction which can be made between different thematic groups is the audiences to which they were addressed. In most cases, this was the government and related agencies (or, where appropriate, the Occupation authorities up to 1952). This was bound to be so in the case of labour legislation, for example, since ultimately it was the government which was responsible for enacting and enforcing laws. On the other hand, in the case of the thematic group 'wages', the target audience was not necessarily the government. Certainly, Nikkeiren *did* lobby the government on wage-related issues, such as civil servants' pay (five lobbying instruments over the period 1948–60) and the minimum wage (seven lobbying instruments). However, it also published other lobbying instruments which were clearly not aimed at government, but at the employing class as a whole. Typical examples would be *The Attitude of Managers towards the Wages Problems that Confront Us* (7 February 1950) and *Our View on the Wages Problems that Confront Us* (4 March 1955).

The fact that Nikkeiren directed part of its lobbying activity towards employers illustrates the relationship it had with those engaged in wage negotiations at grass roots level in the enterprises. While Nikkeiren became deeply involved in certain labour disputes, whose outcomes it felt were so crucial that they simply had to be won, it was beyond its capacity or intention to participate directly in each and every instance of wage bargaining. As noted earlier, Nikkeiren's structure was a federation of employers' associations. This meant that it had only indirect links with enterprises, at one remove from the regional and industrial associations to which they directly belonged. Hence Nikkeiren's relationship with the mass of employers was not structured in a way that would have permitted the issuing of orders to obedient followers. Instead, it had to rely on persuasion through argument and leading by example. Lobbying employers thus played a vital part in the twin processes of cementing Nikkeiren's organization and achieving its goals through influence and persuasion (Nikkeiren 1958: 1–3; 1963: 44–9).

Publishing

Shortly after its formation, Nikkeiren started to publish the *Nikkeiren Times* in August 1948. This appeared on a regular weekly basis and served both as a vital means of communicating with the membership and as a mouthpiece for presenting Nikkeiren's views to a wider public. As early as February 1947, the Kantō Managers' Association had launched a monthly called *Manager*. Nikkeiren subsequently took responsibility for this journal and used it as a vehicle for longer and more discursive articles on managerial themes than those carried by the *Nikkeiren Times*. Nikkeiren's third regular publication was *Labour Economy Law Reports*. This commenced publication in August 1950 and appeared once every ten days. Its purpose was to provide up-to-date coverage on recent cases which had set legal precedents in the realm of labour law.

In addition to these periodicals, Nikkeiren also published large numbers of books and booklets. In all, there were 218 titles published during the period 1948–60 (including four items published by the Kantō Managers' Association in a series which was taken over by Nikkeiren in March 1949, renamed *Materials on Labour* and which had reached Number 62 by August 1960). Perhaps symbolizing the changing priorities of employers as this period unfolded, the first title was *On the Illegality of Production Control*, which appeared in June 1948, and the last, published in December 1960, was *The Modernization of the Wages System and Job Analysis*.

While it would occupy too much space to give details of all the intervening titles, some of the principal themes can be picked out. There was a host of publications on labour management, including the 'Japanese way' of handling this (e.g. *The Tradition of Japanese-style Labour Management and Its Problems*, March 1960), labour relations (e.g. *Various Problems Connected with Labour–Management Cooperation*, March 1954), labour agreements (e.g. *A Dictionary of Revising Labour Agreements for Managers*, October 1948) and collective bargaining (e.g. *The Reality of Collective Bargaining in Our Country*, April 1955). Predictably enough, wages problems were well represented in the forms of both general treatments of the subject (e.g. *Stable Wages*, November 1959) and texts on particular aspects, such as efficiency pay (e.g. *The Wages System and Efficiency Pay*, August 1949). One important initiative was the launching of a series, *Nikkeiren's White Papers on Wages*, in 1959. This series had reached 17 volumes by 1968. During the period that concerns us here, the two volumes published in this series were *The Present State of Our Country's Labour Economy and Wages Problems* (January 1959) and *The Question of Achieving Stable Growth in the Japanese Economy and Wages Problems* (January 1960). Analyses of unions (e.g. *The Actual Circumstances of Enterprise Labour Unions in Our Country*, June 1954), labour disputes (e.g. *Workplace Struggles and Countermeasures against Them*, October 1955) and the Communist Party (e.g. *How Should Managers and Unions Fight against the Communist*

Party?, January 1950) were also frequent additions to Nikkeiren's list. It should also be noted that even prior to starting to publish *Labour Economy Law Reports* in August 1950, there was already considerable demand from employers for information on labour law in a readily usable form. From an early stage, Nikkeiren sought to meet this demand with its *Management Lawyer Series*, which commenced in March 1949 with *Collection I* and was swiftly followed by *Collection II* in July 1949. Then in July 1949 a series on *Collected Legal Precedents and Court Decisions Connected with Labour* was initiated. By August 1950 *Collections I–IV* in this series had been issued in rapid succession (Nikkeiren 1958: 264–5; 1963: 94).

Although the account given here of Nikkeiren's publishing activity has itemized only a fraction of its output, hopefully it has conveyed the scale of its efforts and given some idea of its content. As far as publishing was concerned, Nikkeiren hit the ground running when it was first established and continued thereafter to accord high priority to this field of activity. Through the printed word, it sought to arm employers with facts, arguments and ideology. While the quality of its material varied, the quantity could not fail to impress.

Issues

As a campaigning organization, during the period 1948–60 Nikkeiren engaged with many issues that affected employers. As a representative selection of these issues, Nikkeiren's efforts to advance the interests of employers in three directions will be considered here. First, Nikkeiren's endeavours to tilt the scales of justice to the advantage of the employers will be examined. Second, the campaign to reform education so as to equip workers with more of the qualities that companies required will be reviewed. Third, Nikkeiren's contribution to the crusade to drive up productivity will be assessed. By looking at these three policy areas in turn, an impression can be gained of the energy and perseverance that Nikkeiren brought to its various campaigns.

Labour legislation

When Nikkeiren was formed in April 1948, it regarded the various laws governing labour relations as overly favourable to the unions and insufficiently enforced even when they did have the potential to discipline the workforce. From its earliest days, it therefore started to lobby the government for the relevant laws to be changed. It has already been noted that Nikkeiren's first national conference, held on 9 September 1948, backed this line. After conferring with employers' representatives on the Labour Relations Commissions in February 1949, Nikkeiren issued the lobbying instrument *An Opinion on the Revision of the Labour Union Law and the Labour Relations Adjustment Law* on 19 March 1949 (Nikkeiren 1958: 1, 10).

Up to a point, Nikkeiren was pressing against an open door, since towards the end of 1948 the government had already legislated to prevent civil servants and the employees of public corporations from striking. As a further step down this path, the government amended both the Labour Union Law and Labour Relations Adjustment Law with effect from 10 June 1949. On the day before these amendments came into effect, Nikkeiren issued *An Opinion on the Enforcement of the Revised Labour Union Law* and *Guidelines Concerning Labour Relations Adjustment* (Nikkeiren 1958: 1). Despite this partially successful outcome to its lobbying, Nikkeiren was dissatisfied with the extent of the 1949 reforms and continued to push hard for further changes to the labour laws. On 23 June 1951 Nikkeiren presented two lobbying instruments to the government, *An Opinion on the Revision of the Labour Union Law and Labour Relations Adjustment Law* and *A Request Regarding the Revision of the Labour Standards Law* (Nikkeiren 1958: 2). Following this, the government asked two deliberative councils (*shingikai*) to look again at labour relations legislation and the Labour Standards Law respectively. Although the Labour Relations Adjustment Law was amended further in July 1952 and the Labour Standards Law was amended repeatedly between mid-1952 and July 1954 (Dower 1988: 340), the results were unsatisfactory from the standpoint of Nikkeiren and other employers' organizations, such as the Japan Chamber of Commerce and Industry. This accounts for the successive lobbying instruments on labour legislation that Nikkeiren continued to issue up until 1956. Not only did Nikkeiren press for the laws to be beefed up, but it also wanted the existing statutes to be enforced rigorously. A resolution to that effect was passed at its extraordinary general meeting in September 1949, for example (Nikkeiren 1958: 11).

One result of the 1952 electricity workers' and coal miners' labour disputes was that on 12 December 1952 Nikkeiren organized a Council for the Realization of a Law Regulating Strikes. Its chief organizer was Shikanai Nobutaka who was seconded from Nikkeiren for this purpose. The Council's objective was to secure legislation that would forbid strikes leading to power cuts in the electricity industry and strikes that jeopardized safety in the mines. This campaign was successful and a law regulating strikes in the electricity and coal industries for a fixed term of three years was passed during a special parliamentary session on 5 August 1953, despite fierce opposition from the unions. Three years later, battle was joined again and Nikkeiren's arguments for making the law permanent were articulated in its *Resolution on Retaining the Strike Regulation Law*, which was published on 19 November 1956. To Nikkeiren's satisfaction, the law cleared its last parliamentary hurdle on 8 December 1956 and became a permanent fixture on the statute book (Nikkeiren 1958: 14–18).

Throughout the decade of the 1950s Nikkeiren kept up the pressure on the government to use the full force of the law when trouble erupted in labour disputes. Nikkeiren was outraged at the affront to property rights when railway workers ran free trains as a tactic in their labour dispute in 1957 (Nikkeiren 1958: 18, 78). On 11 June 1958 its Executive Council issued *The New Stage and Our Views*, in which it lobbied the newly elected government of Prime Minister Kishi Nobusuke to 'establish law and order so as to normalize labour–management relations and reform the law in a way that would be based on the principle of equality between labour and management' (Nikkeiren 1963: 6). The following month, a serious dispute broke out at Ōji Paper, which was to last 145 days and involve violent clashes. Nikkeiren's extraordinary general meeting on 17 October 1958 was held against the background of the Ōji Paper dispute and again the demand was conveyed to the government that law and order be enforced. Similarly, the backdrop to Nikkeiren's annual conference on 21 April 1960 was the dispute at the Mitsui Miike Coal Mines. A *Resolution on the Eradication of Collective Violence* was passed as an emergency motion, in addition to the lobbying instrument *Our View on Coping with This Turning Point*, which called, among other things, for the enactment of 'a just law on labour–management relations' (Nikkeiren 1963: 9; 1981: 357–8). It is also worth noting that, starting in 1949, each November Nikkeiren organized a conference of labour lawyers. These conferences were the occasion for listening to reports on the latest developments in labour relations and discussing how to obtain the maximum leverage from the law. In 1959 strikes, lockouts and wages questions were examined as, legally speaking, the most urgent problems of the day. In 1960 the main items on the agenda were union splits, secondary unions and various types of labour and strike activity (Nikkeiren 1963: 10).

Nikkeiren was never afraid of the rough and tumble of direct confrontation and, on such occasions, was hardly a stickler for the law. Nevertheless, it was well aware of the power of the law and therefore of the importance of using it to the employers' advantage. This was the motivation behind its sustained efforts to wring the maximum benefit for employers from the labour laws.

Education

Nikkeiren took a typically philistine, employers' attitude towards education. It regarded education not as an end in itself, but as a process of instruction whereby workers could be equipped with skills that would increase their productivity. It was with this objective in mind that on 23 December 1954 it issued *A Request Concerning the Improvement of the Current Education System*, in which it criticized university education for leaning too much towards arts subjects and the law. In order to correct this imbalance, Nikkeiren wanted to see a shift towards technical education. Nikkeiren had set up a Special Committee on Education as early as September 1949 and this had studied ways of forging links between school education and the workplace (Nikkeiren 1958: 12). In 1956 this special committee was supplemented by a Technical Education Committee whose brief was to look into scientific and technical education. The result of its deliberations was *An Opinion on Technical Education to Meet the Demands of the New Era* which was presented to the government on 9 November 1956. This lobbying instrument recommended that a comprehensive system of scientific and technical education be established, extending right the way through from early schooling to university level. The purpose behind this was to produce technicians and skilled workers in sufficient numbers to meet the needs of businesses. The government responded positively and in 1957 asked the Central Educational Deliberative Council to suggest ways of promoting scientific and technical skills (Nikkeiren 1958: 17). While the deliberative council was working on this, Nikkeiren kept up the pressure with its *Opinion on the Promotion of Scientific and Technical Education* which it issued on 25 December 1957 (Nikkeiren 1958: 3). Nikkeiren's lobbying can therefore be considered as one of the factors that lay behind the passing of a Vocational Training Law on 2 April 1958 and the Central Educational Deliberative Council's report on 28 April 1958 which was entitled *A Plan for Promoting the Education of Working Youths*.

In addition to pressurizing the government to reorient education towards the needs of businesses, Nikkeiren encouraged other initiatives to provide technical training for the workforce in commercial companies. Perhaps the initial motivation for getting involved can be traced back to Nikkeiren's annual conference in April 1954. Employers at this conference complained about the education and training that was available to their workers. After the conference, an Industrial Training Subcommittee of Nikkeiren's Special Committee on Education looked into these shortcomings and recommended setting up a Japan Industrial Training Association (*Nihon Sangyō Kunren Kyōkai*). This suggestion was acted on and the Japan Industrial Training Association commenced operations in July 1955. Although Nikkeiren facilitated its creation, the association's formal status was an associate body that was legally and financially independent. At its formation, it was sponsored by 168 companies who then benefited from the on the spot training that the association provided. The fact that, by the end of 1957, the number of subscribing companies had risen to 416 was evidence of the need that the Japan Industrial Training Association fulfilled (Nikkeiren 1958: 17; 1981: 442). Rather confusingly, after the Vocational Training Law came into force, an existing body known as the Japan Association for Nurturing Skilled Workers (*Nihon Ginōsha Yōsei Kyōkai*) was reorganized in December 1958 to become the Japan Vocational Training Association (*Nihon Shokugyō Kunren Kyōkai*), with Nikkeiren again playing the role of facilitator. Eventually, the Japan Industrial Training Association and the Japan Vocational Training Association were to amalgamate, but that would be in 1965 and thus outside the period discussed here (Nikkeiren 1963: 7–8; 1981: 442–4).

For Nikkeiren, the reason behind education was not to widen human horizons and still less to encourage critical thought. Instead, Nikkeiren was wedded to a narrow view of education, which saw it as furnishing the means to produce better trained and therefore more productive workers. There was thus a considerable overlap between Nikkeiren's highly instrumental approach to education and its enthusiasm for productivity, the third example of a policy issue with which it engaged.

Productivity

In 1950s Japan 'productivity' was a term that was used to refer to both the concrete project to make Japanese commodities more competitive by reducing costs of production and the ideology that different social classes shared a common interest in improving economic efficiency by these means. Nikkeiren's first publication on the subject was *A Policy for Raising Labour Productivity in the Factory* (1951) and others followed, such as *The Movement to Raise Productivity and Labour Problems* (1955) and *Technical Change and Productivity* (1958) (Nikkeiren 1958: 264–5; 1963: 94). On 14 June 1954 Nikkeiren also initiated classes on productivity. Nikkeiren's enthusiasm for raising productivity was by no means unique, but was shared by the employing class generally. Hence not only Nikkeiren but also Keidanren, the Comrades' Association and the Japan Chamber of Commerce and Industry all backed the formation of the Japan Productivity Council (*Nihon Seisansei Kyōgikai*) in the spring of 1954 (Nikkeiren 1958: 16). The Ministry of International Trade and Industry proved no less enthusiastic and government funds were made available for what became virtually a national crusade. Indeed, there was an international dimension too, since the productivity movement fitted in with the USA's ambition to win over Japanese unions to its foreign policy tool, the International Confederation of Free Trade Unions, which had opened an office in Tokyo in 1953 (Gordon 1998: 50). It was thus with the blessing of numerous powerful supporters that a new body, the Japan Productivity Centre (*Nihon Seisansei Honbu*), was set up on 14 February 1955.

Productivity became fashionable in the middle of a decade when Nikkeiren's main priority was to defeat militant unions and win back the employers' 'right to manage'. It was therefore with good reason that Nikkeiren was perceived as a belligerent and confrontational organization that was ever ready to sally forth and do battle. However, just as the best prizefighters are those who combine brains with brawn, so Nikkeiren understood that labour could be more effectively tamed if there were carrots on offer as well as sticks. It was in this spirit that Nikkeiren related to productivity. It argued that the movement to raise productivity was the means to create a 'system of national cooperation' in which labour and management would work together for the common good and where the fruits would be split between capital, workers and consumers. If the quality of manufactured goods was raised, costs reduced and international competitiveness improved, each social group would benefit, since national income would grow, employment would be expanded and the standard of living would rise (Nikkeiren 1981: 315–17).

In contrast to Nikkeiren's pursuit of legal and educational reform, it did not need to pressurize the government on the issue of raising productivity. The government was as committed to the policy as anybody else, so lobbying would have been superfluous. In addition, it is fair to say that Nikkeiren's arguments in favour of raising productivity were not particularly original. To a large extent, its case was the same as that advocated by other enthusiasts for the idea. If there was anything distinctive about Nikkeiren's approach, it was its combination of soft words and harsh deeds. At the selfsame time that Nikkeiren was uttering honeyed words about the virtues of raising productivity and denying that this was a ploy for intensifying labour, it was involved in a succession of bitter labour disputes where companies invariably sought an outcome allowing for more work to be extracted from fewer workers. It was this irreducible gap between what Nikkeiren said and what it did that threw an illuminating spotlight onto productivity as a campaigning issue. Thanks to Nikkeiren, the real nature of productivity became clearer than it otherwise would have been.

Fighting Nikkeiren

In the remainder of this chapter, a number of labour disputes in which Nikkeiren became closely involved will be examined. In addition, an account will be given of the part played by Nikkeiren in the political repression from July 1950 onwards known as the 'red purge'. Then, from 1955, unions started to employ the strategy of *shuntō* ('the spring-season wages struggle') and accordingly Nikkeiren was forced to react. Nikkeiren's attempts during the latter half of the 1950s to devise a strategy to contain *shuntō* will therefore also be evaluated.

The Tōhō Film dispute

As noted earlier, the eruption of this dispute virtually coincided with the formation of Nikkeiren. It was this coincidence that made the Tōhō Film dispute such an 'important test case', as Nikkeiren itself put it (Nikkeiren 1981: 201). It was a test both of Nikkeiren's ability to mobilize its organization so soon after its formation and of whether securing 'the right to manage' was anything more than posturing and bluster. In addition, the dispute at Tōhō Film was significant in that the company's problems were typical of the difficulties facing so many enterprises in 1948. Tōhō Film was burdened with debt, considered itself to have too many staff and had no prospects of making profits without drastically overhauling its operations. It was the fact that so many companies could identify with this combination of circumstances that made Tōhō Film a 'symbol of enterprise reorganization' (Nikkeiren 1981: 220).

Although Tōhō Film had much in common with the predicament of innumerable other companies, what distinguished it was the management's determination to push ahead with restructuring the enterprise, even if this meant taking on the union. The employers announced a package of staff cutbacks on 8 April 1948 and it was this decision that ignited the dispute. The Sanbetsu-aligned union resisted Tōhō Film's move to slim down the workforce, whereupon the company cranked up the dispute with the announcement of further redundancies on 22 and 23 April (Rōdōshō Rōseikyoku 1979: 45). Nikkeiren backed Tōhō Film's uncompromising stand to the hilt and used this particular labour dispute as a peg on which to hang its general case for securing 'the right to manage'. Tōhō Film's involvement in the popular film industry gave it a high profile and Nikkeiren took advantage of this so that the *Opinion on Securing the Right to Manage*, which it issued on 10 May 1948, would create more of a stir. In phrases which conveyed Nikkeiren's resolve to stand full square behind Tōhō Film, the argument presented was that:

> The same company has been on the receiving end of an intense labour offensive by the union and, in the name of full employment, has to carry surplus staff over and above the limits that management can approve of. Let alone cutting back staff, they have not even been able to transfer them rationally. As a result, there has been a growth in unproductive business, a decline in efficiency and hence a one-way path to rising costs.
>
> (Nikkeiren 1981: 221)

Nikkeiren's conclusion was that: 'even though the Tōhō problem is nothing more than a single, unexpected instance of enterprise restructuring, the current measures taken by this company are a legitimate exercise of the right to manage for the purpose of company self-preservation' (Nikkeiren 1981: 233–4).

On 1 June the company formally closed its Kinuta Studio in Tokyo's Setagaya Ward, but the workers refused to vacate the property and occupied it instead. On 16 August the Tokyo District Labour Relations Commission put forward an arbitration plan, but this was rejected by both sides. Three days later the workers were driven out of the Kinuta Studio by the intervention of 1,800 armed police, backed by several hundred American troops, some of whom were in armoured vehicles (Fujita and Shiota 1963: 666). With this overwhelming force pitted against the employees, the outcome was no longer in doubt. Although the dispute dragged on for 195 days in all, when it was resolved, on 19 October 1948, victory clearly lay with the company. Despite the fact that Nikkeiren's support was indispensable for enabling Tōhō Film to win, for the most part it kept in the background. Nevertheless, the role it played was not lost on perceptive observers. Long before he became a renowned animator, Kawamoto Kihachirō was one of the occupiers at Tōhō Film. When questioned more than 50 years later, he recalled:

> Nikkeiren was the enemy . . . We were interested in making good films. Nikkeiren was interested in breaking the union. So there was no meeting of minds. We were on different wavelengths and couldn't talk to one another. The people Nikkeiren drafted in didn't know the first thing about film-making.
>
> (Kawamoto 2001)

When Nikkeiren looked back on the events at Tōhō Film in a similarly retrospective fashion, its conclusion was that 'managers learnt a great deal from this dispute' (Nikkeiren 1981: 234). Apart from the victory at Tōhō Film demonstrating to employers who had previously lost confidence that such disputes could be won, perhaps the most important lesson was that the Occupation authorities would now cooperate fully in breaking unions that were aligned with Sanbetsu, the union federation that was strongly influenced by the Communist Party. With their confidence boosted by the Tōhō Film victory, employers were only too ready to weed out 'uncooperative elements' within their workforce when the unfolding Cold War precipitated the red purge.

The Red Purge

The red purge was the name given to the waves of dismissals that swept through a succession of industries in the months following the outbreak of the Korean War in June 1950. Yet, although the purge properly so called did not get under way until after the Occupation authorities had banned 24 members of the Communist Party's Central Committee and 17 members of the editorial staff of the Communist Party newspaper *Akahata* (Red Flag) from holding office at the beginning of June 1950, unofficially it had commenced as early as 1949 (Nikkeiren 1981: 244). The ostensible targets of the purge were defined by Nikkeiren in *On Countermeasures for Excluding Red Elements* (2 October 1950) as follows:

1 Communist Party members
2 Secret members of the Communist Party (including those members who have faked their exit from the Party, estranged Party members and those expelled)
3 Those who, by their words and actions, can be recognized as fellow travellers of Communism.

(Shiota *et al.* 1984: 367)

By thereby casting the net widely enough to encompass anybody with a past, present or even suspected association with the Communist Party, the stage was set for a veritable witch hunt of whomever the employers wished to eliminate.

There is plenty of evidence that this is exactly how most employers chose to interpret the drive to weed out the 'reds'. When Hagio Tadachi, Head of Labour Affairs at Tōshiba, reported to Nikkeiren's National Conference of Personnel Managers on the long-running dispute in 1949 that involved the same company declaring about 6,000 workers redundant, he explained:

> When it came to reducing the number of staff, we made every effort to avoid inappropriate labour practices and did not consciously make members of the Communist Party the targets of redundancy. Instead, the ones we dismissed were those whom we considered unsuitable from the viewpoint of managerial efficiency (so-called uncooperative individuals).
>
> (Nikkeiren 1981: 245)

The following year, Hitachi announced more than 5,500 redundancies on 8 May 1950 which led to a labour dispute that lasted three months at the height of the red purge. Again, the company targeted 'uncooperative individuals' rather than Communist Party members as such, although Hitachi's President, Kurata Chikara, admitted that the purging of the Communist Party's leadership created a situation in which it was easier to implement the redundancies (Nikkeiren 1981: 246–7). In general, whichever the company, 'uncooperative individuals' was essentially code for Leftists of all persuasions and, above all, militant unionists. As the head of SCAP's Labour Division, Theodore Cohen, admitted in later years, 'although the reasons given for the discharges were uniformly for communist activity, the real reason is that those discharged were often the most energetic and effective union activists' (Cohen 1987: 449–50).

The red purge started properly on 25 July 1950 when 704 individuals in 50 companies in the newspaper, communications and broadcasting industries were dismissed. The following month, more than 2,000 workers in the electricity industry were sacked and from there the ripples spread to virtually all industries so that, by November 1950, more than 11,000 workers had been purged in private enterprises (Fujita and Shiota 1963: 670–1 and Rōdōshō Rōseikyoku 1979: 83). There was also a purge of government employees, but that need not concern us here, since Nikkeiren's role was to coordinate the purge in the private sector. In its official *10 Years' History*, Nikkeiren described its role with considerable pride:

> As for dealing with the red purge, Nikkeiren had prepared carefully. Via its industrial and regional associations, it could with speed and accuracy send out information on aims, methods, intelligence and so forth. Since it had devised scrupulous measures for achieving the ideological unity of managers, this huge operation could be completed in an unex-

pectedly orderly fashion. The reason why all the managers' associations could act as one body, with Nikkeiren at the centre, and complete this difficult undertaking within a short time was because each association had been through the previous two stages [see below] and strengthened their comradely unity. It is not too much to say that it could even be described as an event which stands out in the history of managerial bodies.

(Nikkeiren 1958: 13)

The types of measures which Nikkeiren recommended enterprises should take were detailed in the document *On Countermeasures for Excluding Red Elements*, which was referred to earlier. They included numerous forms of snooping, manipulation and repression, such as: 'keeping records of people's personal explanations', 'investigating and evaluating trends within the union', 'as far as possible, taking an understanding attitude towards healthy [sic] elements within the union', 'being on the lookout for careless attitudes, unguarded promises, inadvertent items of evidence and so on', 'positioning in the workplace employees who can be trusted' and 'securing all means of external and internal communication (telephones, etc.)' (Shiota *et al.* 1984: 368). Truly, at times it was difficult to know whether Nikkeiren was offering advice on how to run a factory or how to organize a prison! Even when the waves of dismissals had passed, Nikkeiren made sure that enterprises did not lower their guard. At a meeting of its Executive Council on 25 January 1951, the decision was taken to launch a movement to defend the workplace against sabotage and disruption. A Special Committee for Defending the Workplace was established and Nikkeiren's efforts included despatching instructors to all regions and publishing pamphlets on security measures (Nikkeiren 1958: 13; 1981: 7).

The goal that Nikkeiren was pursuing by means of the red purge is revealed by the way in which it periodized its early years. Whereas it identified April 1948 to September 1949 as 'the period of establishing the right to manage' and September 1949 to June 1950 as 'the period of the self-strengthening of management', it designated June 1950 to September 1951 as 'the period of establishing order within the workplace' (Nikkeiren 1958: 9–14). Even though all these descriptive labels overstate the concrete achievements, they convey Nikkeiren's ambitions accurately enough. One effect of the hammer blows that fell on combative unions during the red purge was that membership of Sanbetsu's industrial federations, which had reached 1.8 million in 1947, fell to 290,000 in the course of 1950 (Satō 1983: 4). In July 1950, Sōhyō was launched as an alternative umbrella organization with the blessing of the Occupation authorities, although it proved to be a less tame replacement for Sanbetsu than they would have wished.

The electric power dispute

The electric power dispute of 1952 has already cropped up at various points in this chapter, sometimes in association with the coal mining dispute with which it overlapped. Here it will be examined again, although the repetition of points made earlier will be avoided as far as possible. It was mentioned above that two reasons why the electric power dispute was so important for Nikkeiren were that the electricity workers' union (*Nihon Denki Sangyō Rōdō Kumiai* or Densan for short) was one of the most powerful unions in the early 1950s and that electricity was such a widely used source of energy throughout the Japanese economy. In addition, there were three further reasons why Nikkeiren was determined to thwart Densan. First, Densan was identified with a method of rationalizing wage rises that was very influential at the time. Second, the electricity workers had mastered a highly effective method of struggle which the employers had previously shown they were unable to counter. Third, Densan was not just powerful, but it was the foremost example in Japan of an industrial union, as opposed to the type of enterprise union with which the employers preferred to deal.

As far back as 1946, Densan had based its wage demands on a 'market basket' of consumer goods, its argument being that this representative selection of prices should be taken into account when calculating wage levels, so that workers would receive sufficient to support 'a healthy and cultured life'. The attraction of this Densan-style (*densangata*) system of wage calculation to workers who were haunted by economic insecurity hardly needs stressing (Kawanishi 1992: 102–4). Workers in many industries sought to emulate Densan's example and, by the time of the 1952 electric power dispute, the principle had already been incorporated into Sōhyō's wages strategy. Needless to say, 'market basket' calculations underpinned the wage claims that Densan put to the employers in 1952 and they similarly informed the parallel demands that the miners' union (Tanrō) put forward. Nikkeiren rejected as unrealistic and utopian the idea that wages should be calculated with reference to providing a healthy and cultured standard of living for workers and their families. One of its constituent industrial associations, the Coal Mining Industry League (*Sekitan Kōgyō Renmei*), told the miners that 'there is no need to mention demands based on the market basket method' and when Nikkeiren's Director, Maeda Hajime, denounced Densan as a labour aristocracy, it was with reference to their 'market basket' approach: 'calculating wages according to the market basket method, as Densan does, would be nothing more than satisfying the demands of a labour aristocracy' (Nikkeiren 1981: 264).

The tactics which Densan employed in 1952 were the same as in previous electric power disputes. It cut electricity supplies repeatedly by pulling out key workers in locations where their absence would have maximum effect. The beauty of these tactics was that enormous disruption and loss of production could be achieved through the absence of relative handfuls of workers. According to Nikkeiren's industrial association in the electric power industry (the Federation of Electricity Enterprises or *Denki Jigyō Rengōkai*) there were 15 waves of strikes over the period September to December 1952 and the total amount of power lost directly as a result of these stoppages was 280 million kilowatt hours. The resulting cost to factories and mines throughout Japan was estimated to be in the region of ¥26 billion. By way of contrast, the per capita loss of wages for those electricity workers directly involved in stoppages was only ¥3,200, which was a trifling amount when shared out among the entire membership of Densan (Nikkeiren 1981: 266–7).

The rapid growth in the union movement from 1945 had been accompanied by the popularization of the idea of industrial unions. Even though in reality many unions were enterprise based, both in their organization and their activity, commitment to an ideal of industry-wide unions which would unite all employees in the same line of work was widespread. Within this setting, where many unions fell short of the industrial model of organization to which they aspired, Densan was a rare example of a union which had thoroughly attained this goal. There were several reasons that accounted for this, but perhaps the principal one was that the electric power industry itself was highly centralized. Although there were different electricity generating enterprises, a single concern handled the distribution of electricity throughout the entire country. In addition, wage bargaining was centralized, with negotiations normally conducted between Densan and a joint employers' body (Kawanishi 1992: 134–44). What this meant was that, if Nikkeiren wished to deal a blow to the ideal and practice of industrial unionism, the nut it had to crack was Densan.

For all these reasons, Nikkeiren was aware of the threat to employers' interests posed by Densan from well before the 1952 dispute. Accordingly, it had organized committee meetings and roundtable discussions, where both the managers of electric power enterprises and specialists in labour law could pool their knowhow (Nikkeiren 1981: 265). The ultimate objective of such meetings was to study the feasibility of limiting the right to strike of electricity workers, a measure which, as we saw previously, was to be legally enforced from 1953. During the course of the 1952 dispute, Nikkeiren encouraged the electric power companies to move away from centralized pay bargaining and agree only to regional negotiations. As the dispute dragged on, Densan's solidarity cracked when first its Kansai section and then other regions opted for separate negotiations. This was to be the first nail in the coffin of Densan's industrial unionism (Kawanishi 1992: 160–2).

One of Nikkeiren's initiatives occurred at a conference of the chairmen of all its industrial associations which was held on 31 October. Out of this conference emerged a memorandum on *Matters of Agreement and Understanding*, which was a truly remarkable instance of class solidarity, particularly in view of the fractures that appeared in Densan's organization.

As was briefly mentioned earlier, the first item in the three point memorandum was that electrical technicians in all enterprises under the umbrella of Nikkeiren's industrial associations were to be mobilized. They would be despatched when necessary, so as to maintain operations in electric power companies as far as possible and minimize the impact of Densan's strikes. Second, the electric power companies committed themselves to make preparations to integrate into their operations the personnel despatched to assist them. Finally, and very importantly for the hard-pressed electric power companies, the expenses entailed in putting this plan into operation were to be borne collectively by all Nikkeiren's affiliated associations. As Nikkeiren rightly described this display of class-consciousness by the employers, these were 'cooperative countermeasures for handling the dispute, based on managers' solidarity' (Nikkeiren 1981: 267).

In addition to its organizational role during the electric power dispute, Nikkeiren engaged in forceful lobbying. Two lobbying instruments, *The Electric Power Dispute Could Continue for as Long as Ten Years* and *Concerning the Current Electric Power Dispute*, appeared on 31 October 1952 and were followed by *Our View on the Electric Power Dispute* on 20 November. The sensational title of the first of these was clearly intended to alarm public opinion, while the last was designed to bolster the employers' resolve to stand together and see the dispute through to a favourable outcome. In connection with the parallel coal mining dispute, Nikkeiren also issued *A Statement on Putting Emergency Regulations into Effect* on 8 December 1952. This was directed at the authorities at a time when the miners were preparing to withdraw maintenance staff in pursuit of their demands. The miners' union Tanrō ordered this step to be taken on 10 December and the government responded with emergency regulations on 15 December, which brought the miners' dispute to an end on the following day, after they had been on strike for 61 days (Rōdōshō Rōseikyoku 1979: 110–11). From these various examples, we can see that Nikkeiren aimed widely in its lobbying, seeking to influence the authorities, the employers and general public opinion.

For Nikkeiren, a key lesson of the electric power dispute was that class-wide solidarity was indispensable for defeating an enemy as formidable as Densan. This lesson was not forgotten when, for example, the employers confronted Tanrō in the epoch-making dispute at the Mitsui Miike Coal Mines several years later (see below). Nevertheless, despite the fact that the employers' solidarity paid off, the confrontation with Densan was a close enough call to reinforce Nikkeiren's determination to use state power in order to handicap strategically placed sections of the working class, such as the electricity workers. This was why, as was explained earlier, even before the electric power dispute was over, Nikkeiren initiated moves that would end in curtailing the electricity workers' right to strike.

The Nissan Motor dispute

The Nissan Motor dispute was by no means the first time that a union split in such a way that a tame alternative union came to eclipse an increasingly beleaguered original union. The Tōhō Film dispute resulted in the emergence of just such a second union and, during the course of the electric power dispute of 1952, second unions split away from Densan in more than one region. However, if one wanted a textbook case of a company (with Nikkeiren in the background) skilfully using these union-splitting tactics so as to encourage the establishment of a compliant second union, while destroying the combative first union, the Nissan Motor dispute would be a prime example. Certainly, one could say that the tactic was perfected by Nikkeiren in the Nissan Motor dispute and was used thereafter whenever required.

In 1953 the Nissan Motor Company was in poor financial shape and, to add to its problems, its workers were organized by Zenji (the *Zen Nihon Jidōsha Sangyō Kumiai* or All-Japan Automobile Industry Union) which had a record of militancy and was affiliated to Sōhyō. From the beginning of the Nissan Motor dispute, there was more at stake than just Nissan's future, since Zenji was an industrial union to which, for example, most workers at the rival Toyota Company also belonged. Hence, from the outset, Nikkeiren was clear that the battle plan at Nissan was to smash the industrial union Zenji so as to be able to redesign labour relations throughout the motor car industry and not just at Nissan. As Nikkeiren's Shikanai Nobutaka put it:

> Since this was the sort of strike that the management couldn't really cope with, the only course of action was to eliminate the union. That was the only way we were going to get anywhere. There was no alternative.
>
> (BBC 1990)

The immediate issues in the 1953 dispute were wages and the control of certain aspects of the production process. To back its demands, Zenji commenced sporadic work stoppages in June and then unlimited strikes in certain departments on 17 July. These latter were sufficient to bring all production at Nissan to a halt because of the integrated nature of manufacturing operations (Cusumano 1985: 149–50 and Nikkeiren 1981: 283). From then the dispute escalated until, on 5 August, the company instituted a lockout. Attempts by Zenji over the days that followed forcibly to open Nissan's factories resulted in some violence and the arrest of union leaders (Sōhyō 1964: 401). The turning point in the Nissan Motor dispute was the establishing on 30 August of a second union, whose very name (the *Nissan Jidōsha Rōdō Kumiai* or Nissan Automobile Labour Union) explicitly recognized its enterprise union character. Not only did Nissan immediately recognize the second union, but also it paid its members 60 per cent of their wages even while the factories remained closed, thereby offering a major inducement to workers who had been impoverished by the lengthy dispute to switch their allegiance from Zenji. No wonder that one of the slogans of the second union was 'those who love the union love the company'. In the face of such tactics, Zenji was forced to agree to the company's terms on 21 September and production resumed on 24 September. By the end of 1953, Zenji had shrunk to less than half the size of the second union and by December 1954 its membership was down to a few hundred and it had no alternative but to dissolve itself (Cusumano 1985: 156–7).

Nikkeiren's support for Nissan was essential in bringing about this sequence of events. As one of the Nissan employers, Ishihara Takashi, recognized: 'Nikkeiren gave us great support. They held meetings with us and advised us on anti-union tactics' (BBC 1990). Part of this advice was provided by Nikkeiren's labour lawyers, who instructed the employers on how to take steps like sacking the leaders of the first union at Nissan without falling foul of the law. Nevertheless, valuable though such assistance was, probably Nikkeiren's most vital role was to safeguard Nissan's market share and supply chain throughout the dispute, so that the company could give its undivided attention to defeating the union, without having to worry about rival companies undermining its prospects. It was Nikkeiren who persuaded Toyota and Isuzu not to step up production of their own models so as to capture sales that would otherwise have gone to Nissan. Nikkeiren also kept Nissan's suppliers in business during the dispute by arranging for other companies to place orders with them (Cusumano 1985: 155). It was thanks to Nikkeiren taking these steps that Nissan was cushioned from the worst effects of what was for any company a punishing dispute. Although the dispute cost Nissan dearly (about ¥650 million by the end of August 1953, according to Nikkeiren [Nikkeiren 1981: 285]; upward of ¥400 million is Cusumano's guestimate [Cusumano 1985: 160]) it was able to bear these losses, and thereby sustain a fight that was in the general interest of the automobile companies, because the arrangements that Nikkeiren set in place guaranteed that it would be able to resume profitable operations once the dispute was over.

A final word should be added about the relationship between the second union and the company. The Nissan Automobile Labour Union was an enterprise union not just in the sense that its organization existed within the same boundaries as the company, but also because of the interpenetration of union and company structures. In the years following the dispute, numerous union officials advanced to important positions within the company. David Halberstam has rationalized this phenomenon in terms of the managerial mind-set of the second union leaders: 'Yes, they were union leaders, but they were white-collar men of middle management, and their ambitions were managerial. They were an extension of management' (Halberstam 1987: 186).

However, this understates the trajectory followed by many of those at the heart of the second union. Michael Cusumano revealed that, in 1979, 10 directors on the Nissan Board had been members of the 'study group' out of which the second union developed, while five others from the same background became presidents of smaller companies affiliated to the Nissan group (Cusumano 1985: 159). These were not white-collar employees or middle-ranking managers, but men who achieved the status of employers. In later years, Nikkeiren would use such examples to fashion the ideology that Japan was a classless society because of the frequency with which union officials became company executives. Such ideological claims will be examined in the appropriate chapters. Here it is sufficient to note Nikkeiren's satisfaction that the outcome of the Nissan Motor dispute was the blurring of distinctions between company and union. This satisfaction was compounded because it was not an outcome that was confined to Nissan alone. The destruction of the industrial union Zenji meant that the separate enterprise unions which replaced it in different companies became the norm throughout the entire automobile industry.

The Ōmi Silk Thread dispute

The dispute at Ōmi Silk Thread was unusual in that many of the leaders of Nikkeiren felt awkward about the stand taken by the company. Although Ōmi Silk Thread was a sizeable company which employed about 13,000 workers, its oppressive paternalism was more typical of the idiosyncratic behaviour of some small enterprises. Its President, Natsukawa Kakuji, was a devout Buddhist who expected his employees to be of the same persuasion. A large Buddhist altar was erected on the company premises and workers were expected to sit in front of it listening to homilies or to the teaching of the priest, who was frequently invited to come and preach. President Natsukawa was convinced that he knew what was best for his mainly young and female workforce, with the result that the protracted strike that broke out at Ōmi Silk Thread on 4 June 1954 was styled a 'human rights dispute'. Among the mill girls' grievances were demands for 'freedom of belief', 'privacy of correspondence' and 'freedom of marriage' (Nikkeiren 1981: 295–307).

The Ōmi Silk Thread dispute lasted 106 days and was only finally settled on 16 September 1954 when both sides accepted the arbitration of the Central Industrial Relations Commission (Rōdōshō Rōseikyoku 1979: 130–1). It involved much bitterness and several violent incidents at Ōmi Silk Thread factories. Although the company employed various tactics which Nikkeiren had developed in previous confrontations, such as promoting a tame second union, this was a dispute that uncharacteristically divided the Nikkeiren leadership. For some, like Maeda Hajime, it was sufficient that the company was in conflict with its workforce. For those who took this view, Nikkeiren was an employers' organization and was therefore duty bound to offer assistance to fellow employers at times of dispute. However, Sakurada Takeshi reacted as follows to Maeda's line of reasoning:

I suppose that was common sense, but, as for me, I couldn't go along with it. I said, wasn't what they were doing opposed to the ideals of management? You know, as proof of that, even his fellow employers in the spinning business were biting in their criticism of what he was doing. That's within the same management camp. So, because Nikkeiren had to take a cautious attitude towards backing the Ōmi Silk Thread management, we ended up taking a neutral stand.

(Nikkeiren 1981: 732)

Even more acerbic in his criticism was Shikanai Nobutaka. Ōmi Silk Thread's President, Natsukawa Kakuji, fell ill during the dispute and was admitted to Hibiya Hospital in central Tokyo. Shikanai visited him there on as many as seven or eight occasions, in an effort to convince him to back down:

The reason I went was to tell him, 'You should give up; this is a dispute you shouldn't be fighting'. I don't know how many times I went to reason with him. But, you know, he was extraordinarily obstinate and bigoted. He wouldn't accept it at all. So, for Nikkeiren, it was a pretty difficult dispute to handle.

(Nikkeiren 1981: 732)

No doubt these divisions within Nikkeiren were partly responsible for the fact that (unusually for this period) victory in this dispute, on balance, lay with the union. For the majority of Nikkeiren's leaders, the Ōmi Silk Thread dispute was painful evidence of the continuing backwardness of much labour management in Japan. They reached this conclusion not because the company was heavy handed in the way in which it treated its employees or because of the intrusive interest it took in their ideas. Such behaviour was often displayed by employers who nevertheless could rely on Nikkeiren's enthusiastic support. Rather it was that Nikkeiren saw the essence of modern labour management as lying in the extent to which employers focused on production as an exercise in profit acquisition. Ōmi Silk Thread was criticized not because its methods were coercive, but because whether its employees entertained Buddhist or other ideas was irrelevant to the business of buying labour power and using it to generate profits. In that sense, the majority of Nikkeiren's leaders saw employers like Natsukawa Kakuji as still ensnared in premodern attitudes, a conclusion which flowed from Nikkeiren's equating of modernity with production for profit.

Shuntō

Shuntō was an abbreviation of *shunki chingin tōsō* (spring-season wages struggle) and was a strategy of coordinating the otherwise disjointed campaigns to raise wages which workers pursued in various industries. Much more will be said about *shuntō* in the next chapter, since it became a major preoccupation of Nikkeiren during the 1960s and later. In the context of this chapter, however, it will suffice to note the emergence of *shuntō* from 1955 and the inadequacy of Nikkeiren's early responses to this new strategy.

Shuntō was reputed to have been the brainchild of a leading union official, Ōta Kaoru, who proposed the idea in late 1954 when he was head of the National Federation of Synthetic Chemical Industry Workers' Unions. As a result, a Joint Struggle Council was organized on 23 December 1954. This was comprised of union federations in coal mining, paper and pulp, the private railways and electric power, in addition to Ōta's synthetic chemicals federation. In January 1955 they were joined by union federations in metalworking and electrical machinery, plus another federation of chemical unions (Kume 1988: 665–6 and Kōshiro 1983: 219). Unions in all these industrial sectors attempted to achieve a coordinated push on the wages front, agreeing to synchronize their work stoppages for added effect. Thus the 'first wave' of strikes was scheduled for 27–8 March, the 'second wave' for early April and so on (Rōdōshō Rōseikyoku 1979: 138). In practice, achieving this degree of coordination across eight union federations comprised of roughly 700,000 workers was not easy, but nevertheless the underlying strategy met with sufficient success for *shuntō* to become a regular annual event thereafter (Sōhyō 1964: 469).

Nikkeiren responded to the first *shuntō* with *Our View on the Current Wages Problems* which was published on 4 March 1955. This lobbying instrument was addressed to the employers and essentially called on them to hold the line on wages. It identified cost reduction as the top priority facing companies in 1955 and argued that, in order to achieve this, productivity had to be improved and 'rationalization of the wages system carried forward' (Sōhyō 1964: 464). However, the outcome was not entirely satisfactory from Nikkeiren's standpoint. Its own survey subsequently revealed that the average wage rise achieved as a result of the 1955 *shuntō* was just over 5 per cent. Although this was about 2 per cent lower than the corresponding figure for 1954, the Sōhyō union confederation (to which most of the unions participating in *shuntō* were affiliated) regarded the outcome as reasonably successful under the circumstances: 'amid calls for a wages freeze, wage rises were achieved to a greater or lesser extent' (Sōhyō 1964: 469). One of the circumstances to which Sōhyō was referring was Nikkeiren's fierce opposition to wage rises.

Nikkeiren's March 1955 call to arms on 'wages problems' set the tone for a stream of similar documents published in anticipation of each *shuntō* over the following years. The message invariably conveyed was that the employers should stand firm on wages and even the titles of these publications were perennially similar to the point of monotony: *Present Wages Policy and Wages Problems* (18 January 1957), *The Current Japanese Economy and Wages Problems* (16 January 1958), *The Present State of Our*

Country's Labour Economy and Wages Problems (20 January 1959) and *The Question of Achieving Stable Growth in Japan's Economy and Wages Problems* (25 January 1960). While Nikkeiren thus responded to *shuntō* with regular exhortatory appeals to the employers, it was caught unprepared by this new strategy and had no real answer beyond exhortation. In the late 1950s, Nikkeiren was still mainly devoting its efforts to securing 'the right to manage' and to what it called 'normalizing labour–management relations'. With its attention primarily focused on these objectives, it had not yet devised an effective counter-strategy for dealing with the new challenges thrown up by the class struggle in the shape of *shuntō*.

The Mitsui Miike coal mines dispute

The epic struggle at Miike in 1959–60 was a fitting end to a period which saw the repeated defeats of combative unions, followed by the imposition of tighter controls on the workforce and the introduction of more intensive working practices. The particular background to the Miike dispute was the so-called 'energy revolution' which involved the switch from coal to cheaper, imported oil throughout much of Japanese industry. For example, whereas in 1955 more than 90 per cent of the electricity generated in thermal power stations was derived from coal, this had fallen to 63 per cent by 1960 and to 45 per cent by 1965 (Samuels 1987: 113). Faced with these relentless market forces, the watchword of the mining companies was 'increased efficiency', which for the miners translated as cuts in their numbers and pressure to increase productivity. While this set of circumstances affected the entire coal mining industry, Miike became the focal point for a showdown for two reasons. First, the Miike mines were owned by the giant Mitsui combine, which occupied a key position at the heart of Japanese capitalism. Second, the local union at Miike was reputed to be among the strongest in Japan at that juncture and hence a jewel in the crowns of both Tanrō and Sōhyō.

On 19 January 1959 Mitsui Mining presented to the unions a plan for roughly 6,000 voluntary redundancies so as to achieve increased per capita output in its mines. Over the following months there was a good deal of sparring between the two sides, with the number of redundancies proposed by Mitsui Mining consistently running into thousands and the unions responding with strikes and other forms of resistance (Fujita and Shiota 1963: 684–6 and Rōdōshō Rōseikyoku 1979: 193–206). What finally brought matters to a head was when Mitsui Mining issued dismissal notices to 1,277 Miike workers on 10 December 1959. The local union refused to accept these redundancies and initially called a succession of 24 hour strikes, but from there the dispute escalated to the point where the company enforced a lockout on 25 January 1960 (Rōdōshō Rōseikyoku 1979: 214–19). What had raised the temperature to boiling point was Mitsui Mining's provocative announcement that, among its planned dismissals, it intended to eliminate '300 obstructors of production who disrupt work-place discipline', a move which Nikkeiren strongly endorsed (Nikkeiren 1981: 351–6). Needless to say, this was a reference to union activists and others whom the company regarded as undesirables. In a development which had by this stage become standard practice in labour disputes, a second union was established on 17 March 1960 and violent clashes occurred with the first union when the former sought to return to work. One of the focal points of confrontation between pickets and the police became the 'hopper', from where consignments of coal to customers were despatched (Sōhyō 1964: 712–19, 763). These clashes built up to massive proportions so that, by July, up to 10,000 pickets were manning the front line daily. Enormous demonstrations were also organized with, in total, about 300,000 unionists from all over Japan turning out to show support at various times during the height of the dispute between March and July 1960 (Nikkeiren 1981: 367 and Sōhyō 1964: 726).

Nikkeiren was quick to realize that there was more at stake at Miike than just the future of the coal industry. While it established on 27 July 1959 an Extraordinary Committee on Policy for Coal to study the specific issues affecting that industry, an emergency resolution was passed at Nikkeiren's extraordinary general meeting in October 1959 which called on the entire organization of employers to deal with the coal problem in a united fashion (Nikkeiren 1963: 9). Accordingly, Nikkeiren urged employers from all industries (and not just coal) to furnish Mitsui Mining with material and moral support. Nikkeiren worked hard to establish a support network for Mitsui Mining and was well placed to do so by virtue of its organizational structure, which included its industrial association in the coal industry, the Japan Coal Mining Industry Managers' Council (*Nihon Sekitan Kōgyō Keieisha Kyōgikai*). Nikkeiren also used its well developed publicity machine to 'arouse public opinion for a just labour movement', as it put it (Nikkeiren 1963: 10). It was mentioned earlier that, with reference to the ongoing struggle at Miike, a *Resolution on the Eradication of Collective Violence* was passed at its annual conference in April 1960 and this was then widely publicized. From the deliberations of the Extraordinary Committee on Policy for Coal emerged *The Future of the Coal Industry and a Policy for Dealing with the Unemployed* which was published on 13 November 1959.

Thanks to the efforts of Nikkeiren and the other companies in the coal mining industry, a formidable support system for Mitsui Mining was constructed. Both Tanrō and Sōhyō were as aware as Nikkeiren of how much was at stake in the Miike dispute. With about 200,000 members, Tanrō was not just one of the largest union federations in Japan, but one of the last representatives of industrial unionism. It was therefore clear that, if its local section at Miike was defeated, it would not only be a major setback for the Sōhyō confederation, to which Tanrō was affiliated, but also would sound the death knell for industrial unions. As a result, the unions dug deep into their reserves to assist the Miike struggle. Tanrō subsequently revealed that, between November 1959 and October 1960, a total of ¥2,145 million was paid out from the strike fund. Although this was a considerable sum, it was only achieved by running up a deficit of more that ¥252 million, while 6,550 members of the first union at Miike had between them incurred debts of more than ¥140 million by the end of the dispute (Nikkeiren 1981: 367). These figures are worth recording because they put into perspective the financial backing that Mitsui Mining could count on via the support system that had been established. A total of eight banks collectively provided the company with three successive tranches of funds: ¥3,300 million at the end of 1959, ¥1,320 million on 27 April 1960 and ¥2,280 million on 28 October 1960 (Nikkeiren 1981: 357). In all, this came to the staggering sum of ¥6,900 million, which completely dwarfed the union's fighting fund. For example, despite its 3.6 million members, Sōhyō was able to contribute only about ¥650 million to the Miike struggle (Sōhyō 1964: 726).

In addition to financial aid, Mitsui Mining also received invaluable material support. A Japan Coal Association existed which essentially consisted of the largest companies in Nikkeiren's Japan Coal Mining Industry Managers' Council. In January 1960, just prior to the lockout being declared at Miike, the Japan Coal Association signalled that it was ready to keep Mitsui Mining supplied with coal and would even bear the costs of transportation. This meant that, even if Mitsui Mining were unable to extract coal at Miike, or were prevented from moving coal off site, its customers would be guaranteed supplies. In effect, since they recognized that the dispute was being fought on behalf of the industry as a whole, rival companies were signalling their readiness to supply Mitsui Mining's customers at their own expense and not make inroads into its market share. It was because such contingency plans had been carefully prepared that Nikkeiren was able to declare 'since a system of both financial and marketing aid has already been established, coupled with the support of public opinion, let us encourage the company to carry through its original intention in a resolute fashion' (Nikkeiren 1981: 356).

The Miike dispute lasted for 282 days. The longer it went on, the more the advantage lay with the employers, owing both to the resources at their disposal and their impressive solidarity. By way of contrast, the local union was fighting on two fronts, since it had lost nearly half its members to the second union by the closing stages of the dispute (Fujita and Shiota 1963: 550). The Central Labour Relations Commission put forward an arbitration proposal on 10 August 1960, which was acceptable to the company, but not to the first union. A revised arbitration proposal was tabled on 28 October and this was signed by both sides the following day. Production was eventually resumed on 1 December 1960 (Rōdōshō Rōseikyoku 1979: 236–41). Although the Miike dispute was settled by arbitration, and despite the relief measures that redundant miners obtained, it was undoubtedly a victory for the employers.

What this chapter has demonstrated is the crucial role that Nikkeiren played in so many labour disputes and other developments that occurred during the period 1948–60, the cumulative effect of which was to strengthen Japanese capitalism in general and the position of the employers in particular. Over the years 1948–60 the employers decisively regained 'the right to manage', while many workers were taught the hard way where power lay and who were the bosses. In achieving its goals, Nikkeiren's effectiveness was bolstered by the background from which it had emerged and which was reviewed in the previous two chapters. In purging the 'reds' and eliminating what were perceived as 'extremists' from the workplace, Nikkeiren's members could draw on years of experience before and during the war, when snooping on the workforce and suppressing radicals had been standard practices. Likewise, relying on state power in order to break strikes, or even to deprive broad sections of the workforce of the legal right to strike, was a practice that was second nature to Nikkeiren's early members and left them untroubled by democratic scruples. From Nikkeiren's standpoint, one of the major achievements of the period 1948–60 was the defeat of industrial unions and their replacement by enterprise unions. These enterprise unions were more inclined to cooperate with the employers than their industrial counterparts and thus represented a step in the direction of the spineless company unions of prewar days. While it would be going too far to say that postwar enterprise unions were simply reincarnations of the prewar company unions, it would be fair to suggest that the company union was an ideal which many Nikkeiren members harboured as they endeavoured to split the combative unions that initially confronted them and replace them with tame 'second' unions. Even the bosses' class consciousness and solidarity, which made such a major contribution towards achieving the successes of 1948–60, could be said to derive from the élitist camaraderie of prewar employers, since this exclusive frame of mind swiftly reasserted itself after the brief flirtation with labourist ideology from 1945 to 1947.

It is true that, as the Ōmi Silk Thread dispute showed, the background from which Nikkeiren emerged was not necessarily consistently beneficial. In that dispute, the legacy of prewar paternalism distorted the employer's business sense and was an obstacle to the effective acquisition of profit. Even Nikkeiren's leadership was not immune to the tensions which flowed from this. Nevertheless, on balance, Nikkeiren's background helped rather than hindered its leading role in the counter-attack which the employers undertook during the period 1948–60. Despite the largely advantageous legacy of Nikkeiren's past, however, the path of capitalism is rarely smooth and by the 1960s Japan was entering a new phase which would require different responses from those for which Nikkeiren's background had equipped it.

5 Simultaneously applying the accelerator and the brake

High speed growth and the attempt to rein in wages (1961–73)

On the face of it, the period 1961–73 should have been a golden age for Nikkeiren. One after another, militant unions had been defeated in the succession of major labour disputes which had punctuated the earlier period 1948–60. With the end of the massive struggle at Mitsui Miike Coal Mines in late 1960, it was difficult to draw any other conclusion than that union strength was no match for the power of the employers, particularly when the latter were led by a determined and resourceful organization like Nikkeiren. In addition, the Japanese economy had already entered a phase of spectacular economic growth by the late 1950s and this was to be maintained, virtually without interruption, throughout the period 1961–73. Only once (in 1965) did the annual rate of economic growth fall below 5 per cent and the annual average compound growth rate for the years 1960–73 was 9.9 per cent, compared to 4.1 per cent in the USA, 4.5 per cent in West Germany and 5.5 per cent for the world as a whole (*Financial Times*: 22 July 1982).

With a string of victories over labour lying behind it, an unprecedented economic boom in full swing and a business-friendly Liberal Democratic Party permanently in office, one might have expected Nikkeiren to be well placed to exercise a controlling influence over the course of events. Why this was not so, and why instead Nikkeiren found itself struggling to adapt to developments that it had not anticipated, will be the theme of this chapter. Only towards the end of the period under consideration here did Nikkeiren start to improvise a strategy that was more in tune with the conditions prevailing within Japanese capitalism between 1961 and 1973. This change of orientation involved moderating the confrontational behaviour which had become its hallmark during the period 1948–60 and had earned it the nickname 'fighting Nikkeiren'. Confrontation would never entirely be abandoned by Nikkeiren, but it gradually learned that, under the conditions created by rapid economic growth, manipulation and mystification could be more effective methods of achieving its goals than a direct assault.

Economic growth

Japan's economic growth in the 1960s and early 1970s was phenomenal, both in terms of its breakneck speed and the length of time over which this headlong progress was maintained. Although there were exceptions to the string of spectacular advances, such as the contraction of the coal industry, the overall performance of the economy resembled an unstoppable juggernaut. The heavy and chemical industries were among the top performers, as the example of shipbuilding demonstrates. While by 1973 Japan represented 8.3 per cent of total world economic production (compared to 26.9 per cent in the USA and 5.4 per cent in West Germany) in the case of shipbuilding, the proportion constructed in Japanese shipyards rose to fully one half of the new tonnage launched throughout the world (*The Times:* 17 January 1973 and *Financial Times:* 7 February 1994).

The prevailing mood in capitalist circles during the 1960s was 'everything for the economy', with an utter disregard for the havoc wreaked on the environment. A public opinion survey conducted by the Prime Minister's Office in 1971 revealed that 60 per cent of respondents believed that their local environment was being destroyed and, by 1973, this was up to 70 per cent, with most identifying industrial waste and automobile exhaust fumes as the chief culprits (Crump 1996: 117). 'High speed growth' and 'income doubling' were the catchphrases of the time and the government endeavoured to arouse popular enthusiasm for every economic milestone that was passed. With much fanfare, the Economic Planning Agency announced on 10 June 1969 that Japan's GNP had surpassed West Germany's and hence was now in second place in what was referred to as the 'capitalist' or 'free' world, behind the USA. At the same time, and rather less flatteringly, it revealed that Japan's ranking was as low as twentieth in the international table for per capita national income (Mainichi Shinbun 1989: 849).

Clearly, high speed economic growth and the soaring profits that accompanied it were good news for Japanese capitalism, but they brought with them associated problems which were less welcome. One of the consequences of Japan's economic rise and its penetration of overseas markets was that it came under considerable pressure (particularly from the USA) to dismantle trade barriers and open up its own market. As the 1960s progressed, Japan's balance of trade first moved into the black and then registered ever larger surpluses. As early as 24 June 1960 a ministerial conference had adopted the goal of liberalizing 80 per cent of trade and foreign exchange over the next three years (Iwanami Shoten 1991: 430) but the flood of Japanese exports ensured that eye-catching targets alone would not be sufficient to placate other nation-states and that pressure on Japan would be maintained for further concrete steps. In just five years between 1967 and 1971, the value of Japanese exports increased by 130 per cent (Nakamura 1985: 89) which set the context for a report on Japan's trade issued by the OECD in September 1969 and the so-called 'Nixon shock' of August 1971.

The OECD report of 1 September 1969 emphasized the need for further liberalization of Japan's market in view of the size of its by now habitual balance of payments surplus (Iwanami Shoten 1991: 470). The 'Nixon shock' referred to the US President's decision, which was announced on 15 August 1971, to suspend temporarily the convertibility of the dollar and to impose a 10 per cent surcharge on imports into the USA (Mainichi Shinbun 1989: 892). Ultimately, the chain of events which this induced led to a long-term appreciation of the yen relative to the dollar. Having been pegged since 1949 at ¥360 to the dollar, the average exchange rate shifted to ¥348 during 1971, ¥303 in 1972 and ¥271 in 1973 (Nikkeiren 1981: 552). Although these moves had the effect of making Japan's exports more expensive in its principal overseas market, they did not eliminate the trade surplus with the USA which, on the contrary, proved to be resistant to American complaints and corrective measures alike (Nakamura 1981: 218).

Lying behind the specific issue of Japan's overseas trade balance was Japanese capitalism's increasing integration into the world economy. The most stunning evidence of the degree to which Japan was vulnerable to events beyond its borders came in October 1973 with the massive increases in the price of petroleum known as the 'oil shock'. Japan was hit harder than almost any other country owing to its lack of appreciable oil reserves and its virtually total dependence on imports. Yet, even without a body-blow such as the oil shock, it had been apparent to Nikkeiren for many years prior to 1973 that, as Japan gradually succumbed to outside pressure to liberalize its trading regime and ease controls on the movement of capital, its enterprises had no alternative but to raise their competitiveness by reducing costs and increasing productivity (Nikkeiren 1963: 12–13). Amalgamation of Japanese companies in order to meet the challenge of foreign competition was another outcome of the same process, with Yawata Iron and Steel and Fuji Iron and Steel providing a notable example when they merged in 1969–70 to form the Nippon Steel Corporation. Yawata and Fuji were the fourth and fifth largest steel producers in the world, with outputs of 15.3 million tonnes and 13.8 million tonnes respectively in 1969. By merging, they were better placed to compete with the then giants of the world industry, United States Steel (31.5 million tonnes) and the British Steel Corporation (24.4 million tonnes) (*The Times:* 26 August 1970).

A second major repercussion of high speed economic growth was the shortage of labour power that Japanese companies experienced. Many companies were deeply worried by this trend and its implications for labour discipline and wage rates. This anxiety was conveyed to Nikkeiren and hence one of its constant preoccupations throughout the period 1961–73 became how to ensure an adequate supply of labour power, equipped with the necessary skills, for industries that were experiencing sustained economic expansion. In response to the tightness of the labour market, in the summer of 1961 Nikkeiren established an Extraordinary Committee for Surveying the Supply of and Demand for Labour. This committee surveyed companies' present and future requirements over the next few years for different categories of workers. It issued a report on 19 June 1962, which was then published on 10 September as Number 72 in Nikkeiren's *Materials on Labour* series, under the title *Prospects for the Supply of and Demand for Labour Power up to 1965*. This report was particularly concerned that enterprises' performance should not be retarded by inadequate supplies of technical and skilled grades of labour power (Nikkeiren 1963: 14, 94; 1981: 19).

The scale and intractability of the problem of companies obtaining sufficient numbers of workers to meet their needs became clear when the issue was again examined at Nikkeiren's annual conference on 22 April 1970. In the report delivered to the conference on the current labour situation it was predicted that, over the next seven years, 17.27 million workers would need to be recruited by Japanese enterprises in order to fill new posts and replace those retiring. The same report's estimate was that, over this period, only 8.3 million young people would leave school or graduate from university, resulting in a shortfall of almost 9 million workers (Nikkeiren 1981: 535). It is true that the methodology on which this report was based was flawed, since it extrapolated past rates of growth into the future, whereas in reality the oil shock lay just over the horizon. Nevertheless, the very fact that the issue of meeting the projected demand for labour power was again tackled at Nikkeiren's 1970 annual conference does provide a useful indication of the extent to which employers were agitated by this corollary of high speed growth.

Nikkeiren's strategy

With the economy booming and labour power in short supply, wage earners were in a sellers' market during most years between 1961 and 1973. In 1961 the average pay increase secured in large enterprises during *shuntō* not only for the first time broke through the ¥2,000 per month barrier, but also was only marginally below ¥3,000 per month. The precise figure was ¥2,970, which was equivalent to a 13.8 per cent rise in average wages in large enterprises. This was a significant improvement on the ¥1,792 average increase (8.7 per cent) achieved in similar enterprises in 1960. From then on, throughout the rest of the period under consideration here, the average percentage increase in wages conceded to workers in large enterprises in successive *shuntō* was consistently in double figures, with the sole exception of 1963 (¥2,237 or 9.1 per cent). Furthermore, owing to escalating inflation, particularly in the early 1970s, wage settlements became locked into an ever ascending spiral. In the 1968 *shuntō*, the average pay increase in large enterprises was ¥5,296 per month (13.6 per cent) which cleared the ¥5,000 hurdle for the first time. In 1972, the ¥10,000 barrier was broken, with an average rise in large enterprises of ¥10,138 per month (15.3 per cent) and the following year a new record was set in the form of an average increase of ¥15,159 per month (20.1 per cent) (Nikkeiren 1981: 653).

Of course, the data which have been referred to here provide only a one-sided picture of the total situation that workers experienced, since they refer merely to nominal wages. The cumulative effect of these nominal wage rises was that, in 1973, the monthly salaries of workers on the permanent payroll of large enterprises were roughly four times as high as they had been at the end of the previous period in 1960 (Kōshiro 1983: 223). Obviously, this did not mean that such workers were actually four times better off in 1973 than they had been in 1960. The rise in consumer prices had a major effect on real wage levels and productivity increases were no less relevant to the total picture, since they affected the relationship between the value that workers produced during their labour and the diminished portion of that value which came back to them in their wage packets. Inflation and productivity are issues that will therefore be examined later in the chapter, but here it is appropriate to focus on nominal wage increases because it was the rising level of these from 1961 that alarmed Nikkeiren and induced it to formulate a hard-line response. Faced with the rising tide of wage increases from 1961, Nikkeiren's reaction was to mobilize the organization it had constructed between 1948 and 1960 so as to control wage costs, raise productivity and improve labour skills. Its justification for doing so was the heightened international competition which it saw Japanese capitalism as facing. This set of attitudes was not confined to Nikkeiren, but was widely shared by Japanese employers. What was distinctive about Nikkeiren was the importance it attached to employers' solidarity and squaring up to labour as the means to bring wages under control. As for raising productivity and improving labour skills, Nikkeiren saw another of its functions as pursuing its management training initiatives, so as to equip managers with the techniques needed to get more out of labour.

Wages

Nikkeiren's opening shot in the 1961 *shuntō* was to publish in January its annual *White Paper on Wages* which was entitled *The New Stage of the Japanese Economy and Wages Problems* and was intended for employers to use as a factual manual and handy source of arguments in the negotiations over wages. Nikkeiren's line was that, despite buoyant economic conditions, caution was needed owing to uncertainty in overseas markets and the threat of foreign competition as Japan's economy was opened up. To this end, Nikkeiren's leadership conferred with the top executives of all the major industries prior to the negotiations over wages, but the outcome of an average 13.8 per cent wage rise in large enterprises was way beyond what it had envisaged. Nikkeiren's disappointment at this outcome was palpable at its annual conference in April 1961, where one of its directors, Maeda Hajime, delivered the report on the current labour situation and referred to 'the wages wrung from us by sheer force' (Nikkeiren 1963: 13).

In response to this setback, Nikkeiren set up a *Shuntō* Countermeasures

Committee composed of 28 executives drawn from 15 industries. After much intense debate, the results of this committee's deliberations were published on 1 November 1961 under the title *Reflection on Wages Problems and the Attitude of Managers*. Its argument was that, despite the presently favourable performance of the economy, employers could not afford to take an easygoing attitude towards the next *shuntō* in 1962 (Nikkeiren 1963: 13).

This message was then reinforced by a new *White Paper on Wages* which was issued in January 1962 and entitled *The Japanese Economy at a Time of Economic Adjustment and Wages Problems: with trade liberalization as the background*. In Nikkeiren's own words, the aim of this White Paper was to 'unify the consciousness of the business world' that a tough line had to be taken on wages (Nikkeiren 1963: 13). The case it presented was that investment had to take precedence over wage rises:

> It goes without saying that the growth in capital expenses is due to the rapid rise in investment in equipment for technical innovation. This is something that is inevitable in order to achieve high growth but, at the same time, it becomes a considerable burden on an enterprise's profits. On the other hand, with the recent strong growth in investment in equipment, wages have shown signs of rising rapidly, with the focus on starting salaries owing to labour power being in short supply. It is a situation where we absolutely cannot deny the danger of widespread cost inflation, over and above the rise in productivity, owing to the spreading effects of these phenomena on rival industries. All this is in addition to the increase in consumer prices. However, on the subject of wage rises, owing to the fact that a rise in capital expenses is unavoidable because of economic growth, it has to be said that the situation does not permit rapid wage increases of the type we have seen in the past, especially in the case of a future economic downturn.
>
> (Nikkeiren 1962: 142)

This statement is a good example of traits which Nikkeiren displayed throughout much of this period. First, it cried wolf about the economic outlook ('in the case of a future economic downturn') whereas, in fact, the economy continued to perform strongly. Second, it implied that wage rises were jeopardizing capital investment, whereas, in fact, throughout this period the percentage of GDP channelled into gross fixed capital formation in Japanese enterprises fluctuated between 30 and 40 per cent, compared to less than 30 per cent in West Germany and around 20 per cent in the USA (*Financial Times:* 4 May 1989). It was on such shaky bases that Nikkeiren urged employers to use the organizational strength they had acquired during 1948–60 in order to buck the market and rein in wages.

Although the average pay rise in large enterprises of ¥2,515 (10.7 per cent) in 1962 (Nikkeiren 1981: 653) should have warned Nikkeiren that it was vainly attempting to counter market forces, it preferred to focus on what it considered to be the positive lesson provided by the steel industry. In 1962 Tekkō Rōren (*Nihon Tekkō Sangyō Rōdō Kumiai Rengōkai* or the Japan Federation of Iron and Steel Industry Labour Unions) could not win sufficient support from its members for a *shuntō* strike. As a result, the steelworkers' pay rise was below average at ¥1,800. In addition, the steel companies introduced an element of wages for the job to their pay structure, thereby diluting the seniority wages system. At its extraordinary general meeting on 18 October 1962, Nikkeiren held up the way in which the giant steel companies had handled Tekkō Rōren in that year's *shuntō* as an example of what employers' solidarity could achieve. In addition, it called on the movement to generalize this solidarity across all industries:

> The big enterprises which occupy a leading position in this particular line of business were united on the important points and faced the opposition in conformity with the agreement not to take even a single step away from the one decided by the industry. This is a method which should be agreed from now on, although what is needed is to extend it beyond a single line of business to the point where there is solidarity crossways with other industries too.
>
> (Nikkeiren 1981: 464)

In the same vein, Nikkeiren issued the lobbying instrument *Request to Managers Regarding the 1962 Year-end Bonuses* on 29 October 1962. This called on the employers to avoid 'easy compromises' in the negotiations over the size of bonuses (Nikkeiren 1963: 13).

In the build-up to the 1963 *shuntō*, Nikkeiren made a major effort to force down the level of wage rises. In the analysis of this *shuntō* which Alice Cook made in 1966, she reported that Nikkeiren first talked in October 1962 of holding down wage increases to about 5 per cent, which would have been less than half of the average settlement in large enterprises in 1962. However, by January 1963 it had set its sights on an even more stringent target of less than ¥1,000 per month (compared to ¥2,515 in 1962) which would have represented less than 4 per cent of the then average monthly wage of ¥24,718 (Cook 1966: 130, note 32). As ever, Nikkeiren published a *White Paper on Wages* in January 1963 and chose the title *Prospects for the Japanese Economy and Wages Problems*. Its Executive Council adopted *An Agreement Regarding the 1963 Shuntō* on 25 January and called on the entire organization to support it. This lobbying instrument

> pledged sternly to prohibit going it alone; to take into account national economic trends and the actual conditions of industries and enterprises; to peg wage rises to a level consistent with a determined rate of increase; to endeavour to establish a mutually beneficial system for labour and management; and – even if confronted by labour disputes –

to act prudently and with good sense, in a spirit of mutual support among managers.

(Nikkeiren 1963: 13)

On paper, it all sounded highly committed and impressively disciplined, but in the real world of companies seeking to minimize lost production, while wary of competitors gaining an advantage by settling with their workforce, it was a different story. Nikkeiren's strenuous efforts in 1962 and 1963 might have played some part in successively reducing average wage rises by a percentage point or two, but the outcome in 1963 (¥2,237 or 9.1 per cent) was more than twice the level intended and thus almost as far removed from its ambitious rhetoric as previously (Nikkeiren 1981: 653).

It is not necessary to give a year by year account of all the subsequent *shuntō*. By the early 1960s a pattern was already established of Nikkeiren setting an impossibly low target for each round of wage negotiations. Underlying this was Nikkeiren's apparently serious belief that employers only had to muster sufficient will for wages to be held in check at levels which suited their purposes. That this is not a caricature of Nikkeiren's approach to setting wages can be illustrated by a quotation from its 1966 *White Paper on Wages* which bore the title *Shuntō Under Conditions of Depression and Wages Problems*:

What is required of managers on the occasion of this *shuntō* is to have the courage of their convictions, break the vicious circle of prices and wages and move towards autonomous wage determination based on the ability to pay, and strive to go back to the basics of management.

(Nikkeiren 1966: 59)

Yet, despite the air of confident authority which pervaded such words, by this stage Nikkeiren was becoming increasingly aware of just how hollow such statements were. In certain years, such as 1964, it was forced to recognize that the average pay rise of ¥3,305 (12.4 per cent) achieved in large enterprises during *shuntō* constituted a defeat. Nikkeiren attributed this outcome to the weakness and lack of resolve shown by the employers (Nikkeiren 1981: 470). To take the 1967 *shuntō* as another example, Nikkeiren was forced to rationalize an almost identical average pay rise in percentage terms (¥4,371 or 12.5 per cent) with the lame comment that 'without Nikkeiren's restraining lead, probably even larger wage increases would have been achieved' (Nikkeiren 1968a: 12).

Clearly, Nikkeiren required some other approach than simply exhorting employers to resist wage demands. One possibility was to support the introduction of an 'incomes policy', whereby the power of the state would be used in order to restrain wage increases. This was a policy that was often adopted in other countries during this period and its merits were widely discussed in Japan's ruling circles, including Nikkeiren. There was, however, no consensus within Japan, or even within Nikkeiren, on the desirability of an incomes policy. On 24 September 1968, a Prices/Wages/Incomes/Productivity Study Group, which had been appointed by the government with Professor Kumagaya Hisao of Ōsaka University as its chair, published a report. Nikkeiren reacted positively to this so-called Kumagaya Report because it demonstrated that there had been a close relationship between prices and wages throughout the period studied (1954–65). Nikkeiren concurred with Kumagaya's interpretation that this was evidence that price rises were caused by wage costs, despite the fact that it was patently an arbitrary conclusion to draw. There were no sound economic reasons for explaining the close correlation between prices and wages in terms of the causative role of the latter. On the contrary, since wages were themselves prices (the prices of different grades of labour power) it was only to be expected that they would fluctuate largely in harmony with the movement of other prices. Hence, the economic causes of the generalized price inflation (including wage increases) which Kumagaya and his group had studied needed to be sought elsewhere than within the realm of prices themselves.

The Kumagaya Report came out in favour of an incomes policy, arguing that this was the means to overcome what it identified as a wages/prices spiral. There were those in Nikkeiren who were prepared to accept this line of reasoning in its entirety (Nikkeiren 1981: 544) but the organization's most influential leaders remained sceptical about the merits of an incomes policy. Sakurada Takeshi, who was then Nikkeiren's foremost director, headed a group of its leaders who embarked on a study tour to investigate economic conditions in western Europe and North America in October 1970. In Europe, the delegation visited Sweden, West Germany, France and the UK and the various incomes policies in force in these different countries were among the main foci of its attention. Even before departing on this mission (which became a regular, biennial fixture [Crump 2000: 87–90]), Sakurada had warned about the dangers of encouraging the state to intrude into areas which Nikkeiren regarded as employers' territory. At Nikkeiren's Top Management Seminar on 30 July 1970, Sakurada had argued:

> In the final analysis, using any type of controls, such as wage controls, price controls, accounting controls and so on, is forceful intervention by means of the power of the state . . . Insofar as we opt for a system based on liberty and democracy, it is undesirable.
>
> (Nikkeiren 1981: 546)

Despite the obligatory references here to 'liberty' and 'democracy', Sakurada was expressing not so much Nikkeiren's commitment to these abstract principles as its anxiety about returning to past practices, when the state had routinely interfered with what Japanese employers now regarded as their prerogatives. It was probably these considerations which led Shinojima Hideo, one of those who had participated in the overseas study tour, to report to Nikkeiren's extraordinary general meeting on 6 November 1970 that it would be 'pretty difficult' to implement an incomes policy in Japan. While Shinojima's report indicated that Nikkeiren should not entirely rule out the option of an incomes policy 'in the wide sense', it stated that 'something along the lines of a guidepost' would be a more suitable means for addressing the problem of uncontrollable wage rises (Nikkeiren 1981: 546). The 'guidepost' to which Shinojima referred here came to be known in Nikkeiren's jargon as the 'productivity standard principle'.

As was shown in Chapter 4, productivity had long been an issue which had engaged Nikkeiren's attention. Likewise, during the current period too, Nikkeiren had frequently stressed the need to establish a link between wages and productivity. Thus, when the unions used wage levels in Europe as a standard against which to measure Japanese wages in the 1963 *shuntō*, Nikkeiren countered that it was 'national economic average productivity' that should be taken as the relevant benchmark when setting rates of pay in Japan (Nikkeiren 1981: 465). However, the productivity standard principle (*seisansei kijun genri*) purported to be something more than the employers' customary playing of the productivity card in negotiations over wages. The productivity standard principle was supposed to be endowed with the authority of science and hence to have the status of an objective standard, which it might be the duty of employers to enforce, but which did not derive from their sectional interests. Indeed, Nikkeiren's contention was that, such was the scientific pedigree of the productivity standard principle, all reasonable people could not fail to recognize its impartiality. This included wage earners, once they were able to shed their own sectional outlook and adopt the wider view of what was best for 'their enterprises'.

The term 'productivity standard principle' was first used to convey the idea of a mechanism for determining wage levels at Nikkeiren's Top Management Seminar in August 1969. The potential benefits of this concept were quickly recognized and it was further discussed at Nikkeiren's extraordinary general meeting in October and at the meeting of its Executive Council in November 1969. A Small Committee for Studying the Productivity Standard Principle was then established and it proceeded to flesh out the concept, producing a first report in October 1970 and a second report in January 1972 (Nikkeiren 1981: 539–40; 1998, vol. 1: 58, 73).

Already in the 1971 *shuntō*, Nikkeiren brought the productivity standard principle into play in its handbook *Wages Problems and the Japanese Economy Faced with a Turning Point: concerning the new development of the productivity standard principle* which was published on 20 January 1971. In this handbook, each industry was urged to work out its average rate of productivity and use this as the basis for determining wage rises while, at the same time, it should consider the effect of its wage offers on other industries and also bear in mind the rate of real productivity in the national economy as a whole. The purpose behind this exercise was supposedly to eliminate the scourge of rising costs and inflation which Nikkeiren attributed to a 'productivity/wages gap'. In an effort to give this argument a scientific gloss, it advanced the formula:

> rate of price rises = rate of wage increases – rate of increase in real productivity in the national economy – rate of increase in labour's proportional share
>
> (Nikkeiren 1971: 11)

Although the argument was further decorated with numerous figures, graphs and tables, the alleged 'productivity/wages gap' on which it hinged was fundamentally flawed, since Nikkeiren unabashedly combined nominal wages with real productivity. Buried within the statistical tables that were appended to the volume were data which proved that real productivity increases had outstripped the growth in real wages throughout the 1960s. Although, for obvious reasons, the information was not presented in such a clear-cut fashion, it could be shown from Nikkeiren's own data that the advance in real productivity in the national economy between 1961 and 1969 (the last year for which figures were then available) was 99.7 per cent, compared to a corresponding growth in real wages of 53.8 per cent in the economy generally and 57.9 per cent in manufacturing industries (Nikkeiren 1971: 133, 145). On this evidence, Nikkeiren's 'productivity/ wages gap' was an ideological construct and could not legitimately serve to explain inflation.

The 1971 *shuntō* resulted in an average wage rise in large enterprises of 16.9 per cent, which was down from 18.5 per cent in the previous year. Nikkeiren wanted to interpret this as a turning point in the upward trend in wages settlements since 1966, but the outcome in 1971 had more to do with a dip in the rate of economic growth than the effect of the productivity standard principle (Nikkeiren 1981: 554). Nevertheless, Nikkeiren continued to advocate strongly the same principle in its *shuntō* publications in subsequent years. In *The Japanese Economy in a Period of Change and Wages Problems*, which was published on 20 January 1972, Nikkeiren called on the employers to 'carry through the productivity standard principle', but also showed that it was seeking to influence another constituency when it talked about 'the defence of the economy by labour and management collaborating' (Nikkeiren 1972: 19, 71). As the yen rose in value against the dollar in the wake of the 'Nixon shock', Nikkeiren set the productivity standard principle within the context of a scenario of class collaboration:

> With the economy of our country being confronted by a serious situation, the issue of the day is nothing other than how to put into effect defence of the economy and defence of the enterprise, which are the bedrock for the mutual prosperity of labour and management.
>
> (Nikkeiren 1972: 20)

The outcome of the 1972 *shuntō* was again downwards in percentage terms (an average wage rise of 15.3 per cent in large enterprises) but that trend was sharply reversed in 1973 (20.1 per cent) despite Nikkeiren's persistent advocacy of the productivity standard principle (Nikkeiren 1981: 653). Hence, it is fair to say that the productivity standard principle was important, not because it delivered any immediate solutions, but because it provided Nikkeiren with an ideological lever whose purchase would be enhanced once the oil shock exerted its effects.

Getting more out of labour power

If attempting to control wages was one side of Nikkeiren's strategy, another was to get more out of labour power by raising productivity and improving skills. Nikkeiren saw the key to the latter as lying in the better management of labour, so that 'managing ability' became one of its favourite catch-phrases during this period. Under the auspices of its Special Committee on Labour Management, a Research Committee on Managing Ability was established in October 1966 and this reported two years later after undertaking numerous case studies. Nikkeiren published its findings in 1969 as a volume with the title *Managing Ability: theory and practice* (Nikkeiren 1981: 38, 432ff.). 'Managing ability' involved identifying talent and further developing skills within the workforce. It also became associated with so-called 'self-management'. Self-management consisted of companies organizing the workforce into small groups, such as quality control circles, which were then expected to pursue productivity improvement and cost reduction targets (Kurokawa 1989: 157 and Gordon 1993: 385).

The wage control and managing ability sides of Nikkeiren's strategy came together when it urged employers to shift the balance of wage determination away from an employee's length of service with the company towards pay geared to individual ability and the job performed. In May 1962 Nikkeiren published *The Road to Paying Wages for the Job* and later the same year a 16-member research team was despatched to the USA to study job-related pay (Nikkeiren 1963: 15, 94). Nikkeiren kept up the pressure for restructuring wages along these lines throughout the period under review here, arguing in 1968, for example, that 'wages based on ability are gradually spreading, but within the wages system plenty of scope for rationalization still remains' (Nikkeiren 1968b: 18).

At Nikkeiren's annual conference on 20 April 1961, various policies were decided in order to improve the economic performance of enterprises. In addition to 'endeavouring to establish order in the workplace', which could be regarded as a hangover from the previous period, these policies included 'raising productivity and cutting costs' and 'achieving the improvement of management in the workplace and developing and training employees' (Nikkeiren 1963: 13). In part, these policies could be implemented by adapting established procedures. For example, it was noted in Chapter 4 that national conferences for personnel managers were initiated by Nikkeiren in 1949 and these had continued approximately biannually ever since. Some of these conferences became the settings in which to discuss how to put into practice the policies adopted at the 1961 annual conference. Hence, the conference for personnel managers that was organized by Nikkeiren in May 1962 discussed changes to the wages system, the role of supervisors in the workplace and so on, while the next conference in November 1962 engaged with issues such as the implementation of wages for the job and how to manage young workers (Nikkeiren 1963: 15). On the other hand, carrying through some of these policies required techniques, such as job analysis and evaluation, which had not been widely used prior to that by Japanese companies. To meet this need, Nikkeiren initiated short training courses in job analysis in February 1961 and, such was the frequency with which these were held, as many as 5,800 individuals were equipped with the relevant skills over the next 20 years (Nikkeiren 1981: 431–2). In September 1964 Nikkeiren established a Job Analysis Centre as a division within its own headquarters organization. The Job Analysis Centre's brief was to keep up to date on developments in this field and dispense know-how throughout Nikkeiren's affiliated associations and companies (Nikkeiren 1968a: 118; 1981: 38).

At Nikkeiren's annual conference on 19 April 1973, Sakurada Takeshi delivered a special report entitled *A Retrospect on 25 Years of Labour Problems and the Outlook from Now on*. Looking back over a quarter of a century of activity, Sakurada characterized the 1960s as a period when, because economic growth had led to shortages of labour power, Nikkeiren had encouraged management to switch 'from quantity to quality'. According to Sakurada, Nikkeiren had consequently put much effort into the education of managers during the 1960s and the prime examples he cited were the establishment of a Centre for the Development of Human Talent in May 1967 and the launching of an annual Top Management Seminar in August 1969 (Nikkeiren 1981: 594).

The decision to establish the Centre for the Development of Human Talent was originally taken at Nikkeiren's annual conference in 1963. The project took four years to complete and, although the centre had a separate legal identity from Nikkeiren, the two organizations worked together closely (Nikkeiren 1968a: 17; 1981: 39). Indeed, the Top Management Seminar was an initiative taken jointly by the Centre for the Development of Human Talent and Nikkeiren. These annual 'seminars' were in fact conferences lasting several days (the first was held from 7 to 9 August 1969 at the Centre for the Development of Human Talent, close to Mount Fuji) where top-ranking employers could meet in an informal setting, engage with the problems that were uppermost at the time and devise the economic responses and labour relations strategies that would best serve Japanese capitalism. By way of example, the theme of the first Top Management Seminar was 'basic questions on the political and economic problems that confront our country and the way to solve them' (Nikkeiren 1981: 31, 40).

It has already been noted that the productivity standard principle emerged from the wide-ranging discussions which this theme stimulated.

While attendance at the Top Management Seminars was restricted to the most powerful and influential stratum of employers, those whose positions at the heart of giant companies gave them the leverage to formulate strategy for Japanese capitalism, much of the management training that Nikkeiren engaged in was aimed at white-collar workers, whose 'manager' titles belied their lack of autonomy. A case in point would be the thousands who took the courses on job analysis which were referred to earlier. In addition to these short courses for job analysts, Nikkeiren listed in its official *20 Years' History*, which was published in 1968, the other types of training programmes it had offered in recent years. These included so-called three-day 'seminars' on labour management policy and labour disputes policy; two-week lecture courses for middle managers; courses consisting of 14 night-time lectures on practical labour management; seminars on a variety of projects connected with wages and personnel management; practical lectures on how to edit intra-company publications; and lectures designed to equip the employees of regional managers' associations with the necessary skills (Nikkeiren 1968a: 18). Those who emerged from such courses could be thought of as the foot soldiers of management, cogs in the mechanisms of control, speed up and enhanced productivity that were installed in Japanese enterprises during the period 1961–73. None fitted this description better than foremen (*kantokusha*). Kumazawa Makoto described those who occupied the position of foreman as the 'noncommissioned officer' of the workforce, whose function was to act as 'company spokesman with broad authority and responsibility to impose the will of the company on his subordinates' (Kumazawa 1996: 132).

Recognizing the vital role played by such foremen in maintaining shopfloor discipline, Nikkeiren started special training cruises for them in 1970. The first such cruise set sail for Hong Kong, Taiwan and Okinawa on 14 November 1970 and there was one or more in each year that followed (Nikkeiren 1981: 40). Although the participants took lessons while on board, the invitation to join such cruises was an attractive perk in a period that predated mass overseas tourism. By sponsoring foremen to join these cruises, enterprises signalled that there were rewards for those who toed the company line. As for Nikkeiren, by putting on the variety of training programmes that have been described here, it was able to maintain its usefulness for Japanese capitalism even in a period when it struggled to stay in tune with the level of wage settlements that many companies were conceding.

Building bridges with the unions

It has been shown that developments within Japanese capitalism during the period 1961–73 impacted on Nikkeiren and influenced its strategy.

Similarly, the unions were affected by changing circumstances and, as a result, significant organizational realignment took place within their ranks. In 1964 Dōmei (*Zen Nihon Rōdō Sōdōmei* or the All-Japan General Confederation of Labour) was formed as a rival to Sōhyō. Although Dōmei, with 1,476,000 members (15 per cent of the unionized workforce) was much smaller than Sōhyō (4,213,000 members or 43 per cent of the unionized workforce) it was strongly represented in the large private-sector enterprises that were affiliated to Nikkeiren (Cook 1966: 90 and Langdon 1967: 108–9). Another noteworthy development in 1964 was the emergence of the IMF-JC (the International Metalworkers' Federation – Japan Council). This was a federation of unions in the steel, shipbuilding, motor car and electrical goods industries. The IMF-JC's presence was more significant than its relatively small membership (540,000 members or 5.5 per cent of the unionized workforce [Gordon 1993: 377]) might suggest, both because of the economic importance of the industries whose workers it grouped together and because it cut across existing confederal structures. Unions belonging to both Sōhyō and Dōmei were connected to the IMF-JC, but this worked more to Dōmei's advantage, since the outlook of the IMF-JC leadership tended to have more in common with that of Dōmei than Sōhyō.

By 1967 the unions aligned with Dōmei were organizing a larger fraction of the workforce in private-sector enterprises than was Sōhyō (Satō 1983: 7). Although Dōmei's total membership remained far smaller than Sōhyō's, its influence was enhanced by the fact that the pace-setters in each *shuntō* tended to be in the more dynamic private sector of the economy, where the unions that were affiliated to it were mainly to be found. It was for the same reason that Nikkeiren took the view that, by 1967, the IMF-JC was more important than Sōhyō in determining the level of *shuntō* wage settlements (Nikkeiren 1968a: 10).

By the time these developments took place within the union movement, Nikkeiren had already failed in the attempt to control wages by diktat. The emergence of Dōmei and the IMF-JC was therefore a factor which eventually induced Nikkeiren to make selective use of unions as it resorted to other means in its endeavours to apply the brake to wages. Dōmei in particular proved to be receptive to Nikkeiren's readiness to build bridges and one can identify several reasons for this. First, Nikkeiren and Dōmei had a common interest in opposing Sōhyō. Dōmei's origins lay in a number of unions disagreeing with and separating from Sōhyō in 1953. They then linked up the following year with that section of Sōdōmei which had refused to join Sōhyō when it was organized in 1950 and together formed Dōmei's predecessor, Zenrō Kaigi (*Zen Nihon Rōdō Kumiai Kaigi* or the All-Japan Labour Union Council). Thus Dōmei's *raison d'être* was, at least in part, hostility to Sōhyō and Nikkeiren was able to turn this inter-union rivalry to its advantage. Moreover, since many of the cooperative 'second unions' which had emerged in the course of Nikkeiren-backed labour disputes had joined Zenrō Kaigi/Dōmei, while the more combative 'first unions' had been affiliated to Sōhyō, it is not surprising that Nikkeiren leaned towards Dōmei.

Second, there was common ideological ground between the Nikkeiren leadership and Dōmei's leaders. Takita Minoru was leader of Zenrō Kaigi/ Dōmei from the founding of the former in 1954 up to his retirement in 1972 (Carlile 1994: 156, note 6). Takita associated the union confederations that he led with the Japan Productivity Centre, arguing that the best way for workers to achieve higher wages was not to get entangled in struggles for a bigger slice of the cake, but to raise productivity and thereby increase the size of the cake itself. He took the view that:

> Those who stress class struggle tend to evade or denounce the raising of the issue of productivity improvement. It is fine to use strength to fight over distribution. However, how will the financial base be expanded? It is here that the issue of productivity, value added and absolute amounts emerge that cannot be dealt with through distributional arguments.
>
> (Carlile 1994: 153)

It is easy to see how this linking of higher wages to productivity increases dovetailed with Nikkeiren's productivity standard principle.

Third, in return for union officials being consulted over company policy, unions affiliated to Dōmei were prepared to discipline their members and prevent production from being disrupted (Totsuka 1984: 4).

As the 1960s progressed, Nikkeiren increasingly talked about achieving more harmonious labour relations:

> Labour–management cooperation up till now has tended to slip into the mould of a vertical, ruler-subordinate relationship. Now the relationship is expected to take a new form based on mature interaction between labour and management, a relationship based on partnership in the shape of labour, as one side of industry, forming a community with management. Even as they occupy their respective positions, labour and management should base themselves on the concept of equal human respect. It is precisely this that constitutes the entirely natural form that relations between enterprise unions and managers should take.
>
> (Nikkeiren 1968a: 9)

'Labour' here meant the unions and, in particular, the type of enterprise union found in Dōmei. With consultation processes blurring the distinction between company and union, and union office often serving as a stepping stone towards promotion within the company's hierarchy, Nikkeiren and Dōmei could agree on a common policy of cooperation at the point of production and 'fair shares' for both sides in line with improved productivity.

A milestone in the process of building bridges with the unions was the inauguration of relatively frequent discussions between Nikkeiren and the leaders of the different labour confederations in 1971. Although from that point on Nikkeiren kept open the lines of communication with all the labour confederations, its meetings with Dōmei tended to be more productive and were more likely to establish common ground. In 1971, representatives of the *Shuntō* Joint Struggle Committee – which embraced Sōhyō and Chūritsu Rōren (*Chūritsu Rōdō Kumiai Renraku Kaigi* or the Liaison Council of Independent Labour Unions) but not Dōmei – presented their demands in person to Nikkeiren's leaders on 18 February and there was a further meeting between the two sides on 13 April (Rōdōshō Rōseikyoku 1979: 519, 522). As for Dōmei, its leaders met with Nikkeiren on 24 March and their discussions at this meeting ranged across wages, prices, pollution and other issues. Then, as the effects of the August 'Nixon shock' became evident, Nikkeiren and Dōmei leaders conferred again on 10 November to discuss how to handle the situation brought about by the weakening of the dollar (Rōdōshō Rōseikyoku 1979: 521, 537). The following year, Nikkeiren's Special Committee on Inflation Problems took evidence from Sōhyō and Dōmei on 8 June and 7 July respectively. On 19 September, Nikkeiren issued a lobbying instrument which called for tax reduction on retirement allowances, increased old age pensions and reform of the health insurance law. It is significant that before publishing this set of requests (*yōbōsho*) Nikkeiren held meetings with each of the labour confederations to exchange views on these issues, starting with Sōhyō on 5 September and ending with Dōmei on 18 September (Nikkeiren 1981: 37–8). In 1973, too, there were numerous meetings between Nikkeiren and officials of the various labour confederations to discuss a range of issues, including the feasibility of establishing a system of two days off work per week, shortening working hours, raising the age of retirement, reducing income tax and countering inflation. By no means all these discussions were fruitful, but cooperative ventures such as the First Labour–Management Counter-Inflation Policy Conference, which Nikkeiren and Dōmei held jointly on 23 October 1973, symbolized the extent to which there was an overlap in the policy orientation of these two organizations (Nikkeiren 1981: 38–9).

One of the most obviously ideological slogans that was floated by Nikkeiren during this period was 'management involving all personnel' (*zen'in keiei*). As Japanese capitalism advanced, its leading companies grew ever larger and more coldly impersonal, so that within them workers felt increasingly powerless and alienated. This was the context within which Nagata Takao, the President of Hitachi Shipbuilding, advocated 'promoting management where all personnel participate in planning' at Nikkeiren's annual conference on 23 April 1969. Despite the fact that the scale and purpose of capitalist production were bound to frustrate such an ambition, the notion of 'management involving all personnel' was attractive to Nikkeiren as a way of further drawing the core workforce into a company-oriented outlook and pattern of behaviour. In a discussion that took place at Nikkeiren's next annual conference on 22 April 1970, the modern workplace was likened to a 'desert', which supposedly had to be reclaimed so that workers could 'love' it and 'take pride' in it (Nikkeiren 1981: 506–7). 'Management involving all personnel' was accordingly one of the themes of the second Top Management Seminar held at the Centre for the Development of Human Talent from 30 July to 1 August 1970. Although the way in which the concept of 'management involving all personnel' was subsequently developed by Nikkeiren belongs to the next chapter, it is worth noting here that the idea appealed to Dōmei's leaders almost as much as it did to Nikkeiren's. In January 1974, Dōmei proposed that the two organizations undertake a joint study of the subject and Nikkeiren readily agreed (Nikkeiren 1981: 509–10). For Dōmei's leaders, 'management involving all personnel' offered possibilities for the increased involvement of union officials in company decision-making and this outweighed the loss of autonomy that its rank and file members would experience as they were increasingly incorporated into enterprise structures and procedures.

Organization, individuals and activity

The developments during 1961–73 which have been described in this chapter occurred against a background where the organization that Nikkeiren had previously built up remained intact, but underwent some modification. Likewise, many of the individuals who had been prominent in Nikkeiren's leadership until 1960 remained influential, although there were some changes of both personnel and operational style. As for activities, while Nikkeiren continued to be involved in the various fields to which it had committed resources during the period 1948–60, the shifting distribution of its efforts reflected the changes that were under way within Japanese capitalism.

Nikkeiren's organizational structure remained the same meshwork of regional business associations and industrial associations as earlier, so that any changes in this regard were merely incremental. Even though Okinawa was under American control until May 1972, an Okinawa Managers' Association was welcomed into Nikkeiren's ranks long before this (Kuribara and Matsuyama 1961: 269) and the number of industrial associations increased with the affiliation of groups such as the Petro-Chemical Industry Association and the Tokyo Printing Industry Association (Nikkeiren 1968a: 117). By March 1973 Nikkeiren was composed of 47 regional business associations (including the Kantō Managers' Association and Kansai Managers' Association, representing Tokyo and Ōsaka respectively) and 48 industrial associations. The total number of companies connected to Nikkeiren via these intermediary associations was 25,952 (Nikkeiren 1974a: 101). Parallel to this expansion, several significant changes were made at Nikkeiren's headquarters. Whereas organizational matters and maintaining contacts had previously been part of the wide remit of the General Affairs Section, a separate Organization Section was established and its range of functions was widened as the 1960s progressed (Nikkeiren 1963: 91; 1968a: 118). This reflected the importance that Nikkeiren attached to consolidating its organization, so that it was strong enough to meet the challenges thrown up by the developments occurring within Japanese capitalism.

Another innovation was the creation of a Culture and Fitness Section whose responsibilities included 'matters concerned with the wholesome diffusion and development of culture and physical education for those working in industry' (Nikkeiren 1968a: 118). In the postwar years, unions and political organizations like the Communist Party had often used cultural activities, such as music clubs and choirs, to build support, which explains Nikkeiren's concern that 'wholesome' alternatives should be provided for the workforce in the companies affiliated to it. Setting up a Culture and Fitness Section within its headquarters went hand in hand with similar grassroots developments. A federation known as Zenbunren (*Zenkoku Bunka Dantai Renmei* or the National League of Cultural Organizations) was established on 29 January 1964, with strong support from Nikkeiren. Its constituent organizations spanned both physical education groups and various artistic and cultural associations. One existing federation which merged with Zenbunren was Onkyō (*Ongaku Bunka Kyōkai* or the Musical Culture Association) and Zenbunren devoted much effort to opposing Leftist 'workers' music' (*rōon*) (Nikkeiren 1981: 38). By 1968 Zenbunren had more than 300,000 members and included 47 regional music associations. The manipulative intentions behind this were clearly stated by Nikkeiren:

> Musical Culture Associations [*onkyō*] were previously established in all districts throughout the country as the managers' organs for promoting cultural activity and physical education . . . In opposition to the ideologically prejudiced 'workers' music' of the workers' side, we try to promote wholesome cultural activity and physical education.
>
> (Nikkeiren 1968a: 16)

Nikkeiren's Labour Economy Section and International Affairs Section were detached from the main organization at headquarters and were given the status of auxiliary bodies, known respectively as the Labour Economy Research Institute and the International Representative Office (Nikkeiren 1963: 91). On the other hand, by 1968 two new 'sections' had been added to the chart of the headquarters organizational structure (Nikkeiren 1968a: 118). One of these was the Job Analysis Centre which was established in 1964 and whose functions have already been mentioned. The other was the Intra-Company Information Centre which came into existence on 1 November 1962 and took over functions which had previously been performed by Nikkeiren's Committee for Studying Public Relations. The Intra-Company Information Centre advised companies on the production of company newsletters and similar matters. It issued a twice-monthly *Intra-Company Information Materials Newsletter*, provided courses on editing at locations throughout Japan, organized an annual national training conference and undertook an annual overseas study trip to see how companies in other countries handled PR (Nikkeiren 1963: 16; 1968a: 18; 1981: 36–7). The motive behind this burst of enthusiasm for propagating editorial skills was that, during the 1960s, the ability to communicate effectively increasingly came to be seen as important for inculcating the right attitudes in the workforce, which in turn could lead to higher productivity (Nikkeiren 1981: 447–8). A different form of 'centre' was Nikkeiren's Video Library Centre which, at its inception on 1 July 1971, had the status of an independent business providing video cassettes on training and other subjects to interested companies and other organizations (Nikkeiren 1981: 36).

As might be expected, *shuntō* affected the way in which Nikkeiren organized itself in various respects. The opening of a *Shuntō* Liaison Office in Nikkeiren's headquarters on 1 February 1973 was a case in point (Nikkeiren 1981: 38). Another example of the influence that *shuntō* exerted on Nikkeiren was the decision taken at its annual conference in April 1973 to defer the conference until May in subsequent years. The objective here was to ensure that *shuntō* had largely run its course by the time that Nikkeiren met, so that it did not distract delegates' attention (Nikkeiren 1998, vol. 1: 60). The appointment of extraordinary committees to deal with pressing issues, such as the *Shuntō* Countermeasures Committee and the Small Committee for Studying the Productivity Standard Principle, has been mentioned. Supplementing these, the system of standing special committees continued, with the addition of several new special committees, such as those responsible for Health and Safety (in 1965), Inflation Problems (1972), Labour Problems in Overseas Enterprises (1973) and Regional Social Problems (also 1973). Each of these newly created special committees was a response to developments within Japanese capitalism. For example, Nikkeiren's decision to establish its special committee on Labour Problems in Overseas Enterprises on 20 April 1973 was a reaction to the tensions that arose as Japanese companies expanded their operations into South-East Asia. It was accompanied by the publication on 1 June 1973 of *Guidelines for Undertaking Investment in Developing Countries* which was issued jointly by Nikkeiren and several other employers' organizations, including Keidanren, the Comrades' Association and the Japan Chamber of Commerce and Industry (Nikkeiren 1981: 39).

As for individuals, the period 1961–73 saw the retirement at different junctures of several who had been influential within Nikkeiren since its formation. Maeda Hajime had been a director (*senmu riji*) ever since 1948 and throughout he had advocated taking an uncompromising line in order to keep wages in check. It may not be coincidental that his retirement in 1969 coincided with Nikkeiren embracing the alternative approach represented by the productivity standard principle (Nikkeiren 1981: 767). Another leader of the same vintage was Moroi Kan'ichi, who retired in 1968 after 20 years as a top director (*daihyō jōnin riji*) (Nikkeiren 1981: 768). Between 1949 and 1962, Moroi had shared this responsibility with Katō Masato and then, in 1960, Sakurada Takeshi was appointed to the same position (Nikkeiren 1981: 762). Although there were thus three *daihyō jōnin riji* for a brief time at the beginning of the 1960s, it was a measure of Sakurada's strong personality and preponderant influence within Nikkeiren that, after Moroi retired in 1968, he functioned single-handedly in this post throughout the rest of the period that concerns us here (Nikkeiren 1981: 764). Certainly, it was Sakurada's championing of the productivity standard principle that helped it to become so firmly entrenched in Nikkeiren's ideology. Sakurada was Chairman of the Nisshin Spinning Company during this period and witnessed the decline in relative importance of textiles within the Japanese economy as the years went by. While this means that Sakurada owed his power within Nikkeiren more to the strength of his personality and his skill as an administrator than to the standing of his company or the dynamism of the industry with which he was associated, there were many others in Nikkeiren's leadership whose positions directly reflected the status of their enterprise or their industry within Japanese capitalism.

To take the chairmen of some of the most influential of Nikkeiren's special committees as examples, it is no surprise to find that, in 1973, those responsible for general affairs, employment, education, labour legislation, public relations and labour problems in overseas enterprises were executives of Mitsubishi Heavy Industries, Kawasaki Heavy Industries, the Nissan Motor Company, Mitsubishi Mining and Cement, Mitsubishi Chemical Industries and Hitachi Shipbuilding respectively (Nikkeiren 1981: 591–2). The dominant position of giant companies and of the heavy and chemical industries within Japanese capitalism is evident from this distribution of posts.

The class struggle obviously did not disappear with the drawing to a close of the Mitsui Miike Coal Mines dispute in 1960. The miners fought a rearguard action as the industry was run down and there were numerous strikes in other sectors during the years 1961–73. Many of these were brief stoppages of work, designed to add muscle to *shuntō* campaigns, but in addition some lengthy strikes were undertaken. One notable example of the latter was the 1972 seamen's dispute over wages and working conditions which lasted for 92 days from 14 April to 14 July (Kawanishi 1992: 84–5). Although Nikkeiren was still prepared to get actively involved in labour disputes, the changing form taken by the class struggle meant that, on balance, its functions shifted to advising employers and providing a consultation service. The opening of the previously mentioned *Shuntō* Liaison Office in 1973 was a symbol of this shift in emphasis. Among the services it provided were consultation on *shuntō*, up to the minute reports on *shuntō*'s progress and the publication of a series on *Shuntō Problems* (Nikkeiren 1981: 38).

Research continued to be an important activity, as the creation of the

Labour Economy Research Institute showed, and the expansion of Nikkeiren's management training programmes was dealt with in an earlier section. Nikkeiren remained a lobbying body, but at a reduced rate compared to the period 1948–60, so that the number of lobbying instruments issued in any one year only once (in 1969) reached double figures (Nikkeiren 1998, vol. 2: 193–5). Education and training together represented the most frequent group of issues on which Nikkeiren lobbied, reflecting employers' concerns during a period when the supply of young workers was tight and they were becoming more difficult to control. Discipline (or the lack of it) was a preoccupation of several lobbying instruments in 1969, when Japanese universities were paralyzed by disturbances and Nikkeiren was fearful about how this might affect the working habits of the next generation (Schoppa 1991: 125). Other issues to which it devoted significant lobbying efforts were pensions and medical expenses/health insurance. In both these cases, Nikkeiren was concerned about the burdens which benefits for workers imposed on companies.

Nikkeiren also continued to publish prolifically. As well as maintaining its periodicals, such as the *Nikkeiren Times* and *Manager*, it frequently added new volumes to its established series, including *Materials on Labour*. Other new series of publications which it launched included *Materials on Wages Problems*, *Handbooks on Editing Intra-Company Information* and *Management and Labour Law* (Nikkeiren 1968a: 120–1).

Behind the continuity represented by its organization and the routine nature of much of its activity, Nikkeiren was forced to refocus its strategy. The change lay not in its objectives, which remained throughout to control wages and get more out of labour power. What altered was Nikkeiren's perception of the best means of achieving these objectives. Confrontation did not work under conditions of rapid economic growth and a sellers' market for labour power. This accounts for Nikkeiren's shift of emphasis towards manipulation and mystification during the years 1961–73.

6 Seizing the opportunity
Turning the oil shock to the bosses' advantage (1974–80)

In 1974 Japan was plunged into an economic crisis precipitated by the oil shock of the previous October. Even after the initial impact of soaring energy costs was absorbed and the threat to oil supplies was circumvented, Japanese companies remained haunted throughout the rest of the 1970s by a sense of their vulnerability to external economic forces over which they had no control. This perceived exposure to the swirling currents of world capitalism was aggravated by the further major rise in oil prices which accompanied the Iranian Revolution in 1979. Naturally, these problems of Japanese capitalism were transmitted to the population at large. The number of unemployed rose and many more workers than were actually dismissed felt the threat of job insecurity as manning levels were reduced in order to recoup profits. In addition, consumers were faced with an unprecedented surge of inflation, which in turn provoked panic buying and empty shelves. Paradoxically, in the midst of this period of first crisis and then protracted uncertainty for Japanese capitalism, circumstances worked to Nikkeiren's advantage. The threat to jobs and livelihoods provided the leverage needed to tighten labour discipline and to drive down wage increases to levels more in tune with the previously formulated productivity standard principle. For similar reasons, many unions were induced to move even further down the road of coopera- tion with the companies in which they were implanted. In a lecture delivered for Nikkeiren in 1991, the Personnel Director of Ishikawajima Harima Heavy Industries recalled how the difficult situation created by the oil shock was resolved by Japanese companies:

> It was tough for the companies, too, but since the unions were also enterprise unions, they could not avoid taking into account the future of the enterprise and the future of the industry. From that standpoint, they cooperated with us, even while shedding tears over the managing of workforce reduction.
>
> (Nikkeiren 1991: 9)

It was cases such as this which a Nikkeiren director, Naruse Takeo, had in mind when he acknowledged retrospectively the role played by cooperative labour–management relations in the process by which Japanese capitalism overcame the economic problems caused by the oil shock (Naruse 1993: 134).

Problems for Japanese capitalism

The immediate effect of the oil shock was to squeeze all growth out of the Japanese economy. Whereas the average annual rate of growth had been 8.2 per cent over the past five years (1969–73), GDP contracted by 0.5 per cent in 1974. This was the first time since reliable statistics had been gathered in the postwar era that a negative rate of growth had been registered and the effect was to send shock waves through Japan's ruling circles. Although growth was restored to the Japanese economy during the following year, and the average annual increase in GDP over the period 1975–80 was 4.2 per cent, there was no return to the spectacular rates of economic expansion which had characterized the 1960s and early 1970s. Moreover, the period ended with another jolt to economic growth when the GDP indicator fell to 2.6 per cent in 1980 (from 5.1 per cent in 1979) owing to the effect of the rise in oil prices brought about by the Iranian Revolution (Nikkeiren 1996b: 186).

In the period immediately following the oil shock, the word 'stagflation' was incorporated into Japanese vocabulary, since the downturn in economic growth was accompanied by rocketing inflation. Retail prices rose 20.9 per cent in 1974 (Nikkeiren 1996b: 186) and 1.3 million people took part in 'Stop the inflation' demonstrations held throughout the country on 31 March (Mainichi Shinbun 1989: 965). Although the government introduced various measures to bring inflation under control, the most important of which was to reduce the money supply, the retail price index did not fall below 10 per cent until 1976 or below 5 per cent until 1978. Subsequently, the rise in oil prices in 1979 filtered through to consumer goods generally in 1980, lifting the retail price index by 7.6 per cent (Nikkeiren 1996b: 186). The disappearance from supermarket shelves of everyday items, such as toilet paper and washing powder, was linked in the popular mind with the manipulation of supplies by powerful companies intent on profiteering by engineering artificial shortages. On 25 February 1974 the President of Marubeni appeared before the Budget Committee of the Lower House of the National Assembly and was pilloried for 'unethical' trading practices, while the same company's hoarding of goods and tax evasion were targets of popular anger in that year's *shuntō* (Mainichi Shinbun 1989: 964).

Another problem for sections of Japanese capital during the period 1974–80 was the continuing strengthening of the yen against the dollar, since this made exports more expensive. At a meeting of its Executive Council on 17 November 1977, Nikkeiren's Chairman, Sakurada Takeshi, called for government action to deal with the appreciation of the yen relative to the dollar. Despite this, the yen continued on its upward trajectory, breaking through the barriers of ¥220 to the dollar on 3 April 1978 and ¥175 to the dollar on 31 October 1978 (Nikkeiren 1981: 45 and Mainichi Shinbun 1989: 1054). It should be noted that reducing the number of workers on the payroll was a favourite means to cut costs and thereby compensate for the appreciation of the yen, so as to retrieve competitiveness in overseas markets (Hasegawa 1993: 28). Hence, although it was workers who bore the brunt, the rise in unemployment can be regarded as another indication of the problems confronting many Japanese companies (typically those in the private sector engaged in manufacturing and targeting a significant proportion of their output at the American market). It is true that unemployment was defined in such a way as to make the number out of work appear far lower than in the USA or western Europe (see Chapter 8). Thus, at first glance, Japan's rate of unemployment remained consistently low throughout this period, rising by less than a percentage point from 1.3 per cent of the workforce in 1974 to 2.1 per cent in 1980 (Nikkeiren 1996b: 185). However, once one grasps that the stringency of the definition of 'unemployment' meant that the statistics would always be artificially deflated, the very fact that there was a 61.5 per cent rise over the years 1974–80 in the proportion of the workforce that met this definition becomes significant, since it provides a more telling indication of the economic stresses transmitted to employees than the misleadingly low figures might otherwise suggest.

Nikkeiren's responses

Nikkeiren tackled these problems confronting Japanese capitalism in the period following the oil shock in a number of ways. Its first priority was to bring wages under more effective control and it pursued this by both organizational and ideological means. Its principal argument for moderating pay increases was that high wages cause inflation, but Nikkeiren also had several other strings to its ideological bow. Of particular note were its arguments that there was a distinctive 'Japanese way' of running capitalism and that Japanese capitalism was uniquely structured because it 'had no rigid social classes'. In this section, the ways in which Nikkeiren mustered its organizational forces so as to block high wage settlements will first be examined. Following this, its major ideological claims will be considered in turn.

Organized action on wages

The period 1974–80 opened with a defeat for Nikkeiren. In March 1974 Nikkeiren had urged that wage rises should be held to less than 20 per cent in the current *shuntō* (i.e., less than the previous year's average settlement of 20.1 per cent in large enterprises). Furthermore, on 4 April 1974, the chairmen's conference of Nikkeiren's regional business associations had called for 20–30 per cent of the increase in wages to be diverted by companies out of pay packets into savings schemes (Nikkeiren 1981: 610). However, neither of these proposals met with success and the outcome of the 1974 *shuntō* was that wage increases reached an all-time high, averaging ¥28,981 per month (32.9 per cent) in large enterprises (Nikkeiren 1981: 653). Nikkeiren's response to this defeat was to set up a Committee to Study where Wholesale Wage Increases Are Leading which met for the first time on 20 May 1974. The importance which Nikkeiren attached to this project was reflected in the committee's composition which included both its current Chairman, Sakurada Takeshi (then Chairman of Tōhō Rayon), and Ōtsuki Bunpei (President of Mitsubishi Mining and Cement) who was to take over the leadership of Nikkeiren in 1979. Also represented among the committee's 20 members were many of the giant companies at the heart of Japanese capitalism, including Kawasaki Heavy Industries, Mitsubishi Heavy Industries, Mitsubishi Chemical Industries, Hitachi Manufacturing, Hitachi Shipbuilding, the Nippon Steel Corporation and the Nissan Motor Company. With the assistance of seven advisors, who were mostly sympathetic academics (such as Professor Kumagaya Hisao of Ōsaka University), the committee pondered the implications of escalating wage increases and produced a report that was published on 5 November 1974 (Nikkeiren 1974b).

With a subtitle *let both labour and management reconsider from the standpoint of the national economy,* the *Report of the Committee to Study where Wholesale Wage Increases Are Leading* set out guidelines for future wage settlements. It recommended that wage rises should be held to less than 15 per cent in 1975 and that they should fall to single digit levels from 1976 onwards (Nikkeiren 1974b: 33). One interesting aspect of these recommendations was the assertion that 'this is a policy which depends on the determination of the country, the enterprise and the individual each to do their bit and tighten their belts in order to avoid aggravating inflation and deepening the economic depression' (Nikkeiren 1974b: 33). Despite this gloss on the policy that Nikkeiren wished to see adopted, it was not apparent how the burden of restraining wages would fall on any other sector than those living on wages.

Be that as it may, the plan to drive down the level of pay rises in a stepped fashion over the coming years flowed from a line of argument which insisted that the conditions that in the past had facilitated high rates of economic growth and therefore wage increases had now changed fundamentally. The changed circumstances which the report cited were that the benefits of previous technical innovation had now been exhausted, abundant sources of cheap raw materials from abroad had dried up, environmental problems had worsened and labour power had become scarcer (Nikkeiren 1974b: 6–8). Following this, the familiar arguments on the relation between prices, wages and productivity were rehearsed in Chapter 3 of the report (9–14) and a fourth chapter (15–20) was entitled 'Wholesale wage rises and enterprise management: who picks up the bill for wage rises?' Here the argument proceeded to outline two alternative outcomes of wage rises. In the first case, increased wages could be offset by companies raising their prices. 'Yet who pays these higher prices?', asked the report. Its answer was that it is wage earners (in their role of consumers) who pick up the bill. In the second scenario, competition could prevent companies from raising their prices, so that the cost of higher wages would have to be absorbed, which would eat into the capital available for re-investment. The report argued that, if such under-investment continued for long, companies would be forced to close down or to undertake other measures that would be equally unpleasant for the workforce. Hence the report demonstrated, at least to Nikkeiren's satisfaction, that substantial wage rises which outstripped productivity increases would supposedly not be in the interest of wage earners.

Other chapters sought to demonstrate that wage rises undermine international competitiveness (21–4) and 'the people's standard of living' through inflation (25–30). The punch-line delivered in the final chapter of the report was that:

> To cut a long story short, since long-term, low economic growth of the Japanese economy cannot be avoided, both labour and management can hopefully grasp the fact that, however much nominal wages are raised, wholesale increases in real wages of the type that occurred in the past are no longer achievable. It is therefore to be hoped that both labour and management can seriously address the question of what to do in order to avoid the vicious circle of wages/prices. The first thing that is needed in order to achieve this is a national consensus. If there is a consensus on the basic issues, then it should be possible to make headway in discussions to solve other questions. On the other hand, if this consensus does not exist, not only will labour–management antagonism intensify, but also it will never be possible to achieve stability and improvement of the nation's standard of living.
>
> (Nikkeiren 1974b: 35)

Even this brief description of the ground covered by the 1974 report indicates that it was full of highly contentious ideology. While several of these ideological propositions will be examined later, here it is appropriate to focus on the intense efforts that Nikkeiren made in order to achieve the report's objectives. More than 68,000 copies of the 1974 report were published and distributed, not just to company executives, but to government officials, the media and (significantly) union officers. This widespread distribution of the report was accompanied by a major campaign by Nikkeiren's leadership and its headquarters staff to promote the report's policy recommendations at meetings held all over the country. These meetings were concentrated during the period from the end of 1974 to April 1975, so as to coincide with the 1975 *shuntō* (Nikkeiren 1981: 635).

Important though such meetings were in building support, the crucial deliberations took place elsewhere in settings that were less exposed to public scrutiny. At a meeting of Nikkeiren's Executive Council, held on 21 January 1975, a discussion took place on the results of a survey undertaken by the Japan Productivity Centre during November 1974. The questionnaires returned by companies in the course of this survey showed that wage increases averaging 22 per cent were anticipated in the approaching *shuntō*. This was way above the guideline of less than 15 per cent that was incorporated into the *Report of the Committee to Study where Wholesale Wage Increases Are Leading*, which accounted for Chairman Sakurada's forthright denunciation at the meeting of Nikkeiren's Executive Council of the attitudes revealed by the Japan Productivity Centre's survey: 'It's like something out of a dream. Reality is different!' (Nikkeiren 1981: 636). By way of contrast, the same meeting of Nikkeiren's Executive Council also considered a position paper submitted by Nishino Kaiichirō, the Chairman of Nikkeiren's Special Committee on the Problems of Small and Medium-sized Enterprises, which was entitled *An Opinion from the Standpoint of Small and Medium-sized Enterprises on the Question of This Spring Season's Wage Increases*. This position paper called on major companies strictly to observe Nikkeiren's guideline when conceding wage rises, thereby reflecting the worries which many smaller companies entertained about the knock-on effects of *shuntō* wage settlements in large enterprises on their own pay structure and therefore business prospects.

Without a doubt, the most crucial meeting of all was the one which Nikkeiren convened on the morning of 18 March 1975 for the chief executives of 10 major companies in the metalworking industries (steel, shipbuilding, electrical goods and automobiles). This provided a forum in which the major players in hard-pressed industries, such as shipbuilding and automobiles, could put pressure on their opposite numbers in the pace-setting steel industry to hold down wages. The meeting ended in agreement that a uniformly tough line would be taken on setting wage rates in the 1975 *shuntō* (Rōdōshō Rōseikyoku 1979: 627). As Kume Ikuo put it, 'firms in the then-booming steel industry felt direct pressure from Nikkeiren to restrain wage increases' (Kume 1988: 673). Furthermore, at a meeting of Nikkeiren's Executive Council on the afternoon of the same day, Chairman Sakurada demanded greater effort to contain the current *shuntō* wage demands (Rōdōshō Rōseikyoku 1979: 627). As an indication of the difficult situation in which many smaller companies found themselves, it is also worth noting that the Executive Council adopted a lobbying instrument *A Request to Large Enterprises Regarding the Question of This Spring Season's Wage Rises*. This expressed the hope that a period of grace would be granted to sub-contracting companies which were embroiled in *shuntō* and, as a consequence, were late in meeting their delivery dates (Nikkeiren 1981: 42).

The metalworkers' unions organized in the IMF-JC objected to Nikkeiren holding a meeting of metalworking industries' bosses on 18 March 1975 and delivered a written protest to Chairman Sakurada the following day. The IMF-JC protested against Nikkeiren's attempts to influence the outcome of individual companies' wage negotiations on the grounds that these should be conducted in an atmosphere where 'decisions about wages take place autonomously'. Sakurada replied for Nikkeiren on 20 March and, while he admitted that the meeting of metalworking industries' bosses had taken place, he denied that a binding agreement had been reached. According to Sakurada, ever since its formation, Nikkeiren had consistently emphasized that wages 'should be determined by autonomous collective bargaining' between labour and management. Moreover, so as to avoid any 'misunderstanding', notification of the contents of Nikkeiren's reply to the IMF-JC was transmitted to the chief executives of the companies which had been represented at the meeting (Nikkeiren 1981: 636–7). The positions which Nikkeiren was attempting to straddle in its refutation of the IMF-JC's criticisms are well displayed in its commentary on this episode in its official *30 Years' History:*

> Just as with labour, managers too recognize the importance of solidarity and unity. More than that, we would not deny that, at a time when guidelines had been put forward, the need for solidarity and unity was even more important than in other years. Nevertheless, in our country, collective bargaining in individual enterprises is the mainstay of wage determination. In that sense, managers' basic approach is to set wages in a case by case fashion.
>
> (Nikkeiren 1981: 637)

After the initial exchange between the IMF-JC and Nikkeiren, it was elements within Sōhyō which kept up the attack. The Sōhyō-aligned Zenkoku Kinzoku (*Zenkoku Kinzoku Rōdō Kumiai* or the All-Japan Metalworkers' Labour Union) regarded Nikkeiren's explanations as sophistry and on 14 April it called on Nikkeiren to retract its policy of wage restraint, so as to allow *shuntō* to proceed on the basis of autonomous negotiations. Nikkeiren replied on 16 April, but Zenkoku Kinzoku remained dissatisfied and therefore appealed on the same day to the Tokyo District Labour Relations Commission that both Nikkeiren and one of its constituent organizations, the Kansai Managers' Association, were engaging in unfair labour practices. On 2 June 1975, 27 other union federations, which (like Zenkoku Kinzoku) were affiliated to Sōhyō, lodged similar complaints of unfair labour practices against Nikkeiren and the Kansai Managers' Association with the Tokyo District Labour Relations Commission (Rōdōshō Rōseikyoku 1979: 630–6). After that, these appeals became bogged down in the commission's time-consuming procedures and eventually petered out in a compromise on 2 July 1976, when both sides affixed their seals to a conciliatory agreement (Rōdōshō Rōseikyoku 1979: 677–8 and Nikkeiren 1981: 43).

More interesting than this inconclusive outcome of union attempts to use official procedures in order to thwart Nikkeiren was that Nikkeiren persisted in asserting that union objections to its behaviour were misplaced. Nikkeiren was adamant that there was no legal case for it to answer because 'even if one talked in terms of a "less than 15 per cent" guideline, there were no means to enforce it and it primarily relied on its persuasiveness' (Nikkeiren 1981: 638). Undoubtedly, Nikkeiren was right on this score. It has been shown previously that its relations with its constituent organizations, let alone with commercially independent enterprises, were never of an order-giving/order-taking nature. At the meeting of metalworking industries' bosses on 18 March 1975, it would never have occurred to the Nikkeiren officials who were present that they should issue orders to the assembled chief executives. Instead, the Nikkeiren approach was to emphasize to the company representatives who attended the meeting where their class interest lay and which course of action would best serve Japanese capitalism.

Just how persuasive this approach was is revealed by the course of events after the 18 March meeting. Commercially independent though they were, the key companies delivered a joint response to *shuntō* wage demands and, moreover, one which observed the less than 15 per cent guideline. In the steel industry, the Tekkō Rōren union federation had taken a 30-year-old worker with 12 consecutive years of employment as their benchmark and demanded an increase of ¥32,000. On 9 April 1975, five giant steel companies responded with a joint offer of ¥18,300 (including the regular increment linked to seniority) for a 35-year-old worker with 12 consecutive years of employment. Significantly, this was equivalent to a 14.9 per cent pay rise. Although the union federations in the steel, shipbuilding, electrical goods and automobile sectors reacted to the steel companies' offer with a collective statement to the effect that they 'absolutely could not accept this response', ultimately they all settled at about this level (Rōdōshō Rōseikyoku 1979: 630). The result was that the average wage rise in large enterprises across the Japanese economy as a whole was ¥15,279 (13.1 per cent) in 1975, which was comfortably within the less than 15 per cent guideline and represented a sea change from the 32.9 per cent peak of 1974 (Nikkeiren 1981: 653).

The success which Nikkeiren enjoyed in 1975 in keeping wage rises below its 15 per cent guideline was repeated in 1976, when the average pay increase in large enterprises was reduced to ¥11,596 or 8.8 per cent (Nikkeiren 1981: 653). This was well within the single digit target zone, which Nikkeiren had identified as an appropriate level of wage increases from 1976 onwards. Given the success of the strategy mapped out in the 1974 *Report of the Committee to Study where Wholesale Wage Increases Are Leading*, it is not surprising that this committee was kept in existence thereafter and continued to issue annual reports. With the disappearance of wholesale wage increases of the order of 20 or even 30 per cent (as in 1973 and 1974 respectively) the committee was renamed the Committee for Studying Wages Problems in September 1975 and there was even discussion within the committee during 1978 whether it should disband now that the average pay settlement in large enterprises had declined to 5.9 per cent (Nikkeiren 1998, vol. 1: 7). However, Nikkeiren's grass roots enthusiastically favoured the committee continuing to function and in 1979 it became the Committee for Studying Labour Problems.

The latter change of name reflected the tendency as the 1970s progressed for the committee to move beyond its original brief to study wages and to make policy recommendations in its annual reports on a range of issues that impinged on labour, such as inflation, unemployment, hours of work, retirement, working conditions, unions and so forth. The contents of some of these reports will be referred to in the discussion of Nikkeiren's principal ideological planks below, but here it is the surge of activity which accompanied each annual publication that will be outlined. For example, more than 115,000 copies of the third report were distributed after its publication on 14 December 1976. From mid-December 1976 to mid-April 1977, during which time *shuntō* was in full swing, more than 250 meetings, attended by more than 28,000 people, were organized by Nikkeiren throughout the length and breadth of Japan in order to popularize the report's recommendations. Likewise, 12 months later, approximately 270 meetings were held between mid-December 1977 and mid-April 1978, with audiences totalling 33,000. More than 125,000 copies of the fourth report were distributed following its publication on 14 December 1977, which was an impressive increase on the roughly 68,000 copies of the first report that had been issued three years earlier (Nikkeiren 1981: 635).

Ideology

In the *Wholesale Wage Increases/Wages Problems/Labour Problems Reports* and other publications issued between 1974 and 1980, Nikkeiren elaborated an ideology that was intended to complement its organizational efforts to bring wage rises under control. In part, this ideology was directed at employers, with a view to reinforcing their solidarity and in order to provide them with ready-made arguments for use in wage negotiations and other situations. However, Nikkeiren was equally aware that there was a wider public (composed of those such as politicians, civil servants, journalists and union officials) whose ideas it would be advantageous to influence. Nikkeiren's ideology was therefore targeted at these two potential audiences, one of which was intended directly to implement Nikkeiren's policy and the other to play a backup role. The main components of this ideology will now be examined in turn.

Inflation

It was shown in Chapter 5 that Nikkeiren arbitrarily attributed rising prices to an alleged 'productivity/wages gap' and in 1969 invented the productivity standard principle as the means supposedly to eliminate the scourge of

Table 6.1 Percentage increases in nominal wages and consumer prices

Year	1975	1976	1977	1978	1979	1980
Nominal wages	13.1	8.8	8.8	5.9	6.0	6.7
Consumer prices	10.4	9.5	6.9	3.8	4.8	7.6

Source: Sako and Sato 1997: 248

inflation by controlling wage rises. While this had little effect prior to the oil shock, the sequence of events from 1975 could give a superficial plausibility to Nikkeiren's analysis, since the levels of wage increases and price increases moved roughly in tandem and mostly downwards (see Table 6.1).

That over the years 1974–80 Nikkeiren played on popular fears about inflation and unemployment is clear even from the subtitles of several of its annual *Wages Problems/Labour Problems Reports: for labour–management cooperation to prevent inflation and expand employment* (December 1976); *mustering all our strength to go forward and solve the employment problem and prevent inflation* (December 1978); *to prevent the resurgence of inflation and solve the problem of employment for the middle and upper age brackets* (December 1979). At the same time, Nikkeiren continually invoked the productivity standard principle as the way to prevent inflation in practice. Its 1974 publication *Basic Materials for Wage Negotiations* already argued that the abnormal situation created by the oil shock provided an opportunity for getting back to the productivity standard principle, whose correctness had allegedly been proved by the current massive increase in prices (Nikkeiren 1974c: 51). Six years later, in the early months of 1980, consumer prices were again rising sharply, owing partly to the effect of another increase in oil prices. Because of these circumstances, the 1980 *shuntō* was nicknamed the '[rising] prices *shuntō*' (*bukka shuntō*) and Nikkeiren's response was to argue for strict observance of the productivity standard principle when setting wages, so as to bring prices under control (Nikkeiren 1998, vol. 1: 87–8).

There were several reasons why Nikkeiren's line on inflation and the productivity standard principle was ideological mystification rather than sound analysis. First, as in the previous period, Nikkeiren continued to 'demonstrate' that a wages/productivity gap existed by comparing nominal wages to real productivity (for example, Nikkeiren 1974c: 48–9). However, as Nikkeiren's own figures show, the increase in real productivity across the entire economy was 20.5 per cent over the period 1974–80, whereas real wages in all industries increased by only 7.6 per cent (Nikkeiren 1996a: 186). Real wages even fell in 1980 when nominal pay rises failed to keep abreast of the surge in inflation. Hence, once like was compared to like, it was impossible to account for inflation by reference to runaway wage increases.

Second, even Nikkeiren was forced to concede that inflation was caused in part by factors that could not remotely be associated with wage rises. In the face of massive increases in oil prices in 1973–4, it could hardly deny that one contributory factor was 'imported inflation' (Nikkeiren 1974c: 52) and yet it still persisted in advocating wage control as the appropriate corrective for this situation (Nikkeiren 1976b: 46–7; 1981: 604–8). When the same thing happened again in 1979–80, Nikkeiren was particularly frank about transferring the burden of externally induced price rises:

> There is no other way to cope with the sudden jump in the price of oil brought about by the Second Oil Shock than to economize in the consumption of goods or, in other words, to adjust the standard of living. Since that portion of the rise in consumer prices caused by external factors should be borne by the national economy as a whole, it must be dealt with by not raising wages to compensate for the loss incurred.
>
> (Nikkeiren 1998, vol 1: 88)

This relatively uncamouflaged statement of Nikkeiren's intention that labour should pay for Japanese capitalism's economic problems reveals the purpose that lay behind its ideological constructs, such as the supposed wages/prices spiral.

Third, even at an empirical level, Nikkeiren's interpretation of the relation between wages and prices was not borne out. If wage increases had been the cause of price rises, there would have been a noticeable lag between the two as the former fed through to the latter. Yet, as the annual percentage changes in nominal wages and consumer prices between 1975 and 1980 show (see Table 6.1), the two moved largely in harmony. This provided further evidence of the point made in Chapter 5, that wages are themselves prices (the prices of different grades of labour power) and therefore cannot serve Nikkeiren's ideological purpose of explaining the movement of prices.

The Japanese way of running capitalism

The 'Japanese way' of running capitalism was an ideological concept that Nikkeiren frequently used in order to justify the policies it advocated. In 1978 Nikkeiren celebrated its thirtieth anniversary and Chairman Sakurada used the occasion to deliver a speech in which he sought to identify some of the supposed differences between the Western and Japanese styles of capitalism. According to him, the differences between Japanese capitalism and the form it took in the West (*ōbei* or, literally, Europe and America) could be attributed to 'the Japanese ethos' (*Nihon no fūdo*) and to the consciousness that 'management is the conduct of human groups' (*keiei to wa ningen shūdan no un'ei*). Summarizing his speech, Nikkeiren wrote:

> Class immobility has disappeared and in postwar [Japan] those exercising rights derived from the ownership of monopoly capital have been eradicated too. In the light of the differences with Western individual-

ism, priority has invariably been given to 'pursuing harmony between the individual and the collective'. Nikkeiren's current stand and its tradition have certainly been based on the distinctive features of our country mentioned above, giving due thought to how to cope with all the different situations.

(Nikkeiren 1981: 29)

Fuzzy ideas, such as 'the Japanese ethos', 'management is the conduct of human groups' and 'pursuing harmony between the individual and the collective', were never clearly explained by Sakurada or any of Nikkeiren's other leaders, because they were held to be intuitively understood by all Japanese, even if difficult for Westerners to grasp. Thus, behind what at face value could look like conceptual sloppiness, there lay a serious proposition that the way in which capitalism was conducted in Japan uniquely suited the sensibilities of the Japanese by catering for their preference for social harmony, their desire for group cohesion and, indeed, their essential 'Japaneseness'. Confronted by the difficulties which beset Japanese capitalism during the period 1974–80, Nikkeiren habitually argued that, in the final analysis, 'we are all Japanese' and that 'we' (meaning employers and employees alike) should therefore look for 'Japanese' solutions to our problems. It was assumptions such as these which underpinned its oft-repeated turns of phrase, such as 'what both labour and management need to consider more than anything else when determining wages' and 'this is something which probably all sections of the nation can agree on' (Nikkeiren 1974c: 51).

There are two ways in which the 'Japanese way' of running capitalism can be exposed as mystification. The first is to show that it was powerless to insulate the Japanese economy from the imperatives (such as the need to maintain profitability at whatever the human cost) that are built into capitalism and outweigh whatever cultural trimmings it might acquire. The second is to demonstrate that by no means all Japanese shared Nikkeiren's enthusiasm for the 'Japanese way' of running capitalism. As far as the first is concerned, Japanese enterprises were hit exceptionally hard by the abrupt increases in oil prices and could only regain their competitive edge by reducing labour costs and taking other steps to improve productivity. Not only does this explain why there was so much emphasis on controlling wage increases following the oil shock, but it also accounts for the drive to reduce manning levels and achieve efficiency savings. 'The international economic environment and Japan's competitive power' (Nikkeiren 1976a: 12), 'personnel expenses which become a major factor in costs' (Nikkeiren 1976b: 29), 'the problem of excess labour power' (Nikkeiren 1978: 8) and similar phrases decorate the Nikkeiren publications of that era and were used to justify the efforts enterprises were making to slim down their workforce and increase the intensity of labour.

The shift away from the seniority wages system (which was noted in

Chapter 5) continued to gather momentum, particularly because many of those who were transferred to less secure and less well paid jobs, often in subsidiary firms, were older workers. Another trend from the earlier period that was adapted to meet the needs of the new situation was 'management involving all personnel'. A small committee was set up to investigate this proposal and it recommended in a report to Nikkeiren's Executive Council on 26 January 1976 'individual direct participation as the basis' for this (Nikkeiren 1981: 43). One of the concrete forms which this took was that in many enterprises workers were required to assess their own capabilities and, in the prevailing atmosphere of job insecurity, were induced to ratchet up their own production targets. Kumazawa Makoto's *Portraits of the Japanese Workplace* is relevant here and can also usefully be quoted in order to illustrate just how negatively some Japanese regarded the 'Japanese way' of running capitalism which elicited such plaudits from Nikkeiren. Referring to the measures introduced after the oil shock, Kumazawa wrote:

> Apologists for the system use lovely rhetoric. Today in the Japanese workplace, they tell us, we are exploring and expanding the potential of human beings. But clearly this system of personnel evaluation via self-assessment compels workers who aspire to secure and stable livelihoods to 'voluntarily' make sales pitches about themselves and compete to work at a furious pace to live up to their promises. If they fail to make good on these commitments for any reason, they cannot count on their continued job security.
>
> (Kumazawa 1996: 78–9)

No rigid social classes

The Report of the Committee for Studying Wages Problems that was published in December 1978 chose to emphasize another alleged difference between Japanese and Western capitalism. It argued that 'in the society found in our country, unlike the various Western countries, there is absolutely no class immobility'. With the breaking up of the prewar conglomerates, monopoly capital was said to have disappeared, so that

> the economic leaders in our country today are people who entered their companies as rank and file recruits and have risen in line with seniority and ability to become directors and presidents of those companies. These people are not 'the capitalist class' that Marx talked about. They are people who were elected at general meetings of the shareholders and have been entrusted with management rights.
>
> (Nikkeiren 1978: 4)

In a further twist to the argument, the report cited a survey of 352 companies undertaken in 1978 which revealed that 66.8 per cent of these companies had at least one director who had previously been a member of its union executive committee. As a proportion of all directors, 15.7 per cent had previously served on the union's executive committee. Hence, it was not too far-fetched to say that 'the union is the womb which nurtures company executives' (Nikkeiren 1978: 5). The ideological purpose behind this line of reasoning was then spelt out, in case it had escaped anybody:

> It must not be forgotten that, looked at from a worldwide comparative perspective, this type of situation found in the Japanese economy today is the most desirable of conditions. It is a boon derived from labour–management cooperation, particularly in enterprises in the private sector. When thinking about how our country should proceed in the future, this is the essential point that must be uppermost in our minds from now on too.
>
> (Nikkeiren 1978: 5)

Although Nikkeiren stressed the supposed uniqueness of this aspect of Japanese capitalism, its claims were exaggerated. The nineteenth-century capitalist class which Karl Marx had described in *Capital* (Marx 1919, vol. 1: 342ff.) was composed mainly of individual mill owners and mine masters, who passed into history in developed capitalist countries as the scale and complexity of capitalist production progressed. Hence there was nothing unusual about the fact that company executives in Japan differed in their personal characteristics from '"the capitalist class" that Marx talked about'. The rise of the joint-stock company had long ago marginalized most owner-managers and it was several decades since commentators, like James Burnham in *The Managerial Revolution*, had drawn attention to the world-wide trend for the management of capital to be separated from its ownership (Burnham 1945). The osmosis between union and company hier-archies to which the 1978 report drew attention certainly was more unusual from an international standpoint (and derived from the enterprise-based structure and outlook of many Japanese unions) but it did not have the sig-nificance that Nikkeiren attributed to it. If Nikkeiren's purpose had been sociological analysis rather than propagandistic expediency, the important question it should have asked was not *who* company executives were (in terms of their social background) but *what* they did (in terms of the func-tions they had to fulfil). When one surveys the full historical and geographical range of capitalist production, it is clear that those who func-tionally constitute the capitalist class have gained access to their privileges and reproduced themselves as a social group by a wide variety of methods. However, when it comes to their role, there is much less variation in the core functions that they have to fulfil. Those who act as the capitalist class are obliged by the competitive nature of capitalism to restrict the use of the means of production to producing for profit and, for the same reason, have to ensure that the accumulation of capital takes precedence over the satisfaction of human needs. If this applied to even such an 'extreme' case as a stratum of party and state bosses running a system of state-operated capitalism in the former USSR (Buick and Crump 1986) it certainly applied to Japan's company executives, no matter that a minority of them came from union backgrounds. Nikkeiren intended to demonstrate that Japanese capitalism operated for the common good because of its unique structure of permeable social classes, but the premises on which this argument rested could not withstand rigorous examination.

Relations with the unions

The previous section throws light on the importance that Nikkeiren attached in its ideology to relations with the unions and this was borne out in practice too. The period under consideration here was not an easy one for the unions and this was reflected in a decline in the rate of unionization from 33.9 per cent of the total workforce in 1974 to 30.8 per cent in 1980 (Sako and Sato 1997: 299). Tension between rival union confederations, such as Sōhyō on the one hand and Dōmei and the IMF-JC on the other, was endemic. This was partly due to a Left/Right ideological split between these two camps, but Kume Ikuo pointed out that it was also connected to the different sections of the workforce which these confederations organized (Kume 1988: 680–1). Dōmei and the IMF-JC were principally composed of unions implanted in large, private-sector enterprises that were typically geared up to produce goods for export. Many of these enterprises experienced an acute deterioration in their balance sheets as a result of the oil shock, which had repercussions for their workforce in terms of manning levels, job security and other negative outcomes. Pressures of this sort put workers on the defensive and increased the readiness of union officials to cooperate even more wholeheartedly with management. On the other hand, much of Sōhyō's membership consisted of government and local authority employees who worked in sectors that were less directly exposed to economic pressures from overseas markets, allowing its union officials more room for manoeuvre.

This analysis certainly squares with the degrees of warmth that Nikkeiren displayed towards Dōmei and the IMF-JC on the one hand and Sōhyō on the other. Throughout the years 1974–80, Nikkeiren maintained its by now established practice of frequent discussions with all the main union confederations, but its relations with Dōmei and the IMF-JC were considerably closer and more productive than with the others. As the 1978 *Report of the Committee for Studying Wages Problems* put it, 'since entering a period of low economic growth several years ago, differences in the way of thinking about the economic situation of our country between us and the union leaders (particularly of enterprise unions in the private sector) have virtually been impossible to detect' (Nikkeiren 1978: 30). Similarly, at Nikkeiren's annual conference in May 1980, Chairman Ōtsuki flatteringly contrasted the behaviour of private-sector unions with their public-sector counterparts:

> Settlement by the major companies at the 6 per cent level is the result of all industries and enterprises making the effort to put into effect the productivity standard principle. At the same time, we should not overlook the fact that among the leaders and members of the private-sector unions the basis consciousness existed that 'we had better not bring about the vicious circle of wages and prices so that we fall into inflation'.
>
> (Nikkeiren 1998, vol. 1: 89)

The leaders of the private-sector unions saw themselves as engaged in a trade-off. Dōmei's leader, Amaike Seiji, stated on 5 September 1974 that 'if the government is sincere in its wish to stabilize prices and assist the socially disadvantaged, and management agrees to cooperate with such policies, labor is also willing to refrain from demanding the real wage increases to which workers are entitled as a result of economic growth' (Garon and Mochizuki 1993: 162). Likewise, on 25 February 1975, Miyata Yoshiji announced that the IMF-JC would be prepared to exercise self-discipline over wage rises if a policy of controlling inflation was put in place (Nikkeiren 1981: 42). What these private-sector union leaders were less candid about was that part of the trade-off was their own incorporation into the policymaking establishment from which they had previously been excluded. The launching on 7 October 1976 of a private sector based Labour Unions' Policy Promotion Council (*Seisaku Suishin Rōso Kaigi*) was symbolic of this (Nikkeiren 1981: 43–4). Various commentators cited the way in which 'private-sector union leaders began to participate in some of the most important economic advisory councils' as a case of 'corporatist inclusion of labor at the industrial and national level' (Knoke *et al.* 1996: 56). Nikkeiren supported these developments, holding its first meetings with the Labour Unions' Policy Promotion Council to discuss economic policy on 14 January and 16 February 1977, for example (Nikkeiren 1981: 44). Nevertheless, even though it had a closer rapport with the private-sector union leaders, Nikkeiren described its relations with the entire union movement as follows:

> From the mid-1970s, meetings between Nikkeiren and all the labour organizations became increasingly frequent. The fact that discussions multiplied, not merely with Sōhyo, Dōmei and Chūritsu Rōren, but with the IMF-JC, the Labour Unions' Policy Promotion Council and so on, means that it would be appropriate to talk about a new trend.
>
> (Nikkeiren 1981: 648–9)

Organization, individuals and activity

Given the limited time span of the period 1974–80, it is not surprising that Nikkeiren grew only marginally over these years. By 1979, it consisted of the same 47 regional business associations as previously, 51 industrial associations (an increase of three) and the total number of companies connected to Nikkeiren via these intermediary associations had grown by 2,677 to 28,629 (Nikkeiren 1998, vol. 1: 67). At the annual conference on 9 May 1974, the decision was taken to change the title of whoever would lead Nikkeiren from then on (Sakurada Takeshi was the current incumbent) from 'Director' (*daihyō jōnin riji*) to 'Chairman' (*kaichō*) (Nikkeiren 1981: 41). As for the headquarters organization, the Video Library Centre did not survive as an independent company beyond 18 September 1974, when the service it provided was taken over by Nikkeiren's head office and then put under the supervision of a Video Library Special Committee on 1 April 1975 (Nikkeiren 1981: 41–2). Several months later, on 17 July 1975, there was a further reorganization of the special committee structure, whereby health and safety was incorporated into social security, and wages into labour economy. At the same time, the special committees on general affairs and labour problems in overseas enterprises were abolished and the ILO (International Labour Organization) Committee, which had been an adjunct of general affairs, was given the status of a special committee in its own right (Nikkeiren 1981: 650–1).

At the time of Nikkeiren's thirtieth anniversary in 1978, Sakurada Takeshi was still Chairman. While (as has been mentioned previously) his roots in the textile industry can be regarded as a hangover from the past, the industrial affiliations of his four Vice-Chairmen were more representative of where power lay within Japanese capitalism at that juncture: Inayama Kazuhiro (steel), Ōtsuki Bunpei (mining and cement), Ishii Ken'ichirō (steel) and Kamei Masao (electrical engineering) (Nikkeiren 1981: 651). Sakurada's retirement one year later, at the annual conference on 11 May 1979, was a landmark in Nikkeiren's history. Although the transfer of power to his successor, Ōtsuki Bunpei, went smoothly, no chairman after Sakurada was ever again to dominate Nikkeiren to the same degree that he had. Sakurada had held important posts in Nikkeiren's leadership ever since its formation in 1948 and led from the front during most of the 1960s and 1970s. Even in his retirement, he became Honorary Chairman until his death on 29 April 1985 (Nikkeiren 1998, vol. 1: 69).

In his speech at the meeting to commemorate the thirtieth anniversary on 19 May 1978, Sakurada enumerated the main fields of Nikkeiren's activity as labour problems, labour relations, employment, personnel management, education and training, labour legislation, social security, health and safety, labour economy, labour culture, publishing and international contacts (Nikkeiren 1981: 28). To these could be added lobbying, which continued throughout the period 1974–80, although the number of lobbying instruments issued in any one year never reached double figures and was as low as two in both 1977 and 1978. Out of the total number of 27 lobbying instruments issued during 1974–80, fully one-third appeared in the crisis year of 1974 as Nikkeiren reacted to the drastic decline in economic growth and other effects of the oil shock (Nikkeiren 1998, vol 2: 195).

As the foregoing account demonstrates, success did not immediately come to Nikkeiren in 1974. However, from 1975 there was a notable improvement in Nikkeiren's effectiveness, as enterprises resolved to drive up productivity, and as job insecurity put workers on the defensive. Nikkeiren combined orchestrated action on wages with an intensive propaganda campaign to interpret such action in ways that were favourable to Japanese capitalism. Of course, Nikkeiren did not accomplish all this unaided and success would have been far more difficult to achieve without the compliance of union leaders. Nevertheless, the course of events during 1974–80 proved once again Nikkeiren's continuing usefulness to Japanese capitalism.

7   No room for doubt

Japan in a class of its own (1981–91)

The years 1981–91 were notable for the high level of self-satisfaction which Nikkeiren displayed. Sakurada Takeshi's foreword to Nikkeiren's official *30 Years' History*, which was published in 1981, was typically self-congratulatory. According to Sakurada, Japan had so far been able to avoid the 'economically and socially diseased condition which it is easy for industrially advanced countries to fall into'. As specific instances, he cited the 'British disease' and the 'Italian disease' (Nikkeiren 1981: 2–3). By 1986, Nikkeiren's annual *Report of the Committee for Studying Labour Problems* was exulting over 'our country's superb economic performance' (Nikkeiren 1986: 42). Three years later, the same committee was reporting:

> Fortunately, Japan has been expanding its economy, with the focus on stable internal demand even under conditions where the yen has been appreciating. Of course, as will be mentioned later, there are still various problems of a structural nature, but we are solving our problems by responding to them with flexibility and good sense, in addition to the diligence and effort of the Japanese.
>
> (Nikkeiren 1989: 3)

Even in 1991, as Japan's economy stood on the verge of its deepest and most protracted downturn since the Second World War, Nikkeiren's publications were still predicting that 'economic growth of more than 3 per cent will continue' (Nikkeiren 1991: 11).

Nikkeiren's sense of well-being derived in part from the steady economic growth that was achieved during this period. While there was no return to the double digit figures registered during the 1960s, neither was there any disruption on the scale of the oil shock. The average annual rate of growth of GDP across the entire period 1981–91 was 4.1 per cent (compared to 2.3 per cent in the USA and 2.5 per cent in West Germany) and particularly during the so-called bubble years of 1987–90 it averaged 5.1 per cent (compared to 2.7 per cent in the USA and 3.6 per cent in West Germany) (*Financial Times*: 8 June 1987 and Nikkeiren 1996b: 236). Although such rates of economic growth were not spectacular by the standard of earlier decades, they signalled that Japanese capitalism continued to outperform its principal rivals in North America and western Europe, despite its exports being affected by the strength of the yen. Following the so-called Plaza Accord between the USA, Japan, West Germany, France and the UK in September 1985, the yen broke through the barrier of ¥200 to the dollar on 25 November 1985 and continued to strengthen thereafter, so that it traded at less than ¥160 to the dollar for the first time on 12 May 1986 (Mainichi Shinbun 1989: 1192, 1223). As before, Japanese companies met this challenge by shedding workers and driving up productivity. For example, in the hard-hit steel industry, the five largest producers shed 22,000 workers between 1986 and 1990, often through early retirement. In addition, by 1990 more than one quarter of their remaining workforce had been relocated into subsidiary companies, a process which frequently worsened wages and conditions for those involved (Hasegawa 1993: 30 and Kumazawa 1996: 154). Although the official (and understated) unemployment rate was virtually unchanged at the end of this period (2.1 per cent) from what it had been at the beginning (2.2 per cent), it reached 2.8 per cent in 1986 and 1987 which was the highest percentage since records began in 1953 (Nikkeiren 2001: 143). As for productivity, while it increased by 30.3 per cent in real terms across the economy as a whole over the years 1981–91, the 36.3 per cent increase in labour productivity achieved in manufacturing industries over the same period gives a better indication of the degree of pressure exerted on their workforce by enterprises targeting overseas markets.

Not only was the general performance of the economy between 1981 and 1991 a source of satisfaction for Nikkeiren, but the state of labour relations was even more gratifying. For the first time since the 1950s, the annual number of labour disputes throughout Japan lasting half a day or longer fell below one thousand to 950 in 1981 (Sako and Sato 1997: 248). Also, for the first time in 17 years, no section of Kōrōkyō (*Kōkyō Kigyōtaitō Rōdō Kumiai Kyōgikai* or the Council of Public Enterprise and Related Labour Unions) went on strike in 1981. This was symbolic of the extent to which the attitudes of the less combative, private-sector unions were being generalized across the labour movement by this stage. Indeed, of all the features of the 1981 *shuntō*, the one that Nikkeiren judged to be the most significant was that it was the private-sector unions which were setting the tone. In particular, the IMF-JC's ready acceptance of a joint offer made by the leading companies in the four metalworking industries (steel, shipbuilding, electrical goods and automobiles) had a major influence on the levels of wage settlements in other sectors (Nikkeiren 1998, vol. 1: 91). After 1981, the number of labour disputes declined to an annual total of 284 in 1990. The total number of disputes rose to 310 in 1991, but resumed its annual, downward trend thereafter (Sako and Sato 1997: 248). As for the preponderant role of the private-sector unions, this was to be formalized by Sōhyō's disbandment and absorption by Rengō in 1989 (see below). Not surprisingly, Nikkeiren welcomed the process leading to this merger, writing in the *Report of the Committee for Studying Labour Problems* that, 'taking the opportunity arising from the birth of Rengō, Japanese labour relations too will be thrust into a new era' (Nikkeiren 1988a: 41).

Wages

Despite the favourable conditions for Japanese capitalism producing a high level of self-satisfaction within Nikkeiren, this did not dispose it to be any more generous as far as wages were concerned. Throughout the period 1981–91, Nikkeiren continued to take a hard line on wages and, to this end, in July 1981 it reconstituted the Small Committee for Studying the Productivity Standard Principle. Before taking that step, the 1981 *shuntō* had been resisted by Nikkeiren on the basis of the policy encapsulated in the *Report of the Committee for Studying Labour Problems* which the Executive Council had approved on 19 December 1980. This report bore the subtitle *driving home the productivity standard principle and raising the efficiency of the public sector*. Predictably, the productivity standard principle was presented there as the panacea for inflation and Nikkeiren was unhappy when the 1981 *shuntō* ran its course and the outcome turned out to be an average rise in nominal wages in large enterprises of ¥13,808 (7.5 per cent). Nikkeiren continued to compare nominal wage increases to real productivity gains, so it was additionally dismayed when the 1981 figure for the latter proved to be under 3 per cent (Nikkeiren 1996b: 186). It was as this sequence of events unfolded that the Small Committee for Studying the Productivity Standard Principle began its work and published in September 1981 a report entitled *On the Productivity Standard Principle*.

Much of the content of this report repeated Nikkeiren's established arguments on the productivity standard principle. It maintained that, if the average rate of wage increases were consistent with the average rise in productivity, 'home-made inflation would become virtually zero'. Furthermore, if inflation were supposedly eliminated in this fashion, the attractive prospect was held out to wage earners that all rises in monetary wages would then translate into equivalent increases in real wages. Externally generated inflation (owing to a rise in the price of oil, for example) could still pose a problem, but this must not be compensated by wage increases, on the grounds that 'the loss in income . . . should be borne by the whole nation, including government, workers and employers'. In addition, the combination of real productivity with nominal wages in Nikkeiren's exposition of the productivity standard principle was well in evidence (Nikkeiren 1998, vol. 1: 73–6).

All these were familiar arguments which have been discussed earlier in this study. The same deficiencies as existed previously were not corrected in *On the Productivity Standard Principle*, as can readily be demonstrated by referring to Nikkeiren's assertion that 'home-made inflation would become virtually zero' in the scenario it postulated. Even if Nikkeiren's ambition to restrict nominal wage rises to the same level as the growth in real productivity had been achieved, an unrelated development, such as an increase in the money supply, would still have had inflationary consequences. In other words, Nikkeiren was positing a simplistic cause and effect relationship between wages and prices, which ignored the other economic factors in the equation. Had the small committee's purpose been less ideological, it might well have directed more attention to the correlation between the 7.6 per cent increase which consumer prices registered in 1980 and the 7.5 per cent rise in average wages achieved in the spring of 1981 (Nikkeiren 1996b: 186–8). These percentages are too close to be fortuitous and are best explained by seeing the 1981 *shuntō* as an attempt by workers to bring the price of labour power into line with the general trend in commodity prices.

Where *On the Productivity Standard Principle* did differ from earlier expositions of the subject was the greater attention that it directed to 'ability to pay' (*shiharai nōryoku*). The productivity standard principle was presented as an 'ideal' or a 'baseline' which should operate at the level of the entire national economy and to which individual industries and enterprises should endeavour to adhere. Nevertheless, despite the productivity standard principle's 'ideal' status, it was conceded that in practice it might be necessary for a particular industry or a particular enterprise to stray from the 'baseline' in accordance with its business prospects and therefore its ability to pay. Ability to pay was presented as what was consistent with the long-term stable prosperity of the industry or enterprise in question. Depending on whether business was booming or otherwise, Nikkeiren envisaged particular wage settlements departing from the baseline across a range whose extremities it described as a moderate 'plus alpha' and an appropriate 'minus alpha'. This advice that companies should bear in mind their ability to pay certainly came closer to the reality of wage bargaining at industry or enterprise levels than did invoking the quasi-scientific rhetoric of the productivity standard principle. However, this concession to reality at the same time opened a chink in Nikkeiren's ideological armour.

Ability to pay revealed the essence of wage determination as a process where each side probed to see what price of labour power the market would bear. In that sense, ability to pay was a fulcrum on which the class struggle pivoted, with the outcome determined by the degree of power and commitment that each side could muster. In the years ahead, Nikkeiren's leaders would frequently urge that wages should be set by 'rationally combining' the productivity standard principle and ability to pay, as Chairman Suzuki Eiji did in his opening address to the extraordinary general meeting on 20 January 1988, for example (Nikkeiren 1998, vol. 1: 175). Despite such glib advice, these two devices frequently pointed in different directions (as the 'plus alpha'/'minus alpha' deviations indicated). Moreover, even Nikkeiren was forced to concede that applying the productivity standard principle relied on data that generally were not available during the rough and tumble of *shuntō* wage negotiations. As the 1985 *Report of the Committee for Studying Labour Problems* admitted:

> At the level of the individual enterprise, it may be difficult when determining wages in a particular year to predict accurately the macro-economic figure for the rate of increase in national economic productivity. So it may be that wage negotiations will take place with the focus on the enterprise's ability to pay (which it is relatively easy to predict) and future business trends. Nevertheless, even in that case, the way of thinking encapsulated in the productivity standard principle should in the end lay the foundation.
>
> (Nikkeiren 1985: 16–17)

As the final sentence of the above quotation reveals, Nikkeiren did not abandon the productivity standard principle as an ideological construct. Without fail, it was invoked in each annual *Report of the Committee for Studying Labour Problems* throughout the years 1981–91. Indeed, Nikkeiren came close to boring to death regular readers of this publication owing to the frequency with which the familiar phrases were repeated, and the talismanic status which it had acquired is conveyed by a passage in the 1986 report to the effect that 'the productivity standard principle . . . is an ideal that should be pursued permanently, whatever the change of economic circumstances' (Nikkeiren 1986: 7). Yet, despite such assurances, Nikkeiren's supplementing of the productivity standard principle with the ability to pay had a corrosive effect on the former. From its origins in 1969, the productivity standard principle had lacked credibility as the objective and impartial method of wage determination that Nikkeiren claimed it to be. During the 1980s it was further undermined by coupling it to the less pretentious yardstick of the ability to pay. This latter never pretended to be much more than an imprecise estimate of likely demand for an enterprise's products and for the labour power required to produce them. On the positive side, ability to pay had the merit of being a step in the direction of reality, but its downside was to expose the ideological hollowness of the productivity standard principle.

Against this ideological backdrop, Nikkeiren kept up its practical efforts to hold down wages. From 1982, the publication of the annual *Report of the Committee for Studying Labour Problems* was moved to January, so that it coincided with the start of *shuntō*. Its adoption in that month by Nikkeiren's Executive Council would trigger a concerted push by its leadership to unite the nationwide organization behind the report's objectives. After *shuntō* had run its course, there would be a post-mortem at the annual conference in May, enabling lessons to be drawn on how best to keep up the pressure on wages next year. For example, Chairman Ōtsuki Bunpei assessed the outcome of *shuntō* in his address to the annual conference on 12 May 1983. The average wage rise achieved by workers in large enterprises in the just completed 1983 *shuntō* was ¥8,855 (4.4 per cent). This was a sizeable reduction compared to the 6.9 per cent average pay rise secured in 1982 and was, in fact, easily the lowest percentage increase in the more than 25 years' history of *shuntō*. Inevitably, the gist of Chairman Ōtsuki's remarks was that, although it was a step in the right direction, the settlement was still overly generous when judged from the standpoint of the productivity standard principle. Hence he urged his troops to be made of sterner stuff the following year (Nikkeiren 1998, vol. 1: 95–6). In the event, market forces resulted in an almost identical settlement of ¥9,236 (4.4 per cent) in 1984 (Nikkeiren 1998, vol. 1: 98).

In addition to this ongoing activity linked to established procedures, such as the publication of the *Report of the Committee for Studying Labour Problems* and the annual conference, Nikkeiren took some new initiatives. One that was directly linked to the importance attached to ability to pay was the introduction in August 1985 of an Ability to Pay Diagnosis System. Nikkeiren's headquarters offered this service with the aim of enabling companies to set wages at levels consistent with their ability to pay (as understood by Nikkeiren). Essentially, the system consisted of analysing a company's performance over the previous five years, clarifying its mid-term and long-term objectives, and devising a management plan which took this perspective into account. On the basis of this plan, the company's ability to pay was then calculated. Following this innovation, Nikkeiren also launched seminars on how to calculate the ability to pay personnel costs. The idea behind these seminars was to equip companies with the appropriate know-how, so that they did not need to rely on the headquarters system. The seminars also had the additional purpose of encouraging companies to think beyond wages alone and to factor into their calculations the entire package of personnel costs (Nikkeiren 1998, vol. 1: 76).

The cumulative effect of these practical efforts to restrict wage increases, in conjunction with the ideological crusade to promote the productivity standard principle and ability to pay, was that real wage rises lagged well behind real productivity gains over the period 1981–91. Although Nikkeiren's comparison of nominal wages to real productivity enabled it to wring its hands histrionically over the illusion that 'wages' were running ahead of 'productivity', it was all a sham. Nominal wages in all sectors rose by 39 per cent (42.4 per cent in manufacturing industries) during 1981–91, which certainly outstripped the rise of 30.2 per cent in the real productivity index for the entire economy (36.3 per cent in manufacturing). However, once the rise in consumer prices of 20.2 per cent that occurred over the same period is taken into account, real wages can be seen to have risen by only 16.4 per cent nationally (19.3 per cent in manufacturing). In other words, no matter whether one surveys the economy generally or focuses on manufacturing specifically, real productivity increases between 1981 and 1991 were more than 80 per cent greater than comparable rises in real pay. No wonder the level of self-satisfaction in Nikkeiren was so high, when employees at the end of this period were receiving in their salary cheques an appreciably lower percentage of the wealth they created than at the beginning.

Uniqueness of Japanese capitalism

Just as the stance on wages which Nikkeiren adopted during these years was an extension of its previous arguments and attitudes, so its praise for the virtues of Japanese capitalism had much in common with its pronouncements delivered in earlier periods. As with wages, the annual *Report of the Committee for Studying Labour Problems* was an important vehicle for this type of propaganda. Japanese capitalism was routinely presented there as less class ridden and more egalitarian than varieties found elsewhere. Another claim that regularly appeared was that Japanese enterprises practised an outstandingly 'human-centred' form of management. This beautification of Japanese capitalism was then rounded off with descriptions of cooperative labour relations and references to the allegedly widespread consciousness that both sides of industry share a common fate.

Part of the evidence advanced in support of the contention that Japanese capitalism was relatively classless and egalitarian pertained to the frequency with which union officials metamorphosed into company executives. This argument had already been mobilized in the period 1974–80, but Nikkeiren conducted a new survey of 313 companies in 1981, which revealed even higher percentages than previously: 74 per cent of these companies had at least one director who had previously sat on their union's executive committee and 16.2 per cent of all directors had experienced this change of role as their careers progressed (Nikkeiren 1982: 5). The moral which Nikkeiren drew from such statistics was much the same as its earlier line of argument:

> These facts demonstrate that classes are not immobile and that, accordingly, the consciousness of confrontation between a working class and a capitalist class is also weak. There is nothing strange about a father who is head of a company or one of its executives having a son who spends his whole life as a union member. Likewise, even when the son of a union offical becomes head of a company or one of its executives, he is not called 'a class traitor' or something similar.
>
> (Nikkeiren 1982: 5–6)

Even ignoring for the moment the overly harmonious image of Japanese capitalism which was depicted here, what Nikkeiren chose to overlook was that this type of behaviour was open to an entirely different interpretation from the one it was keen to draw. Far from signifying the amicable symbiosis of labour and management, it could just as well be taken as evidence of the extent to which particularly enterprise unions in the private sector had been manipulated by the companies in which they were implanted to the point where they were no longer recognizable as working-class organizations. By the same token, the spectacle of company executives and union officials co-existing without rancour could be interpreted as illustrating the extent to which union leaders had been incorporated into the web of structures that maintained capitalist domination. As if to confirm this, Nikkeiren wrote:

> Unlike the industrial and occupational unions found in the West, in the case of enterprise unions, the union leadership well understands from its own experience the actual situation in the workplace and the enterprise's standpoint. As a result, the union leaderships in our country know intimately the economic condition of their company and can empathize with the managers. These factors lay the basis for the consciousness that all are in the same boat and for relations of trust between labour and management.
>
> (Nikkeiren 1982: 4)

An additional argument that was deployed in order to demonstrate the exceptionally egalitarian nature of Japanese capitalism was based on the narrowing income differential between heads of companies (*shachō*) and new recruits. According to data which Nikkeiren presented in successive issues of the *Report of the Committee for Studying Labour Problems*, the gap had narrowed dramatically in postwar years to the point where it was only 14.5 times greater in 1980 (or merely 7.5 times greater after tax had been deducted), whereas in the prewar era the annual income of the head of a company had typically been more than 100 times higher than the salary of a new recruit who had just left university (Nikkeiren 1982: 6). Nikkeiren contrasted this relatively narrow band of incomes with the multiples of between 30 and 50 which it said were common in the West when payments to heads of companies were compared to the salaries of newly recruited graduates. It also referred to a survey which showed that the comparable multiplier in what it called 'the Communist bloc' was of the order of 15 (Nikkeiren 1984: 40). Nikkeiren's underlying purpose in pursuing this line of argument was revealed in the 1985 *Report of the Committee for Studying Labour Problems*, where a selection of the above statistics served as a lead-in to the proposition that:

> The formula of a capitalist class confronting a working class, which the Leftists put forward before the war, has lost its ability to explain labour relations in our country today. In our country, 90 per cent of the nation has middle-class consciousness and heads of companies and rank and file company employees alike are called 'salarymen', whereas in many foreign countries occupations are still hereditary and it is difficult to get out of the constrictions of class consciousness. When we compare the two, we need to be mindful of the fact that this weak existence of class consciousness, which is something that foreigners cannot easily imitate,

is the background to the egalitarian and excellent labour relations found in our country.

(Nikkeiren 1985: 42)

Nikkeiren's official *50 Years' History* was also revealing in its explanation of why the *Reports of the Committee for Studying Labour Problems* paid so much attention to distinctive features of Japanese labour relations, such as the relatively low income differential, the high percentage of company executives who had been union officials and weak class consciousness. According to this publication, the function which this exercise fulfilled was 'to deepen the understanding of the nation'. It then continued:

Also, these figures [the percentages and multiples referred to above] were useful as material for explaining labour relations in our country to those connected with labour relations abroad and so on. However, when foreigners listened to these explanations, they all showed in their expressions that they could not believe them. Pointing out these facts seemed to be truly shocking to them, so we can think of these figures as having that degree of persuasive power.

(Nikkeiren 1998, vol. 1: 79)

In fact, despite these remarks, how those abroad regarded Japanese labour relations was of limited concern to Nikkeiren. The real target of these remarks was influential people within Japan itself, such as employers, government officials, journalists and union leaders. The rationale for making pointed contrasts with practices in other countries was to cultivate the impression within Japan that, as Japanese, they were blessed with a form of capitalism that operated exceptionally fairly and harmoniously. However, there were several reasons why the supposed egalitarianism of Japanese capitalism was less convincing than Nikkeiren intended. First, even accepting Nikkeiren's figures, an income differential of 7.5 times (750 per cent) was far removed from a situation of equality. Even if it were true that the income differential was narrower in Japan than in other parts of the world, it is arguable that, once a multiple of several hundred per cent exists, people's consciousness is already conditioned by unequal distribution and that further excesses beyond this make little difference to perceptions. In other words, there was no automatic reason why (as Nikkeiren assumed) an income differential of 7.5 times (750 per cent) should result in more placid labour relations than in countries where differentials extended up to 50 times (5,000 per cent).

Second, it was appropriate that Nikkeiren chose to contrast Japan not merely with the West, but also with so-called 'Communist' countries. Nikkeiren claimed income differentials of about 15 times (1,500 per cent) in the latter but it was common knowledge that, in countries such as Russia and

China during this era, inequality far exceeded differences in declared salaries, owing to the privileges and perks that came with positions (Buick and Crump 1986: 58–62). There was a clear parallel between such arrangements and the situation that existed in many Japanese companies. By focusing on declared incomes alone, Nikkeiren ignored the chauffeur-driven limousines, membership of exclusive golf clubs, expense account feasting and whoring, and the other spin-offs that accompanied the top positions in Japanese companies (*Financial Times*: 31 January 1994). It did so because to have mentioned the numerous privileges and perks enjoyed by company executives would have undermined its assertion that relative egalitarianism resulted in cooperative labour relations.

Third, and most importantly, there was the functional role that company executives had to fulfil, irrespective of the rewards they received for shouldering this responsibility. As explained in Chapter 6, for Japanese enterprises to survive, they had to accumulate capital at a rate that was at least equivalent to their competitors at home and abroad. As a condition of retaining their positions, company executives had to supervise this process, no matter whether the personal benefits they derived from it were lucrative or otherwise. It was this unremitting pressure that drove company executives to pursue productivity gains and to control the wages bill, just as Nikkeiren urged them to do. Quite independently of any egalitarian feelings and inclinations that company executives allegedly harboured, this was a process which left no room for humanity. For this reason above all others, Nikkeiren's notion of Japanese-style, 'human-centred management' (Nikkeiren 1989: 28) was vacuous ideology. If the becalming of labour relations could not be explained by Nikkeiren's depiction of these supposedly unique features of Japanese capitalism, the reasons had to be sought elsewhere.

Relations with Rengō

When Rengō (*Nihon Rōdō Kumiai Sōrengōkai* or the Japanese Labour Union Confederation) was formed on 21 November 1989, it was the largest confederation in the history of Japanese unions, both in an absolute sense (8 million members) and in a relative sense (65 per cent of the 12.3 million workers then organized in unions). It easily dwarfed Zenrōren (*Zenkoku Rōdō Kumiai Sōrengō* or the All-Japan Labour Union Confederation) which was launched at the same time as Rengō by unions aligned with the Communist Party and had up to 1.4 million members. Shortly afterwards, on 9 December 1989, assorted Leftists set up Zenrōkyō (*Zenkoku Rōso Renraku Kyōgikai* or the All-Japan Labour Union Liaison Council) but this was even smaller, with at most 500,000 members (Kawanishi 1992: 423–4). However, at least as significant as Rengō bringing 65 per cent of the members of all unions under the same umbrella organization in 1989 was the fact that, in the same year, the rate of unionization declined to only 25.9 per cent. In other words, Rengō's 65 per cent of total union membership looked considerably less impressive when it was expressed as a mere 17 per cent of all workers. Nor did Rengō's emergence halt the long-running downward trend in the proportion of the workforce found in the unions. In 1991 the rate of unionization (24.5 per cent) fell below one quarter for the first time in Japan's postwar history and it continued to shrink thereafter (Sako and Sato 1997: 299).

Rengō's formation in 1989 was the culmination of a sustained campaign by the leadership of Dōmei and other predominantly private-sector union confederations to bolster their strength within the union movement as a whole and ultimately to eliminate Sōhyō. At a conference on 14 December 1982, Zenmin Rōkyō (*Zen Nihon Minkan Rōdō Kumiai Kyōgikai* or the All-Japan Private-Sector Labour Union Council) came into existence. Nik-keiren held its first exchange of views with this new body on 17 March 1983 and there were three further meetings during the same year. No doubt it was this type of development that Nikkeiren had in mind when it said that, from 1982, the frequency of its meetings with labour organizations increased and started to be conducted on a regular basis throughout the year, rather than just being a feature of the *shuntō* period, as had tended to be the case previously (Nikkeiren 1998, vol. 1: 80).

The swing of the pendulum away from Sōhyō gathered momentum on 20 November 1987 when Private Rengō (*Zen Nihon Minkan Rōdō Kumiai Rengōkai* or the All-Japan Private-Sector Labour Union Confederation) was established. Not only was this the successor to Zenmin Rōkyō, but it for-mally incorporated Dōmei and Chūritsu Rōren, which had both disbanded on the previous day, and attracted private-sector unions from Sōhyō's ranks. Private Rengō had a more centralized structure than its predecessor, Zenmin Rōkyō, and, with a membership of 5.6 million, it was larger than Sōhyō had been even at its peak of about 4.9 million members (Genseki 1990: 5).

The writing was clearly on the wall for Sōhyō and, on 3 February 1988, after conferring with Rengō's leaders, its leadership agreed on a plan to take Sōhyō's public-sector unions into an expanded Rengō by the autumn of 1989. This decision was endorsed at Sōhyō's conference on 26 July 1988, although minorities within Sōhyō's ranks opted to enter Zenrōren or Zenrōkyō in preference to joining Rengō when realignment took place at the end of 1989. Nikkeiren did not attempt to hide its elation as the union movement's long-standing mould was broken. As it commented in the handbook it produced for the 1988 *shuntō*:

> Taking advantage of the opportunity created by the birth of 'Rengō' [Private Rengō] in this way, it is to be hoped that, from now on, the form of Japanese labour–management relations will be such that, on the important questions, it will be a case of 'together arguing about those things that should be argued about and cooperating on things where there should be cooperation'. As for Nikkeiren, it believes it is necessary to have in-depth discussions on macro policy with 'Rengō'

and to cooperate to arouse public opinion and try to promote policies on questions where both sides' views coincide.

(Nikkeiren 1988b: 147)

One of the chief factors in Sōhyō's elimination was the privatization of nationalized industries, a policy which the government and employers pursued tenaciously throughout much of the 1980s. The changes in established practices and manning levels that accompanied privatization undermined Sōhyō's core constituency in the public-sector unions and eventually drove the majority of these unions into Rengō's arms. For example, in the process of privatizing Japan National Railways (JNR) the main Sōhyō-affiliated union was severely mauled between 1981 and 1988, owing to its intransigence over the issue of privatization. This was Kokurō (*Kokutetsu Rōdō Kumiai* or the National Railway Workers' Union) which had 245,000 members in 1981, when the drive to privatize public corporations got under way, and less than 34,000 members by 1988, after privatization had run its course (Mochizuki 1993: 189; Sako and Sato 1997: 220). Conversely, the leadership of the train drivers' union Dōrō (*Kokutetsu Dōryokusha Rōdō Kumiai* or the National Railways Locomotive Workers' Union) abruptly withdrew its opposition to privatization in 1986 and disaffiliated from Sōhyō. By amalgamating with the Dōmei-affiliated union Tetsurō (*Tetsudō Rōdō Kumiai* or the Railway Workers' Union) in 1986, Dōrō transformed itself from a small union of 44,000 members in 1981 into an important constituent of Tetsudō Rōren (*Zen Nihon Tetsudō Rōdō Kumiai Sōrengōkai* or the All-Japan Railways Labour Union Confederation) which embraced 132,000 members (67 per cent of all unionized railway workers) by 1988 (Fukuda 1992: 32; Mochizuki 1993: 189; Sako and Sato 1997: 221). One reason for the adroit footwork of Dōrō's leadership was that it received assurances from management in 1986 that the brunt of job losses following privatization would fall elsewhere, as proved to be the case when Kokurō members were treated more harshly than those in more cooperative unions (Mochizuki 1993: 184–90). Tetsudō Rōren joined Private Rengō when it was formed in 1987.

Nippon Telephone and Telegraph (NTT) was another public corporation that was targeted for privatization. In NTT's case, a single union known as Zendentsū (*Zenkoku Denki Tsūshin Rōdō Kumiai* or the All-Japan Telecommunications Workers' Union) prevailed and its leadership executed an opportunist about-turn on privatization in 1982. Zendentsū then went on to provide Rengō with Yamagishi Akira as its first Chairman in 1989 (Mochizuki 1993: 192–4).

Privatization and administrative reform were policies which Nikkeiren backed strongly, as did Keidanren and the other employers' federations. The overt aims were to prune the government's financial liabilities, overhaul the state's administrative machinery and inject greater economic competition into the delivery of services such as the railways and telecommunications.

Public corporations such as JNR and NTT were prime targets, on account of the chronic losses incurred by the former and the low productivity achieved by the latter (Mochizuki 1993: 192). Such poor economic performance was considered by the bulk of employers to impose an unacceptable tax burden on Japanese companies in an era of relatively low economic growth like the 1980s, while they regarded the public sector's allegedly lax attitude towards wages as setting a bad example to workers in the private sector. It was within this context that the government appointed Dokō Toshio, a former leader of Keidanren, as Chairman of the Provisional Commission for Administrative Reform on 21 January 1981. Following this, on 13 February 1981, the main employers' federations (including Nikkeiren) set up a Five Man Committee to Promote Administrative Reform which issued a lobbying instrument *What We Expect from the Provisional Commission for Administrative Reform* in March to coincide with the Provisional Commission getting down to work (Nikkeiren 1998, vol 1: 82). At later stages, Nikkeiren leaders played important roles in the successive deliberative councils which promoted administrative reform. Ōtsuki Bunpei became Chairman of the second Provisional Deliberative Council to Promote Administrative Reform from 21 April 1987 and Suzuki Eiji chaired the third of these deliberative councils from 31 October 1990 (Nikkeiren 1998, vol. 2: 227–9).

Nikkeiren identified with the general line taken by employers on privatization and administrative reform, but its particular concern for labour relations enabled it to recognize the possibilities for taming uncooperative unions that were inherent in these policies. Virtually every annual *Report of the Committee for Studying Labour Problems* issued between 1981 and 1991 lent support to the general thrust of policy, with repeated calls for the reform of the executive and legislative branches of government, the restructuring of government finances, the loosening of government economic controls (deregulation) and the overhauling of the public sector of the economy, so as to make it more competitive. However, what was distinctive about Nikkeiren's approach was the attention it focused on wages and personnel management in the public sector. Hence the *Report of the Committee for Studying Labour Problems* that was published on 19 December 1980, in readiness for the 1981 *shuntō*, included a chapter on 'Labour problems in the public sector'. This was critical of what Nikkeiren regarded as the overly generous treatment of public employees and of the way in which the National Personnel Authority (*Jin'jiin*) calculated wage increments. In particular, it objected to the expectation that there should be parity of pay between the private and public sectors of the economy, such as the profitable private railways and the loss-making national railways (Nikkeiren 1998, vol. 1: 105–6).

The 1982 *Report of the Committee for Studying Labour Problems* returned to these themes in chapters on 'The question of administrative reform' and 'Three problems of labour relations'. In the latter chapter, Nikkeiren referred to salary statistics for 1980, which it cited as evidence that central and local government employees were more favourably treated than those working in the private sector. Nikkeiren wanted an overhaul of the machinery that was responsible for setting the pay and conditions of government employees, rightly pointing out that this was a case of administrative overlap, involving not only the National Personnel Authority, but also the Prime Minister's Office, the Ministry of Finance and the Administrative Management Agency (Nikkeiren 1982: 12–22). The 1983 *Report of the Committee for Studying Labour Problems* maintained the pressure and, in its concluding chapter, forthrightly attacked the record of the National Personnel Authority (which was responsible for government employees' wage levels) and the Public Corporations and Government Enterprises Labour Relations Commission (which had similar responsibility *vis-à-vis* the national railways and other nationalized concerns) (Nikkeiren 1983: 36–7). Nikkeiren's ambition to rein in wages in the public sector was also clearly stated in the lobbying instrument *A Proposal Regarding the Wage Responses of the Three Public Corporations and Four Government Enterprises*, which Chairman Ōtsuki submitted to Prime Minister Nakasone on 19 April 1983 (Nikkeiren 1998, vol. 1: 108).

In their comparative study of policy networks affecting labour issues, David Knoke and his co-workers were struck by the degree of cooperation that existed between Nikkeiren and Private Rengō (and its predecessor, Zenmin Rōkyō) during the years when administrative reform was being pursued and which led to the privatization of JNR and NTT. Analysing attitudes towards 22 separate legislative measures that directly affected labour, they found that Nikkeiren and Private Rengō were twice as likely to be in agreement (on 10 out of the 22 legislative items) than they were to be opposed (five out of 22). On the remaining seven items, Private Rengō and its predecessor were noncommittal (Knoke *et al.* 1996: 171). Knoke and his co-workers' judgement was that, in networking terms, Private Rengō was far closer to Nikkeiren than it was to Sōhyō (which opposed 21 out of the 22 legislative items considered) and that 'this alignment indicated that the FEA [Nikkeiren] and the PTU [Private Rengō] supported one another in reaching compromises within an otherwise highly polarized polity' (Knoke *et al.* 1996: 213). The reasons for this collaboration between Nikkeiren and Rengō's predecessors are not difficult to discover. In addition to the employers' determination to raise the efficiency of public corporations and union leaders' aspirations to use privatization as a vehicle for further integrating themselves into the policymaking process (Tsujinaka 1993: 207–11; Sako and Sato 1997: 200–5), where their interests particularly coincided was their ambition to crush Sōhyō. The old adage that 'my enemy's enemy is my friend' comes to mind here and certainly this convergence of interests between employers and union leaders better explains the becalming of labour relations in the 1980s than do the supposedly unique qualities of Japanese capitalism, as Nikkeiren would have us believe.

Nevertheless, while collaborating with Nikkeiren, union leaders still had to carry their membership with them and could not afford blatantly to neglect their interests. Nikkeiren provided an escape route from this potentially tricky situation by developing a line of argument which insisted that the problems confronting working people derived not from the relations of production within enterprises, but from inequities within society at large, which were allegedly unfair to labour and management alike. Prices were too high (particularly the cost of housing, owing to astronomical land prices), taxes were too onerous, social security contributions were forever increasing and so on. Furthermore, these were problems for society generally, because – so the argument ran – we all buy goods, we all pay taxes and we all fall sick and grow old.

Thus, when Rengō was formed in November 1989, Suzuki Eiji announced, as Nikkeiren's Chairman, that he 'wanted to push ahead with the joint study of policy issues where we share a common understanding, such as the inflation problem, the land and housing problem and the social security problem, and endeavour to solve such problems' (Nikkeiren 1998, vol. 1: 177). This was the continuation of practices which had already been established during the period of Private Rengō's existence. For example, during 1988 Nikkeiren and Private Rengō conducted a joint investigation into the prices of Japanese commodities, drawing comparisons with the cost of living in the USA and West Germany, and on 19 October they jointly sponsored a symposium in Tokyo on the obstacles frustrating salaried workers' aspirations to acquire their own houses (Nikkeiren 1998, vol. 1: 191). This symposium resulted in the two organizations together directing to the government a lobbying instrument entitled *A Joint Appeal on the Land and Housing Problems of Salarymen in the Metropolitan Area* (Nikkeiren 1998, vol. 2: 196, 228). After Private Rengō was enlarged into full-scale Rengō, it issued with Nikkeiren on 2 July 1990 a report that emerged from their Joint Project on the Problem of Prices. On the basis of this report, Nikkeiren's and Rengō's Chairmen jointly addressed a lobbying instrument to Prime Minister Kaifu, requesting that he take steps to eliminate the gap between Japanese prices, which were kept high by restrictive practices, and the lower prices of many of the same items on the world markets (Nikkeiren 1998, vol. 2: 228–9).

As an accompaniment to this active collaboration between Nikkeiren and Rengō, the former kept up a constant barrage of propaganda that the wages struggle was *passé* and that attention ought to be switched instead to correcting prices, housing costs and other problems. The *Report of the Committee for Studying Labour Problems* asserted in 1988 that 'it is clear that the era of pursuing higher nominal wages has already come to an end' and that 'raising living standards by lowering the level of prices and bringing down land prices' is the way ahead (Nikkeiren 1988a: 32, 35). Likewise, the 1989 issue of the same publication declared:

Nominal wages have reached the highest level in the world and what is needed now to make the living standards of the Japanese truly affluent is completely to revise how we regard the level of consumer prices. Their rate of increase must not merely be brought down to zero, but has to be reduced to a minus figure.

(Nikkeiren 1989: 6)

While the hope had been expressed that Nikkeiren and Rengō should proceed 'together arguing about those things that should be argued about and cooperating on things where there should be cooperation', it is clear that cooperation became the predominant mode in their relations owing to the strategy of sidestepping the wages struggle in favour of other concerns.

Organization, activity and individuals

During the period 1981–91, Nikkeiren continued to grow, albeit unspectacularly. In 1986, the middle year of this period, it consisted of the same 47 regional business associations as previously, but the number of industrial associations had increased to 55. The number of companies affiliated to Nikkeiren by virtue of belonging to these regional and industrial associations was about 31,000, an increase of some 2,000 over the previous seven years. After 1986 there was no change in the number of regional business associations and, although the Japan Printing Industries Federation and the Japan Ford Service Association joined Nikkeiren in 1987 and 1990 respectively, their entry was counterbalanced by the withdrawal of the Japan Aluminium Federation (the aluminium industry was a casualty of Japan's high energy costs) and the dismembered Japan National Railways (Nikkeiren 1998, vol. 1: 67, 157). One innovation in 1985 was the holding of an annual meeting of the chairmen of all the regional business associations and industrial associations. This was intended to serve as a grass-roots forum and its timing in November enabled each approaching *shuntō* to be discussed (Nikkeiren 1998, vol. 1: 163).

Some of the anniversaries that occurred during the years 1981–91 indicate Nikkeiren's persistent activity in many different fields: the 20th annual National Intra-Company Information Conference was held on 5 November 1981 to discuss the theme 'Japanese-style management and the role of intra-company information'; on 2 October 1984 a lecture meeting was organized to mark the 20th anniversary of the Job Analysis Centre; on 8 October 1985 the 70th National Personnel Managers' Conference engaged with the subject 'The new industrial revolution and enterprises' response'; and on 7 November 1985 the 60th National Conference on Management Law considered the topical issue of 'Enterprises' response to the Equal Opportunities Law on Male/Female Employment' (Nikkeiren 1998, vol. 2: 224–6). The Top Management Seminars had been held annually in August ever since 1969. They had originally been conceived as 'internal study meetings', where top executives could discuss issues away from public scrutiny. However, as their 20th anniversary drew near, it was decided in 1988 to raise their profile by issuing a 'statement' in which Nikkeiren's views across the political, economic and social spectrum would be presented at the close of each seminar. In keeping with this decision, from 1988 the Top Management Seminars were also used more consciously to formulate Nikkeiren's direction and policies (Nikkeiren 1998, vol. 1: 165–6).

Training and education remained important areas of concern to Nikkeiren. The Centre for the Development of Human Talent (often referred to as the Fuji Training Institute because of its location at the foot of Mount Fuji) was enlarged and refurbished in 1983. Several hundred training events, attended by tens of thousands of participants, were held there each year (Nikkeiren 1998, vol. 1: 137). Many companies also continued to regard the cruises for foremen as important, not only for the practical training they provided, but also for their role in integrating lower supervisory grades into management's way of thinking. The maiden voyage of a newly constructed, luxury passenger ship, which was acquired for this purpose, took place between 9 and 23 November 1991 (Nikkeiren 1998, vol. 2: 229).

Many of the issues in which Nikkeiren became involved during this period have been touched on in the foregoing account, including reference to several of the lobbying instruments that Nikkeiren produced, either independently or in conjunction with other organizations, such as Rengō. However, in order to obtain a more accurate picture of Nikkeiren's lobbying activity, it is useful to make a distinction between the former half of the period (1981–5) and the latter half (1986–91). During 1981–5, lobbying remained at the same low ebb as it had done for many years previously, with less than five instruments released annually on average. By way of contrast, the number of lobbying instruments leaped into double figures in 1986 and remained at a relatively high level thereafter, reaching a total of 62 for the years 1986–91 (Nikkeiren 1998, vol. 2: 1, 195–6). This spurt of lobbying activity was connected to the problems which Nikkeiren perceived Japanese capitalism to be facing. One example was the ageing of Japanese society, brought about by the low birth rate and increasing longevity of the population. Nikkeiren's alarm at this trend explains why the number of lobbying instruments connected with old age and its attendant problems (pensions, retirement and health expenses among others) was on a par between 1986 and 1991 with those relating to perennial issues of concern to Nikkeiren, such as taxes.

The ageing of Japanese society was also well represented in Nikkeiren's publishing activity, which continued unabated throughout 1981–91. *Health and Welfare in an Ageing Era: guidelines and concrete policies* (1982) and *Aiming at the Construction of an Ageing Society that Is Affluent and Full of Vitality: the challenge to realize a society of lifelong welfare* (1990) are representative publications from this period. Nevertheless, by virtue of it being the most widely read of Nikkeiren's publications among policy-making circles, it was probably the annual *Report of the Committee for Studying Labour Problems* which exerted the most influence on decisions connected to ageing and other issues. Two of these other policy areas which received extensive coverage in the *Report of the Committee for Studying Labour Problems* were the position of women in the workforce and the reduction of working hours. These questions respectively moved up the policy agenda in the context of the passing of an Equal Employment Opportunities Law in 1985 and the amendment of the Labour Standards Law in 1987. Conscious of Japan's image abroad, the Ministry of Labour exerted 'administrative guidance' to encourage enterprises to change their practices in these areas and Nikkeiren reacted with startling belligerence. For example, a section of the 1986 *Report of the Committee for Studying Labour Problems* was entitled 'From the labour offensive to the Ministry of Labour offensive'. The argument presented there proceeded from the obser-vation that both Nikkeiren and the regional business associations had originally been organized to counter 'the labour offensive' in the postwar years. However, since then the union movement had been in long-term decline, with the rate of unionization falling below 30 per cent in 1983. Since this signified that 'the labour offensive' had now receded, one might have expected membership of employers' organizations to be registering a parallel decline to that experienced by the unions. According to Nikkeiren, the reason why this was not so could be attributed to 'the Ministry of Labour offensive' which took the form of a succession of initiatives in areas such as shortening the working week and equality for women. It was to meet this new challenge from the Ministry of Labour that companies were still enrolling in employers' organizations in increasing numbers, even though the threat from the unions had subsided long ago (Nikkeiren 1986: 44–7).

As for the roles of prominent individuals, Ōtsuki Bunpei remained as Nikkeiren's Chairman until the annual conference on 13 May 1987, when he was replaced by Suzuki Eiji. Suzuki held the position until Nikkeiren's annual conference on 15 May 1991, when he in turn was replaced by Nagano Takeshi. Remarkably, Ōtsuki, Suzuki and Nagano all came from Mitsubishi backgrounds, being chief executives of Mitsubishi Mining and Cement, Mitsubishi Chemical Industries and Mitsubishi Materials respec-tively. In view of Nikkeiren's contention that heads of companies were just as much 'salarymen' as were ordinary, rank and file employees, it is instruc-tive to quote Albrecht Rothacher's *The Japanese Power Elite* for a thumb-nail description of Nagano:

> Takeshi Nagano himself hails from one of Japan's gilded clans, which includes his late father, the former transportation minister Mamoru Nagano, his late eldest son Iwao, who was an Upper House member, and his late uncle, Shigeo Nagano, a former president of Japan's Chamber of

Commerce and Industry who played an active role as one of the Big Four in *zaikai* business circles in the 1970s.

(Rothacher 1993: 227)

Following established precedent, Ōtsuki became Honorary Chairman when he retired in 1987, while a change to Nikkeiren's statutes at the 1991 annual conference allowed Suzuki to be appointed Special Advisor when he stepped down as Chairman. When Nagano took over in 1991, few could have guessed that the new Chairman was leading Nikkeiren into a period that would see its demise as an independent organization.

8 Economic downturn and its consequences

Labour quiescence and Nikkeiren's extinction (1992–2002)

In 1992 the fortunes of Japanese capitalism took a dramatic turn for the worse. Growth was virtually squeezed out of the economy, with the GDP index registering a mere 0.4 per cent rise. This was the poorest economic performance since the oil shock of 1974, but in 1992 there was no external calamity on which to pin the blame. Alongside the paltry GDP increase, 1992 produced an array of equally negative economic statistics. Productivity decreased marginally within the economy as a whole (0.3 per cent) and more severely in the manufacturing sector (where there was a decline of 2.9 per cent in labour productivity). Wholesale prices fell by 1.5 per cent, which was the second annual drop in what would prove to be a succession of five consecutive years (1991–5) of falling prices. The official rate of unemployment edged up to 2.2 per cent, initiating an upward trend that would continue remorselessly throughout the 1990s and beyond, to reach 5 per cent in 2001. As for real wages, in 1992 they generally stagnated at 1991 levels, but in the manufacturing sector they even declined by 0.9 per cent (Nikkeiren 2001: 142–5 and Kamada 2002).

Although there was a resemblance between some of these negative economic statistics and those which had accompanied the oil shock in 1974, there was to be no swift recovery in Japan's fortunes in the 1990s corresponding to the way in which the Japanese economy had rebounded in 1975. Already by 1993 one of Nikkeiren's directors, Naruse Takeo, was writing that the current depression was the most protracted in Japan's postwar history, but Nikkeiren at that stage had no inkling of just how severe and prolonged the downturn in the economy was to be (Naruse 1993: 132). During 1992–4 annual growth of GDP remained marginal (0.5 per cent on average) and wholesale prices declined cumulatively by 6.1 per cent. There was a false dawn in 1995–6, when average annual growth of 3.7 per cent suggested temporarily that recovery was under way (Nikkeiren 2001: 144). However, in the event, the Japanese economy actually contracted in 1997 and 1998. There was then feeble growth in 1999 and 2000, but in 2001 the economy contracted once again (Nikkeiren 2001: 144 and Nikkei 2002). Wholesale prices also resumed their downward slide in 1998. Other economic indicators were equally depressing. Consumer expenditure in wage-earning households was in decline from 1997, which was a consequence of both the fall in real wages from that year and the rising level of officially recognized unemployment from 3.5 per cent in 1997 to 5.0 per cent in 2001 (Nikkeiren 2001: 143–5 and Kamada 2002).

Not only was Japan's economic performance from 1992 far inferior to its past record, but also it was uncharacteristically outclassed by its principal rivals within world capitalism. Japan's average annual rate of growth in GDP during the period 1992–9 was a mere 0.9 per cent, which was only one-quarter of the 3.6 per cent average achieved in the USA and even lagged behind Germany's sluggish 1.4 per cent average (Nikkeiren 2001: 213). Whereas in 1974 it was the precipitous rise in the international price of oil that had disrupted the economy, the economic downturn from 1992 was primarily due to the reckless expansion in which many Japanese companies had engaged during the so-called 'bubble' years, 1987–90. Fixed capital formation by companies in the private sector increased on average by a massive 12.3 per cent annually during those years (Nikkeiren 2001: 152–3). To put this into perspective, whereas the investment rate was running at about 20 per cent in most other major economies during 1987–90 (20.2 per cent in West Germany, for example) in Japan the average proportion of GNP channelled into investment over this period was 30.7 per cent (*Financial Times*: 26 April 1993). As a result, the dilemma facing Japanese companies in the 1990s was that they were burdened with a level of productive capacity that was vastly in excess of what the markets could profitably absorb.

Given its importance within the Japanese economy, the motor vehicle industry can serve as a particularly striking example of overcapacity. Whereas at its peak in 1990, domestic production reached 13.5 million units, by 1995 this had contracted to 10.2 million and, by 2000, to 10.1 million (Autoindustry 2003). Typically, the Nissan Motor Company possessed the capacity to produce 2.3 million motor cars, but in 1998 it sold only 1.53 million (*Financial Times*: 27 May 1999). It is cases such as this which lend credibility to estimates that as much as 25 per cent of Japan's industrial capacity was lying idle in 1995 and that only 35 per cent of Japanese companies were making profits in 1998 (*Financial Times*: 2 June 1999). From 1992 successive governments unleashed one fiscal package after another, running into trillions of yen, in an effort to reinvigorate the economy by means of tax reductions and public spending. While this policy had the effect of driving the level of government debt considerably higher than total GDP, it made little impression on the dead weight of overcapacity and failed in its purpose of ending the recession.

Organization, individuals and activity

Against the background of this unprecedented and totally unpredicted downturn in the economy, much of Nikkeiren's activity in the 1990s continued along by now well-established lines, using the organization it had built up over the postwar decades. In 1998 it reviewed its half-century of activity with the publication of two volumes of self-celebration entitled *Nikkeiren's 50 Years' History*. At this juncture, Nikkeiren consisted of the same 47 regional business associations as before and 58 industrial associations (a net increase of three since 1986). The accession of industrial associations such as the Information Services Industry Association in 1992 and the Japan Human Resources Placement Association in 1995 revealed as much about the direction in which Japanese capitalism was moving as did the lapsing of the Japan Silk Thread Manufacture Association (Nikkeiren 1998, vol. 1: 157). Standing at the apex of these regional and industrial networks, in 1998 Nikkeiren summarized the extent and limits of its relations with its constituent associations as follows:

> Nikkeiren's objectives in its activity are mutual communication and co-operation between managers' groups, surveys and research into labour problems, publishing resolutions and views on labour problems, and so forth. Nikkeiren does not have a negotiating function and, of course, it has no right to issue directive orders to member groups. However, while it is a fact that Nikkeiren has neither negotiating rights nor the function of regulating negotiations, it is well known that it exerts a major influence on labour–management relations.
>
> (Nikkeiren 1998, vol. 1: 5)

As these remarks make clear, Nikkeiren's *raison d'être* in the 1990s continued to be that of an employers' organization specializing in handling labour problems. This way of characterizing itself was something which had remained unchanged from earlier periods, despite the changes that had affected Japanese capitalism over the decades since Nikkeiren's formation, not least in the field of relations with the unions.

Under its statutes, the annual conference was Nikkeiren's highest decision-making body, supplemented by the deliberations of the Executive Council between conferences. However, in reality, power had come to lie in the hands of a much more compact group, known as the Policy Committee. Originally created to deal with any emergencies, the Policy Committee had acquired extra authority owing to its composition. It consisted of Nikkeiren's Chairman and Deputy Chairmen, the chairmen and deputy chairmen of its regional and industrial associations, the chairmen of its special committees and its Director (*senmu riji*) (Nikkeiren 1998, vol. 1: 5). Naturally enough, many of the leading players within Japanese capitalism were represented among the Policy Committee's 34 members, including in 1998 Toyota, NTT, Fuji Bank, Mitsubishi, Hitachi, Matsushita and Tōshiba (Nikkeiren 1998, vol. 2: 198).

Apart from the predominant role of the Policy Committee, the special committees remained the backbone of Nikkeiren's organization, in that they were charged with formulating policy and drafting lobbying instruments in their respective areas. In addition to the Committee for Studying Labour Problems, which was responsible for issuing annually the flagship policy document, the special committees covered publishing, employment, labour management, education, environmental safety, social security, labour legislation, industrial regeneration/small and medium-sized enterprises, regional/organizational regeneration, international affairs, structural reform, improvement of national life and labour relations (Nikkeiren 1998, vol. 2: 199). Some of these special committees had long been in existence, while others were newly formed in response to problems arising from the economic depression. Those with responsibility for structural reform, improvement of national life and labour relations were examples of the latter, since they were all established at Nikkeiren's annual conference on 15 May 1997 in the face of worsening economic conditions (Nikkeiren 1998, vol. 2: 234). Other committees of a more ad hoc nature were also formed as occasion demanded, such as a committee to undertake a 'Research Project into a New Japanese-style Management System etc.', which started work on 6 December 1993 with Nikkeiren's then Chairman, Nagano Takeshi, as its convenor. This eventually published its report, *'Japanese-style Management' for a New Era: the direction we should strive for and the concrete measures entailed*, in time for the annual conference on 17 May 1995 (Nikkeiren 1995).

During the period under examination here, Nikkeiren experienced two changes of leader. Chairman Nagano stepped aside to become a special advisor at the annual conference in 1995 and was replaced by Nemoto Jirō. Nemoto was Chairman of Nihon Yūsen, the largest shipping company in Japan, and he occupied Nikkeiren's top post for the next four years. It was under his direction that Nikkeiren endeavoured to formulate an adequate response as the gravity of Japan's economic situation became increasingly apparent. Then, at the 1999 annual conference, Okuda Hiroshi was elected as the new Chairman. As President (later Chairman) of the Toyota Motor Corporation, Okuda was one of the most powerful industrialists in Japan and the fact that each spring the wage settlement at Toyota had a major influence on the outcome of *shuntō* was a further qualification for leading Nikkeiren. It was during Okuda's period of office that negotiations between Nikkeiren and Keidanren were conducted in 2001, leading to the two employers' federations merging in 2002. The reasons for Nikkeiren and Keidanren amalgamating will be discussed later. At this point, suffice it to say that, for Nikkeiren, the trauma of losing its separate identity was cushioned when Okuda became the first Chairman of the new organization. It was launched on 28 May 2002 under the name Nippon Keidanren (*Nippon Keizai Dantai Rengōkai* or the Japan Federation of Economic Organizations).

Over the years from 1992, Nikkeiren continued to carry out its various roles, such as publishing house, lobbying body, training organization and research institute. Looked at in that way, the various functions Nikkeiren fulfilled could be said to be unchanged from previous periods. On the other hand, a more issues-based analysis of Nikkeiren's activity better reveals where the balance of its efforts now lay and throws light on some changes of emphasis that occurred within the general pattern of continuity. In December of each year, the *Nikkeiren Times* summarized, under a number of headings, Nikkeiren's activity over the past 12 months. These summaries were interesting, both for what they included and what they omitted. The list of headings invariably included 'Wages', 'Employment', 'Labour management' and so on but, by this stage, 'Labour disputes' were conspicuously absent. This omission was a clear indication that the days when Nikkeiren regularly intervened in disputes and fulfilled the role of strikebreaker had long since disappeared. There was no longer any need for this because of the dwindling level of labour unrest as the years passed by. In 1992 the number of labour disputes throughout Japan had already been reduced to 788, involving no more than 410,000 workers and a mere 231,000 days lost. Low though these figures were, by 1999 the corresponding totals were down still further: 419 disputes, involving 106,000 workers and 87,000 days lost (Nikkeiren 2001: 205). In Nikkeiren's annual summaries of its activity, residual confrontation between labour and management was most visible in the column headed 'Labour law', which principally dealt with court decisions on issues affecting labour. In earlier years, labour disputes and labour case law had both been of vital concern to Nikkeiren but, by the 1990s, only the latter involved its activity to any appreciable extent.

The inclusion from 1998 of a 'NR Housing Association' heading (*Nikkeiren Times*: 3 December 1998) and from 1999 of a 'Social security' heading (*Nikkeiren Times*: 13 December 1999) reflected other changes of emphasis in Nikkeiren's range of activities. The NR Housing Association had been established in June 1991 with the aim of providing affordable rented accommodation for employees, but it did not start business (with Nikkeiren's Chairman as its Managing Director) until March 1994. From 1998 the *Nikkeiren Times* reported each December on the progress of this scheme. Although the NR Housing Association was a new venture, launched in the 1990s, it nevertheless had its roots in the strategy that Nikkeiren had already developed in the previous period. This attempted to deflect workers away from the wages struggle, by arguing that finding a solution to high prices (particularly of housing) was more important than pursuing pay increases. The fact that 'Wages' continued to appear among the headings incorporated into the annual report on Nikkeiren's activity shows that this strategy was not entirely successful, but the equal space afforded to the 'NR Housing Association' demonstrates the effort that Nikkeiren put into the strategy.

As for social security, this was an issue which increasingly preoccupied Nikkeiren as the 1990s advanced. It argued that enterprises were caught in a pincer of falling profits and rising costs deriving from an excessively generous social security system. Nikkeiren sought to cut the costs borne by enterprises by shifting the burden of pensions, health care and other benefits towards the individual. Its mounting concern with this issue from the mid-1990s, as the economic situation worsened, is one reason why Nikkeiren's annual tally of lobbying instruments increased sharply from eight in 1994 to 17 in 1995 and remained in double figures for several years thereafter (Nikkeiren 1998, vol. 2: ii–iv). It also explains why by 1999 'Social security' had become an independent heading, rather than being bracketed with other issues, as in earlier annual summaries of Nikkeiren's activity.

Handling labour

During the period 1992–2002, Nikkeiren's efforts to control wage rises followed its established procedure. Each year, the line which it recommended employers to adopt during the coming *shuntō* would be set out in the *Report of the Committee for Studying Labour Problems*. This would be endorsed at an extraordinary general meeting held in January. To take 1996 as a more or less typical year, about 800 employers attended the extraordinary general meeting, which was held in Tokyo on 12 January. Chairman Nemoto gave the opening address to the meeting, following which Director (*senmu riji*) Fukuoka Michio presented the report to the meeting and gained approval for it from the assembled employers. As the following issue of the *Nikkeiren Times* put it, the report 'demonstrated the basic thinking of Nikkeiren regarding this spring's labour–management negotiations' (*Nikkeiren Times*: 18 January 1996). After this morale-boosting exercise, Nikkeiren would publish the *Handbook for the Spring Season Labour–Management Negotiations* (in 1996 this was published on 20 January). This was a reference work of analysis, arguments and copious statistics which was intended to provide the employers' representatives with handy ammunition in the approaching wage negotiations.

The next stage of the proceedings would be a roundtable discussion between Nikkeiren's and Rengō's leaders at the national level (in 1996 this was held on 6 February). The action would then switch to individual industries and enterprises, where the detailed bargaining would take place. From that point on, Nikkeiren's main function would be to act as an information clearing-house. During February and March the weekly *Nikkeiren Times* would report on the demands tabled by the unions in major companies and in the trend-setting industries. In this way, levels of expectation across the economy as a whole and within different industries could be discerned, although in many cases there would be a good deal of transparent posturing by unions which had no intention of pursuing their claims resolutely, let alone striking in support of them.

To stick with 1996 as the example, the *Nikkeiren Times* reported on 7 March that demands had been tabled in more than 50 per cent of large companies and that the average claim for wage increases was ¥13,027 (4.35 per cent). One week later, claims had been submitted to 70 per cent of large companies and the fact that the sum and percentage had barely altered (¥12,991 or 4.36 per cent) indicated that a trend had clearly emerged as far as the level of wage demands was concerned (*Nikkeiren Times*: 14 March 1996). By this stage, it was also clear that in 1996 the crunch in wage negotiations in major companies in the trend-setting, metalworking industries would come around 21–2 March. Once the major companies in the metalworking sector had announced their level of wage increases, others swiftly followed suit, so that Nikkeiren already calculated on 26 March that the going rate in the 153 companies which had settled by that date was ¥8,209 or 2.69 per cent (*Nikkeiren Times*: 28 March 1996). As soon as it became clear that wage settlements among the trend-setters were averaging just over 60 per cent of the pay rises demanded by the unions, the dust swiftly settled in most large companies. By 9 April Nikkeiren calculated that agreement had been clinched in 85 per cent of large companies and that the average settlement had shifted only marginally to ¥8,559 or 2.78 per cent (*Nikkeiren Times*: 11 April 1996).

The focus of attention would then switch to small and medium-sized companies which typically settled their wage increases in the wake of the large companies and usually at a marginally lower rate. 1996 was a typical year in these regards. At the point where 85 per cent of large companies had settled (9 April) only 24 per cent of small and medium-sized companies had announced their wage increases (*Nikkeiren Times*: 11 April 1996). By May the stragglers among the large companies would have reached decisions and it would therefore be possible for Nikkeiren to announce the definitive statistics for large companies in time for its annual conference, where a post-mortem on the current year's *shuntō* would be conducted. In 1996, these statistics were announced on 15 May, the day that the annual conference opened, and revealed an average wage increase of ¥8,628 (2.81 per cent) in large companies throughout the economy as a whole. In addition, Nikkeiren provided equivalent figures for 24 different industrial sectors, where average wage increases among large companies varied between ¥4,531 (1.54 per cent) in the steel industry and ¥15,054 (3.54 per cent) in the newspaper industry. A similar exercise was carried out for small and medium-sized companies, but in their case the statistics were provisional, because only about 60 per cent had concluded wage settlements by 15 May (*Nikkeiren Times*: 16 May 1996).

After the annual conference, wage negotiations would typically continue among small and medium-sized companies right the way through until the summer. They would thus overlap with the onset of negotiations over summer bonuses in leading companies. The *Nikkeiren Times* would report on both types of negotiations as they progressed, with a view to keeping employers informed of the going rates for bonuses as well as wage increases. In 1996, it reported that by the end of May about 80 per cent of large companies had already settled their summer bonuses, while more than one-quarter of small and medium-sized companies were still undecided on *shuntō* wage increases (*Nikkeiren Times*: 30 May 1996). As a result, Nikkeiren was unable to announce in 1996 the definitive statistics for average wage increases in small and medium-sized companies until 17 July. The global figure for small and medium-sized companies in all sectors was ¥6,665 or 2.72 per cent which was almost ¥2,000 less than in large companies, but only marginally behind in percentage terms (*Nikkeiren Times*: 18 July 1996). As for year-end bonuses, negotiations would normally get under way in October and would continue right through mid-December, with large companies settling first as usual. In 1996, Nikkeiren produced its first list of 116 large companies which had reached agreement on their year-end bonuses on 15 October (*Nikkeiren Times*: 24 October 1996). By 26 November, 80 per cent of large companies had settled (*Nikkeiren Times*: 28 November 1996) but the process was more protracted elsewhere and it was not until 17 December that Nikkeiren was able to release definitive statistics (*Nikkeiren Times*: 1 January 1997). By this stage, of course, it would almost be time for Nikkeiren to start the annual cycle once again, since the next year's *shuntō* would be fast approaching.

The extended process described above derived from times past, when the Japanese economy had been far more buoyant and the outcome of wage and bonus negotiations less predictable. Under such circumstances, the custom had developed of the *Nikkeiren Times* giving extensive coverage of negotiations which occupied much of the year and whose outcome was a matter of consuming interest. In those days, the paper's atmosphere had sometimes resembled a racing sheet, with tips on likely winners and losers beforehand and high excitement as the results came in. Although the pattern persisted after 1992, it no longer conformed to the realities of a situation where the economy was almost permanently depressed and real wages were frequently static or even falling. In these new circumstances, it was questionable how useful was Nikkeiren's blow by blow account of negotiations whose outcome held few surprises. Nevertheless, Nikkeiren persisted with this practice, as it also did with reciting the mantra of the productivity standard principle and the ability to pay in the annual *Report of the Committee for Studying Labour Problems*. Since the economic downturn from 1992 drove the annual rates of productivity increase lower than they had ever been (with the exception of the 1974 oil shock) it was inevitable that Nikkeiren would conclude with monotonous regularity that there was no scope for wage increases.

Unemployment

If there was a large slice of *déjà vu* in all this, the new development that impinged on wages was the ever-rising level of unemployment. The official rate of unemployment repeatedly broke postwar records, passing the 3 per cent milestone in 1995, 4 per cent in 1998 and 5 per cent in 2001. However, there were several reasons why the official figures seriously understated the real numbers out of work. First, the method used by the authorities to estimate unemployment consisted of surveying a highly restricted sample of the workforce, which did not necessarily produce authentic results. Second, the stringent definition of 'completely unemployed' which the authorities utilized excluded anyone who had secured even the briefest spell of casual work during the previous 30 days. Third, pervasive social pressures served to channel many women, young people and older workers who could not find employment into forms of non-participation in the labour market which did not register on the unemployment statistics. For reasons such as these, even Nikkeiren's leaders recognized that there were many more jobless than the official statistics indicated. Chairman Nemoto admitted to a British journalist in 1996 that the then official rate of 3.4 per cent would have been more like 6 per cent if measured by UK criteria (*Financial Times*: 6 February 1996) although even this higher figure might itself have been a considerable underestimate.

While there was room for argument about what the real incidence of joblessness was at any particular juncture, what is beyond dispute is that from about 1994 unemployment and its threat became an increasingly potent weapon for the employers to use. This development was all the more striking because it contrasted with earlier concerns about finding sufficient supplies of labour power, which had been a feature of the 'bubble economy' in the late 1980s and persisted into the early years of the period under consideration here. Such was the competition among enterprises to recruit new graduates from high schools and universities that, in the 1992 *Report of the Committee for Studying Labour Problems*, Nikkeiren expressed alarm about the upward pressure on starting salaries. Nikkeiren claimed that initial salary levels had increased by about 90 per cent over the past three years and was worried about the knock-on effects of rises at this end of the pay scale on the wages paid to established staff (Nikkeiren 1992: 44). As well as urging companies to get a grip on starting salaries, the 1992 *Report of the Committee for Studying Labour Problems* carried a copy of an agreement to regulate the timing of the recruitment of new graduates, the purpose of which was to damp down competition among enterprises to snap up those entering the labour market (Nikkeiren 1992: 35). Initiated in February 1991, this agreement eventually suffered the same fate as earlier attempts by Nikkeiren to buck the labour market and was scrapped in January 1997 as changed economic circumstances made it unworkable (Nikkeiren 1998, vol. 2: 229, 234). Despite the failure of this agreement to survive, the prominence it was given in the 1992 report indicated that at that point the perceived problem was shortage of labour power rather than unemployment. This was still the case in 1993, when the *Report of the Committee for Studying Labour Problems* addressed the issue of employment primarily in terms of the predicted tightness of the labour market (Nikkeiren 1993: 29ff.).

Nikkeiren's outlook on unemployment shifted perceptibly from 1994. The *Report of the Committee for Studying Labour Problems* that was published on 12 January 1994 was subtitled *long-term depression which is getting more severe and a labour–management response aimed at maintaining employment*. While the view presented there was still balanced by the belief that, in the mid- to long-term, finding adequate supplies of labour power could be problematic, it still recognized that the immediate prospect was rising unemployment:

> In the current harsh economic downturn, all means must be used to avoid aggravating employment problems, starting with checking the rise in personnel costs. Maintaining employment is the most important issue in enterprises where management professes to be human-centred (respecting human beings). Even in enterprises which cannot avoid moving production operations and so forth overseas, due to rapid appreciation of the yen, it is to be hoped that serious consideration will be given to employment problems, including the impact on small and medium-sized enterprises, such as those which have a sub-contracting relationship.
>
> (Nikkeiren 1994: 29)

Using these turns of phrase, Nikkeiren asserted that right-minded employers were as committed as workers to avoiding unemployment. However, it also made clear that the price to be exacted for this offer of solidarity over maintaining jobs was, in the first place, 'checking the rise in personnel costs'. Unsurprisingly, this was a price that the Rengō leadership was prepared to pay. Nikkeiren and Rengō issued a joint appeal *Looking to Maintain/Create Employment* on 2 March 1994, which was timed to coincide with the crunch point in the *shuntō* wage negotiations. As Nikkeiren later commented appreciatively, this had a major effect in ensuring that wage settlements were kept lower than in the previous year (Nikkeiren 1998, vol 1: 183). What it did not achieve, however, was the claimed maintenance or creation of employment, since the rise in the number out of work continued unchecked, as previously noted.

In subsequent *shuntō*, the supposed choice between wage increases or jobs became as much a part of Nikkeiren's regular stock in trade as the productivity standard principle and the ability to pay. The course of events was to show just how hollow this choice was, since the outcome was neither appreciable wage increases nor job security. Taking all factors into account, real wages across the economy as a whole increased by only 2.6 per cent during the seven years 1992–9 (a minuscule annual average of 0.37 per cent). Over the same period, the official unemployment rate rose from 2.2 to 4.7 per cent (Nikkeiren 2001: 142–3). Despite the empty phrases about human-centred management and respecting human beings, Nikkeiren encouraged employers to use the threat of unemployment as an alibi for

freezing wages. Even during the false dawn of 1995–6, when annual productivity increases improved temporarily to 3.0 and 3.5 per cent respectively,
Nikkeiren still argued that employers should resist wage increases:

> The wage level in our country is the highest in the world. A further rise
> in wage costs, linked to a loss in international competitiveness, can only
> further accelerate the industrial hollowing out that is under way. What
> should concern us is the actualization of excess employment in industry
> and enterprises. Under these circumstances, the maintenance and
> stabilizing of employment becomes the most important question for our
> country as a whole. Fundamentally, further wage rises will cause
> difficulty.
>
> (*Nikkeiren Times*: 18 January 1996)

One unusual development was that even some employers found Nikkeiren's
hard line on wages counter-productive at that juncture. Imai Takashi, the
Chairman of Nippon Steel, distanced himself from Nikkeiren's position and
Kawamoto Nobuhiko, the President of Honda Motors, warned that freezing
wages could undermine employees' readiness to work (*Financial Times*:
27 January 1996). Nevertheless, Nikkeiren did not waver in its opposition
to wage increases then or subsequently.

Stratification and 'flexibility'

In addition to squeezing wages, Nikkeiren also saw the economic downturn
and consequent rise in unemployment as creating conditions for weakening
the position of many of those who remained in work. This was first system-
atically spelt out in the previously mentioned publication *'Japanese-style
Management' for a New Era* (1995). Although dressed up with expressions
such as 'respecting the subjectivity of individual employees' (Nikkeiren
1995: 27), what Nikkeiren advocated was increased insecurity for wider
sections of the workforce by means of more extensive stratification. In itself,
there was nothing new about stratification. It always had been a feature of
'Japanese-style management', with major fault lines between those working
for big companies and those employed in small and medium-sized enterprises, between male and female employees, and between permanent
workers and the rest in large companies. Owing to these entrenched divisions, the lifetime employment, seniority wages and enterprise union
package which was intrinsic to 'Japanese-style management' always had
been more of a normative concept than an accurate description of the conditions most workers experienced. Yet, even taking this into account, what
was new about the proposals Nikkeiren put forward in 1995 was that they
entailed extending sub-divisions into the permanent, male (and, one might
add, unionized) workforce in large companies. Nikkeiren's plans still
allowed for something approximating long-term security for a much

slimmed down aristocracy of labour, but beyond that there were to be increasingly peripheral strata with decreasing levels of job security.

In *'Japanese-style Management' for a New Era*, Nikkeiren urged that only a core group within the workforce should henceforth be provided with secure tenure. This group would be comprised of those such as managers, key technicians and workers with accumulated expertise. They would be on permanent contracts and would enjoy a range of benefits, such as generous bonuses, incremental salaries, company pensions and comprehensive welfare provision. At the other end of the scale were those whose status was described as 'flexible', which became Nikkeiren's codeword for insecurity. These workers would be on fixed-term contracts, would not be provided with company pensions and would be treated as inferiors in various other ways. For example, their bonus and welfare entitlements would be significantly worse than those enjoyed by the core group and their wages would not rise incrementally. Sandwiched between these two poles, there would be an intermediate stratum made up of those equipped with specialist skills which were currently in demand. They too would be on fixed-term contracts, would not be provided with pensions and would have access to only limited welfare. On the other hand, their pay and bonus entitlements would be better than those available to the 'flexibly' employed (Nikkeiren 1995: 32).

Nikkeiren offered the above model of a revamped 'Japanese-style management' not as a precise blueprint, but as a guide to the direction in which companies should move. Although Nikkeiren illustrated its arguments by reference to only three strata, as outlined above, there was no doubt that in reality the layering of the workforce would be more complex than this. Hence, Nikkeiren recognized that each company would have to work out its own 'employment portfolio', corresponding to the precise mix of different types of labour power that it required (Nikkeiren 1995: 33). Nevertheless, as a generalization of the employers' strategy, the model was useful for conveying how Nikkeiren envisaged companies could bolster their competitive strength and be brought back to profitability. In essence, to achieve this, costs had to be driven down and productivity driven up. Further stratifying the workforce would contribute to these goals in several ways. First, it would permanently cut costs by worsening the benefits available to a significant proportion of the workforce. Second, at times of economic upswing, it would allow companies to take on workers 'flexibly' without incurring long-term obligations. Third, whenever the economy slipped into recession, it would enable companies to offload at will those who were 'flexibly' employed. Fourth, whatever the economic circumstances, stratification could be expected to enhance overall performance by playing off each stratum against the others. This would be so because the model provided for movement between the different strata, thereby stimulating each and every worker to compete, as some sought promotion by raising their performance and others strove to avoid demotion by the same means.

The model's influence was evident in various Nikkeiren policy statements issued over the years, starting with the *Report of the Committee for Studying Labour Problems* in 1996. In this report, the model featured in a section dealing with how to make the labour market more flexible (Nikkeiren 1996a: 28–30). In a passage that was studded with the inevitable clichés about respecting workers as human beings and individuals, the model was invoked as beneficial to employees and enterprises alike:

> From the angle of personnel management, in order to realize the ideal of 'human-centred (respecting human beings) management', one should aim at a system which invigorates the entire enterprise and workplace, while all along respecting the subjectivity of individual company employees. Looked at in a different way, there is diversification of employees' sense of values and the personnel system from now on needs to aim at a mechanism which matches the need for work of employees with the need of enterprises to diversify employment.
>
> (Nikkeiren 1996a: 29)

While the advantages to companies of stratification and 'flexibility' were obvious, Nikkeiren never adequately explained how making workers more insecure amounted to treating them with respect or how cutting their benefits contributed to their subjectivity. In the years that followed, Nikkeiren adhered to the basic approach encapsulated in the model, but tweaked it so that schemes such as work sharing were added to the range of types of employment which it urged companies to pick and mix. While Nikkeiren never ceased to insist that the model would deliver benefits to labour and capital alike, the fact that phrases such as 'including a reduction of the sum total of labour costs' were woven into the discussion of 'flexibility' did little to allay suspicions that the outcome would be disproportionally beneficial to one side (Nikkeiren 1999: 50).

Cooperation with the unions

Despite the pressure which Nikkeiren encouraged the employers to exert on wages and conditions of employment, relations with Rengō and the IMF-JC remained essentially cooperative. The 1992 *Report of the Committee for Studying Labour Problems* expressed hope that 'labour and management, as partners in industry, should become a stabilizing presence within the economy and society' (Nikkeiren 1992: 45) and Rengō in particular duly obliged. The habit of arranging a roundtable discussion between Nikkeiren's and Rengō's national leaders early in the year, so as to set the framework for *shuntō*, has already been noted and, as the 1990s advanced, the holding of an equivalent year-end meeting became routine. To mention some concrete examples, on 24 December 1996, Nikkeiren and Rengō delegations, led by Chairman Nemoto Jirō and Chairman Ashida Jin'nosuke respectively, exchanged views on employment and other problems. They also used the occasion to put the finishing touches to a report based on jointly conducted research into the development of new industries and job creation. At the same time, a joint lobbying instrument was issued to Prime Minister Hashimoto (*Nikkeiren Times*: 1 January 1997 and Nikkeiren 1998, vol. 2: 234). The following year's meeting, on 11 December 1997, included the first press conference ever jointly organized by Nikkeiren and Rengō. Each side fielded its Chairman and a Vice-Chairman and the occasion was used to unveil *A Request for the Revival of the Japanese Economy and the Elimination of Fears about Employment*, a joint lobbying instrument which urged the government to stimulate the economy with a package of measures totalling ¥5 trillion (*Nikkeiren Times*: 1 January 1998). On 10 December 1998, a three-way meeting (including government ministers) to discuss employment policy was held in Tokyo. Nikkeiren's and Rengō's leaders gathered for a preliminary discussion on the morning of the same day, so as to agree on a common line. The result was another joint lobbying instrument, addressed to Prime Minister Obuchi, which this time called on the government to create 1 million jobs (*Nikkeiren Times*: 1 January 1999).

As these cases demonstrate, cooperation between Nikkeiren and Rengō involved joint research and frequent joint lobbying of the authorities. The research projects ranged across a wide spectrum of issues, including housing, information technology, the environment, health and welfare, employment, social security and education. More often than not, agreement was reached on the policy initiatives required to address these problems, so that, to take the period 1994–8 as a typical example, at least 14 lobbying instruments were issued in the names of both Nikkeiren and Rengō during these five years alone (Nikkeiren 1998, vol. 1: 191–2; 1998, vol. 2: 232–5; 1999: 5). In addition, there were at least two lobbying instruments, on the question of the 'hollowing out' of manufacturing industries, issued jointly by Nikkeiren and the IMF-JC during 1994–5 (Nikkeiren 1998, vol. 2: 231–2). Although Nikkeiren and the major union confederations together constituted a powerful lobby, they did not always achieve the desired response from the government, which could lead to other forms of cooperation in pursuit of their common goals. For example, advertisements in the names of Nikkeiren, Rengō and Kenporen (*Kenkō Hoken Kumiai Rengōkai* or the Federation of Health Insurance Unions) were inserted in the *Asahi*, *Yomiuri* and *Nihon Keizai* daily newspapers on 21 January 1998. In an attempt to influence public opinion, these advertisements protested about the 'unfairly increased burdens placed on salarymen and enterprises' (Nikkeiren 1998, vol. 2: 235).

The wide-ranging cooperation between Nikkeiren and union confederations such as Rengō and the IMF-JC did not mean that they saw eye to eye on everything. The ritual shadow boxing on wages was staged annually during *shuntō*, since without it many rank and file members would have wondered what was the point of belonging to a union (the rate of unionization had dwindled to 22.2 per cent by 1999). Nevertheless, even at the height of the rhetoric, Nikkeiren and the union leaders flashed placatory signals at one another and the wage settlements were inevitably about midway between the initial bargaining points of the two sides. In 1996, for example, Rengō's Chairman Ashida was one of the invited speakers at the National Conference of Personnel Managers which Nikkeiren held in Tokyo on 17–18 January. At this conference, Ashida revealed Rengō's *shuntō* shopping list, which included an average wage increase of ¥13,000, shorter hours and the implementation of what he referred to as 'policies and a system which would give adequate consideration to life'. Yet, alongside the patently overambitious wage demand, Ashida was at pains to emphasize:

> We won't completely oppose everything Nikkeiren puts forward. Regarding the regulation of employment and other concrete policies, we'll discuss with the management side and make efforts to reach agreement between labour and management. It is not our intention to change the approach that we have adopted up till now.
>
> (*Nikkeiren Times*: 25 January 1996)

As noted in an earlier section, in the face of the Rengō demand for a ¥13,000 (4.4 per cent) wage increase, Nikkeiren squared up with the equally unrealistic assertion that pay rises were out of the question. An editorial in the *Nikkeiren Times* particularly took issue with Rengō's contention in its policy document *Rengō's White Paper* that a wage increase of the order it was demanding would boost the annual rate of economic growth to 3 per cent. Nikkeiren's counter-arguments asserted that pushing up productivity levels and reducing high prices would be more effective than chasing wage increases. Nevertheless, despite this difference of opinion, Nikkeiren had no intention of allowing it to overshadow the wide areas of agreement that existed between the two sides. True to that spirit, the *Nikkeiren Times* editorial continued:

> In the 'Rengō White Paper', apart from the foregoing, improving the standard of living and creating employment, making progress on the relaxation of regulations so as to encourage new industries, the necessity of reforming the financial system and so on are all mentioned. This perception is fundamentally in agreement with Nikkeiren's. Hence the importance of labour and management uniting in a joint effort to realize these objectives.
>
> (*Nikkeiren Times*: 1 February 1996)

As seen earlier, the oucome of the mutual posturing on wages was a predictable compromise, averaging ¥8,628 (2.81 per cent) in large companies. Nikkeiren's and Rengō's leaders could wring their hands over this, respectively complaining that it was too high or too low, while all the while mutually supporting each other on a far wider range of issues than the few on which they publicly disagreed.

Planning and ideology

Faced with the economic downturn from 1992, Nikkeiren sought to devise ways to extricate Japanese capitalism from its problems. However, since Nikkeiren's plans for alleviating Japan's economic woes inevitably entailed hardship for the workforce, they had to be provided with an ideological gloss so as to rationalize the sacrifices involved. Hence, planning and the manufacture of ideology were not separate activities in which Nikkeiren engaged, but inseparable aspects of a single process. Nowhere was this clearer than in the preposterously named Bluebird Plan Project, whose ideological features certainly gave it an 'over the rainbow' quality. The origins of the Bluebird Plan Project can be traced back to a press conference in April 1996, when Chairman Nemoto mentioned the idea of a 'made in Japan road map' for taking the country into the twenty-first century (Nikkeiren 1998, vol. 1: 231). This idea was developed at the Top Management Seminar in August 1996, where it was specified that the search was for 'a "third way" that was different from the advanced countries of Europe and America' (*Nikkeiren Times*: 15 August 1996). Following this, the Bluebird Plan Project took its course and a report was submitted to the powerful Policy Committee which approved it on 17 December 1996. This cleared the way for the Bluebird Plan to be presented and formally endorsed at Nikkeiren's extraordinary general meeting, held in Tokyo on 14 January 1997 (*Nikkeiren Times*: 1 and 17 January 1997).

Nikkeiren declared that important aims of the Bluebird Plan were to stabilize employment and to bring about the qualitative improvement of people's lives. It argued that the only way to achieve these objectives was to bolster the international competitive power of Japanese enterprises and that this depended on a three-way partnership between government, the employers and labour, who should jointly pursue an action programme over the three years 1997–9. Nikkeiren's package of measures for boosting international competitiveness ranged across economic structural reform and reforms of the administrative, financial, tax and social security systems. For example, as far as reforming the economic structure was concerned, this was to involve nurturing new industries, closing the gap between domestic and overseas prices, deregulation, and correcting what Nikkeiren called high structural costs by taking action to address low productivity in some sectors and high public charges. It is not necessary to list Nikkeiren's equally wide-ranging proposals in the areas of administrative, financial, tax and social security reform, but it should be noted that one of its key recommendations relating to these was to peg the projected rise in tax and social security payments. In the face of an ageing population, Nikkeiren sought to restrict the rise in the combined tax and social security burden to less than

50 per cent (and ideally less than 45 per cent) of national income (*Nikkeiren Times:* 1 January 1997).

Stabilizing employment was to be tackled by another raft of reforms. Some of these overlapped with suggestions for boosting competitiveness (such as promoting new industries) but prominent among them was making the labour market more flexible. The small print of the Bluebird Plan also stressed the need for measures such as controlling the wages bill in ways that Nikkeiren had long advocated and combining diverse forms of employment in a fashion reminiscent of *'Japanese-style Management' for a New Era*. Proposals for qualitatively enhancing people's lives included aiming to make housing available for an outlay of ¥20 million (roughly four times the average annual per capita income of employees). Another section of the Bluebird Plan was concerned with establishing enterprise morality and management ethics. One of the principal facets of this quest to uplift morals was described as 'to establish correct human relations within the enterprise' (*Nikkeiren Times*: 1 January 1997 and Nikkeiren 1998, vol. 2: 184–90). Overarching these various components of the Bluebird Plan was its ultimate ambition to give Japanese capitalism a unique identity which would distinguish it from the socio-economic norms that prevailed in the other leading capitalist countries. Thus, in his opening address to the Top Management Seminar on 8 August 1996, Chairman Nemoto defined the aim of the Bluebird Plan as 'groping for a Japanese model that is distinct from the European and American moulds' (*Nikkeiren Times*: 15 August 1996).

The most glaring omission from the Bluebird Plan was an adequate analysis of the roots of the current economic problems. If the Bluebird Plan was to be Nikkeiren's medicine for Japan's economic ills, the prescription had to be based on a correct diagnosis. However, there was no mention of Japanese enterprises' excessive productive capacity, resulting from the reckless overinvestment of the 'bubble' years. Clearly, it was Nikkeiren's character as an employers' organization that made it incapable of honestly reflecting on the past decisions and actions of its members which had precipitated the present economic malaise. Perhaps this was understandable in terms of human psychology, but it did put into perspective Nikkeiren's gall in advocating measures that would impose heavy costs on those who bore no responsibility for past mistakes.

Behind its veneer of high-minded reform and concern for the people's welfare, the Bluebird Plan was full of proposals that were bound to impact negatively on ordinary men and women. For example, its call to raise the level of productivity could only mean squeezing more out of the workforce. Nikkeiren particularly targeted white-collar workers in this regard and claimed that enterprises had 'large numbers of excess personnel' on their books (Nikkeiren 1998, vol. 2: 185, 189). How shedding these workers would help counter unemployment was just one among many perplexing questions woven into the Bluebird Plan. Controlling the wages bill and increasing the 'flexibility' of employment were established Nikkeiren policies that were patently more advantageous for enterprises than for the workers they employed. The recommendation to restrict social security expenditure was another issue on which Nikkeiren had long campaigned, with the aim of shifting the costs of old age and illness onto the shoulders of those affected. Four years earlier the *Report of the Committee for Studying Labour Problems* had declared:

> The most important aspect of how to respond to the ageing society is for all the people to possess a spirit of making efforts to help oneself. The greater the reliance on the state and local authorities, the higher is the burden borne by tax payers. If that is so, there is no hope of realizing a society brimming with vitality.
>
> (Nikkeiren 1993: 21)

The Bluebird Plan echoed these sentiments and was equally of the opinion that the vitality of a society was synonymous with the balance sheets of its enterprises. Even the unsubstantiated promise of making housing available for ¥20 million threw an unfavourable light onto Nikkeiren's notion of improving the quality of people's lives. Again, the small print of the Bluebird Plan made it clear that the type of accommodation which it envisaged workers purchasing for this sum was an apartment measuring 80–100 square metres. Who, other than an employers' organization, would describe accommodation of these dimensions for a working-class family as 'realizing a life of ease and abundance'? (Nikkeiren 1998, vol. 2: 185, 189).

The attempts to dress the Bluebird Plan in the trappings of a 'third way' of running capitalism or a 'Japanese-style model' (*Nikkeiren Times*: 17 January 1997) were as unconvincing as the plan itself. The term 'third way' was used in order to distinguish Japanese capitalism from two other ways in which capitalism was said to operate. One of these was primarily identified with the USA and the second with the countries of western Europe, such as Germany and France. Nikkeiren contrasted these allegedly American and European ways of running capitalism by reference to their degrees of reliance on the free market, their levels of social security provision and so forth, but pointed out that both tolerated high levels of unemployment (*Nikkeiren Times*: 11 April 1996 and 23 May 1996). By proclaiming stable employment as one of its key objectives, the Bluebird Plan was supposed to embody a 'third way', just as references to 'management which respects human beings' were incorporated so as to give it the flavour of a 'Japanese-style model' (Nikkeiren 1998, vol. 2: 185). Ironically, it was the workings of Japanese capitalism itself which exposed these elements of the Bluebird Plan as ideological froth. The very reforms that Nikkeiren recommended helped push up unemployment in the years after the publication of the Bluebird Plan. By 1999 even the understated, official rate of unemployment was higher than in the USA and, far from Japanese capitalism behaving differently from Europe and America, Nikkeiren was quoting their experiences in self-justification:

As the examples of Europe and America show, the unemployment rate rises temporarily as structural reform goes ahead. However, if there is no reform, the situation will get even worse. Our choice is to do everything we can to prevent unemployment as we press ahead with reform.

(*Nikkeiren Times*: 21 January 1999)

To unemployment as an inevitable feature of capitalism could be added job insecurity, inadequate benefits, poor housing, real wages lagging behind productivity and authoritarian structures. Each of these inherent aspects of working-class life could be glimpsed between the lines of the Bluebird Plan. Whatever ideological spin Nikkeiren attempted to put on the Bluebird Plan, those working for wages in Japan were in essentially the same position as wage earners find themselves under any form of capitalism. This essential sameness provided no leeway for the construction of Nikkeiren's stridently proclaimed 'third way' or 'Japanese-style model'.

Merging with Keidanren

As noted earlier in this chapter, Nikkeiren and Keidanren joined forces on 28 May 2002 to become Nippon Keidanren. As of 18 June 2002, the new organization consisted of 47 regional business associations, 127 industrial associations and 1,232 directly affiliated companies (Nippon Keidanren: 2002). Looked at in this way, the benefits of merging are immediately apparent, since Nippon Keidanren was more powerful than either Nikkeiren or Keidanren had been separately. However, the logic of numbers was not a sufficient explanation for Nikkeiren and Keidanren deciding to amalgamate in 2002, since arithmetic alone would have led to the same conclusion many years previously and yet had been steadfastly rejected. Both Nikkeiren and Keidanren were proud organizations, jealous of their independence and accustomed to operating in separate spheres. Typically, Nikkeiren had indignantly asserted in 1968 that it was quite wrong to regard it as merely the labour section of Keidanren (Nikkeiren 1968a: 12). So what were the additional factors which made the logic of numbers irresistible in 2002?

Three reasons can be identified. First, Nikkeiren had gradually lost its *raison d'être*. An employers' organization specializing in labour problems was of doubtful value in a period when labour was increasingly quiescent. In part, Nikkeiren's success over the decades since its formation had ultimately undermined the reason for its existence. However, in the period under consideration here, it was the effects of economic downturn (such as the threat of unemployment) which put labour on the defensive, rather than any victories scored by Nikkeiren. Handling labour problems had ceased to require an employers' organization dedicated to this task and could be subsumed into the general business of managing capitalism. As the *Nikkeiren Times* remarked in 2001, 'it has become difficult to deal with labour problems separately from economic problems' (*Nikkeiren Times*: 1 January 2001).

Second, while Nikkeiren's original purpose had become increasingly superfluous, so Keidanren's influence was much reduced. By the beginning of the twenty-first century, it was difficult to believe that less than 20 years earlier Rob Steven had written:

> Keidanren . . . is a unique institution, since, unlike the Confederation of British Industries, it includes and speaks for monopoly capital alone. Its ability to direct government policy on wages, prices, investment, interest rates, employment, economic growth, regional development, trade, foreign policy, taxation, education, police powers, and almost every facet of the nation's life is widely documented even in the conservative Japanese press.
>
> (Steven 1983: 55–6)

Even allowing for a degree of hyperbole in Steven's remarks, Keidanren's influence had undoubtedly waned since then. This was due to a number of reasons, including the widening gap between Keidanren's national focus and the multinational interests of powerful Japanese companies and changes in the ways in which political parties were funded, which gave Keidanren less leverage than previously over Liberal Democratic Party governments. Whatever the reasons, to compensate for their loss of individual clout, it made sense for Nikkeiren and Keidanren to speak with one voice when they lobbied the government on issues that concerned them both, such as reforming social security (Kikuchi 2000: 45).

Third, as the economic recession dragged on, many companies' finances were put under increasing strain, which made it difficult for them to continue paying membership dues to both Nikkeiren and Keidanren. Figures on withdrawals from Nikkeiren and its constituent associations for this reason are difficult to obtain, but it is known that 42 companies and economic organizations resigned from Keidanren during the months immediately preceding the founding of Nippon Keidanren. These included some famous names, such as McDonald's Japan and Mitsui Mining (Asahi 2002). The need for economic structural reform was at the heart of the Bluebird Plan, but Nikkeiren probably never imagined when it published that document in 1997 that it would be a victim of the same process just five years later.

9   Conclusions
Nikkeiren and Japanese capitalism

It was argued in Chapter 1 that the prevailing interpretations of Japanese capitalism by Western commentators have largely ignored the roles played by class power, manipulation and mystification. As a corrective to these blind spots, the hypothesis was advanced that the employers' federation Nikkeiren could best exemplify the organized power of capital and its techniques of coercion, manipulation and mystification. In the chapters that followed, an account was given of Nikkeiren's organization and activity, from its formation in 1948 until its merging with Keidanren in 2002 to become Nippon Keidanren. This history of Nikkeiren was set within the context of the different periods through which Japanese capitalism has passed since 1945. To what extent has this account of Nikkeiren's history provided evidence to support the contention that class power, manipulation and mystification fulfil vital roles in the operation of capitalism in Japan?

Class power

Coercive class power was most strikingly visible during the period 1948–60, when Nikkeiren was leading the employers in a concerted campaign to regain 'the right to manage'. In one bitterly fought labour dispute after another, Nikkeiren impressed on whichever company was involved that the battle was not just about the immediate issues, such as wage increases and working conditions, but about annihilating the enemy in the shape of independent unions with the guts to challenge management. Shikanai Nobutaka's maxim that 'when it comes to a dispute, it's the last five minutes that count' (Nikkeiren 1981: 749) expressed Nikkeiren's determination not merely to win the immediate struggles, but to inflict crushing defeats from which the enemy could not recover. This was a strategy of class war, which is an apt term to use, not merely because of the belligerence which Nikkeiren displayed, but also because it was able to forge solidarity between the employers by appealing to their collective interest. In labour disputes such as those involving Nissan in 1953 and Mitsui Mining in 1959–60, commercial rivals were well positioned to expand their share of the market and make additional profits at the expense of the companies directly involved. Under normal circumstances, the pursuit of profit would have dictated such a course of action, but Nikkeiren was able to convince the employers that their collective interest in seeing a militant union humbled outweighed their separate efforts to maximize sales. Hence, as was explained in Chapter 4, Nikkeiren persuaded Toyota and Isuzu not to expand production during the Nissan dispute, while it encouraged the coal mining companies collectively to keep Mitsui Mining in business even when the labour dispute disrupted its commercial operations. In the case of the electric power dispute in 1952, classwide solidarity among employers was even more impressive, since it extended beyond the electricity generating companies to involve other industrial sectors. Under the terms of the memorandum *Matters of Agreement and Understanding*, which was approved at a conference of the chairmen of Nikkeiren's industrial associations on 31 October 1952, enterprises throughout the economy offered to mobilize electrical technicians at their own expense to assist the electricity generating companies (Chapter 4). In each of the labour disputes mentioned above, the widespread support from other employers, which Nikkeiren orchestrated, enabled the companies directly involved to fight on to the point where the union they were confronting was effectively broken.

It is true that the 1959–60 Mitsui Miike Coal Mines dispute was a watershed, after which pitched battles between capital and labour largely disappeared. Nevertheless, trench warfare over wages and conditions continued, with Nikkeiren attempting to unify companies' strategy, since it realized that a united response to workers' demands would best serve the interests of employers. This approach worked more effectively in some periods than others, depending on the state of the economy. Under conditions of high speed growth, when the demand for labour power was intense, discipline among employers tended to be lax as they competed to recruit and retain workers by raising wages and improving conditions. In this situation, Nikkeiren's call for wage restraint was little more than a voice in the wilderness and its continuing usefulness to the employers lay in management training and similar services that it provided (Chapter 5). By way of contrast, sharp downturns in the economy provided both the opportunity and the need for employers to close ranks in order to rein in wages and other personnel expenses. One example of the latter set of circumstances was the oil shock and its aftermath which led Nikkeiren officials to hold a meeting on 18 March 1975 with the top executives of 10 major companies in the metalworking industries. As explained in Chapter 6, out of this meeting a consensus emerged to keep wage increases within Nikkeiren's guideline of 15 per cent. The metalworkers' unions objected that Nikkeiren had no right to set wage levels, but this missed the point that Nikkeiren had no need to dictate on such matters (nor, indeed, the power to impose its will on independent companies). At the meeting on 18 March 1975, it was sufficient to state the case for pegging wage increases to less than 15 per cent and to let the collective interest of the assembled employers do the rest. The fragile state of the economy at that time meant that the previous sharp competition for labour power had eased, thereby removing the factor which could have set company against company and undermined class solidarity. In these circumstances, there was no impediment to employers pooling their strength in order to achieve common objectives which flowed from shared interests. Undoubt-edly, Nikkeiren was a useful catalyst in bringing this about, but it was successful only because employers stood in the same relation to the means of production and hence had a collective interest in restraining wage rises as part of their strategy for bringing enterprises back into profitability. The employers' exercise of class power on occasions such as this did not mean that they had *carte blanche*. They always had to operate within the limits set by economic circumstances. Nevertheless, when they acted in concert with economic trends, the employers could use their formidable power, which derived from their control of the means of production, to impose their will on the workforce in ways that were facilitated by Nikkeiren.

Manipulation

It was shown in Chapter 4 that destroying militant unions was only one half of the strategy that Nikkeiren developed for taming labour. The other half was to encourage the emergence of cooperative unions, whose outlook and organization would be firmly set within the mould of the enterprise. Unions of the latter type were not exact replicas of the company unions of prewar days, but their enterprise character made them sufficiently similar to predis-pose employers in their favour (Chapter 2). In order to shift the union movement's centre of gravity in this direction, Nikkeiren's standard advice to employers when labour disputes occurred during the period 1948–60 was to engineer a split in the workforce and then to discriminate in favour of the 'second' union at the expense of the recalcitrant 'first' union (Chapter 4). In later periods too, different types of unions were treated in similarly discrim-inatory fashion, an obvious example being the preferential handling of the more cooperative unions in the breaking up of Japan National Railways (Chapter 7). Unions of the preferred type were appreciatively described by Nikkeiren as 'healthy' because of their propensity to cooperate with company policy (Chapter 4) and as 'the womb which nurtures company executives' because of the frequency with which union officials moved on to management posts (Chapter 6). It was this type of enterprise union that formed the backbone of the Dōmei and Private Rengō labour confedera-tions, which were formed in 1964 and 1987 respectively. Increasingly, cooperation between Nikkeiren and first Dōmei, then Private Rengō and (from 1989) full-scale Rengō became the norm (Chapters 6 and 7). Although the annual shadow-boxing over wages during *shuntō* was main-tained so as to lend credibility to the unions' image, partnership between Nikkeiren and the major labour confederations came to characterize their relations far more than opposition (Chapter 8).

If it was the exercise of coercive class power that destroyed combative unions, it was techniques of manipulation which often brought 'second' unions into existence and which helped them and other enterprise unions to flourish by divisive treatment of the workforce. Manipulation also took the form of Nikkeiren pursuing joint initiatives with the major labour confederations over issues such as the reform of prices, taxes and social security, in the expectation that this would be effective in damping down the wages struggle (Chapter 7). There are those who would argue that what has been described here was not manipulation, because the unions were able to turn these developments to their advantage by gaining access to the policymaking process (for example, Kume 1988). However, such views hold water only if the interests of the unions are equated with the interests of their leaders. Undoubtedly, over recent decades, the leaders of cooperative labour confederations have been drawn into deliberative councils and other fora where policy is formulated. Yet, while union leaders gained influence and prestige in this manner, the workers whom they claimed to represent saw no change to the established pattern of Japanese capitalism, where real productivity increases across the economy as a whole continued to outstrip any improvement in real wages. In addition to their wages representing a shrinking portion of the wealth they created, workers were the targets of innumerable manipulative projects advocated by Nikkeiren, ranging from 'management involving all personnel' (Chapters 5 and 6) to 'flexible' forms of employment (Chapter 8). While the details of each project differed, what they all had in common were the intentions to set worker against worker and to play on employees' sense of insecurity, so that they would be induced to ratchet up their own exploitation 'voluntarily'. As if manipulation during their working hours was not enough, Nikkeiren was also anxious to channel workers' leisure activities in 'wholesome' directions via its promotion of Zenbunren (Chapter 5). Manipulation was thus a pervasive mode of operation, extending far beyond the handling of unions into every aspect of workers' existence.

Mystification

The so-called productivity standard principle can be taken as a prime example of the mystification in which Nikkeiren engaged, both because of the prominent part it played in campaigns to restrain wage increases and owing to the regularity with which it was paraded over the more than 30 years that followed its invention in 1969. Despite the aura of objectivity and science which Nikkeiren was at pains to bestow on the productivity standard principle, it was flawed from the outset by utilizing a formula which incorporated nominal wage increases alongside real productivity advances (Chapter 5). This had the convenient effect of enabling Nikkeiren perennially to complain that wage settlements were too high, even though (as noted above) real productivity increases generally kept ahead of any rises in real pay. In addition to this failure to compare like with like, the productivity standard principle also proceeded from the unproven assumption that rising prices were caused by wage increases, another convenient way of making it look as though it were labour's selfishness that created the scourge of infla-tion. As was argued in Chapters 5 and 6, this assumption was unwarranted because it overlooked the facts that wages are themselves prices, are suscep-tible to the same economic forces which act on all prices and are accordingly ill equipped to serve as the explanation for price movements. The fact that Nikkeiren retained the productivity standard principle despite its obvious defects was evidence that it had been invented primarily for an ideological purpose, rather than as an aid to serious economic analysis.

Apart from specific instances of mystification, such as the productivity standard principle, the idea that there was a distinctively Japanese way of running capitalism was assiduously promoted by Nikkeiren at every oppor-tunity. This idea could be traced back to the widely held view among prewar employers that Japanese labour–management relations were uniquely har-monious (Chapter 2) and it persisted throughout the various periods examined in this study, right through to the groping for a 'third way' in the Bluebird Plan of 1997 (Chapter 8). Nikkeiren's belief in a peculiarly Japanese way of operating capitalism exhibited the kind of imprecision which typically accompanies notions of Japanese uniqueness (Dale 1986: 25–37). At times, Nikkeiren attributed the distinctiveness of Japanese capitalism to the attitudes that allegedly suffused it. Nikkeiren's frequent ref-erences to 'human-centred management' and 'respecting subjectivity' were cases in point (Chapter 8). On other occasions, it was claimed that certain structural characteristics distinguished capitalism in Japan from elsewhere. Nikkeiren cited the supposed absence of rigid social classes (Chapter 6) and narrow income differentials (Chapter 7) in support of this contention. As yet another variation on the same theme of distinctiveness, Nikkeiren some-times implied that what made Japan different was primarily the aspiration to achieve a yet-to-be-discovered 'Japanese-style model' of capitalism (Chapter 8).

Whichever of these various interpretations of Japanese distinctiveness was employed by Nikkeiren at any one time, the defect which they all suf-fered from was their failure to explain how attitudes or structures or aspirations could make capitalism work differently from its inherent ten-dency to put the acquisition of profit before human welfare. Although Nikkeiren had no answer to this conundrum, it was paradoxically this very tendency of capitalism (in Japan as elsewhere) to ride roughshod over people as profits are pursued which accounted for the effort that Nikkeiren expended on ideological mystification. Wherever it exists, capitalism is not only about the process of extracting surplus value from workers and ploughing it into capital accumulation. It is also about integrating workers into the system by persuading them that the way in which things are orga-nized in 'their' company and 'their' country caters for their sensibilities as

'Japanese' or 'Americans' or whatever. It was in order to meet this need that Nikkeiren employed the notion of a distinctively Japanese way of running capitalism. It was a useful concept in general, but particularly so when harsh conditions risked further alienating workers. Thus, as was shown in Chapter 8, even as unemployment climbed ever higher in the 1990s towards American and European levels, so Nikkeiren declared that Japan must discover 'a "third way" that is different from the advanced countries of Europe and America' (*Nikkeiren Times*: 15 August 1996). Similarly, even as Japanese employers borrowed from Western business practices in order to survive in the harsh environment of the world market, so Nikkeiren's leaders delivered anodyne homilies, such as that 'an Asian sense of value, which attaches importance to flexibility, harmony and cooperation, is taking root' (*Nikkeiren Times*: 1 January 1998).

Unions

The unions have figured prominently in this account of Nikkeiren's history and have already been dealt with in this chapter in the course of discussing class power and manipulation. Some of the unions against which coercive class power was mobilized were industrial unions, while the labour confederations which allowed themselves to be manipulated by Nikkeiren were largely composed of enterprise unions. This could give the impression that industrial unions are the more steadfast champions of workers' interests, although more likely to be drawn into glorious but unwinnable struggles. Conversely, the conclusion could be drawn that the collaborative behaviour of most Japanese unions is rooted in their enterprise structure and outlook. It has been shown at several points in this study that Nikkeiren held the latter view and contrasted Japanese enterprise unions favourably with trade or industrial unions in other countries. In one typical instance, Nikkeiren argued that, 'unlike the industrial and occupational unions found in the West, in the case of enterprise unions, the union leadership well understands from its own experience the actual situation in the workplace and the enterprise's standpoint' (Nikkeiren 1982: 4). However, despite Nikkeiren's eagerness to assert that Japan has been blessed with an exceptionally cooperative form of unionism and unusually tractable union officials, collaboration between unions and the institutions of capitalist society is a general rather than a specifically Japanese phenomenon. Such collaboration can take many forms and, while the Japanese practice of union officials metamorphosing into company executives might be unusual in a country such as the UK, their transformation into government Ministers or members of the House of Lords has been anything but exceptional in Great Britain. This being the case, the question arises how such widespread behaviour by union officials can be explained, both in Japan and in many other countries.

First, it is necessary to establish what the fundamental purpose of unions is. Unions are organs of struggle formed by workers to defend and, where possible, advance their wages and working conditions. In most countries, when unions are first formed, they exhibit the type of militance that many Japanese unions showed during the period 1945–60. Nevertheless, no matter what their origins or their organizational structure, there are consequences for unions which arise from their ultimate function of negotiating on behalf of their members with the representatives of capitalist enterprises. Negotiations between a union and a company over issues such as wages and working conditions can be likened to a game of poker. Each side strives to outsmart the other and, in order to do so, engages in bluff and other tactics. Each side must also decide which cards to play and in what order. As any poker player could confirm, one cannot play cards effectively by behaving with a scrupulous regard for democracy and getting approval from those looking over one's shoulder for each move one makes. To behave in that fashion would spoil one's game and undermine one's chances of winning. At the end of the day, it is the player holding the cards who has to take responsibility for how the cards are played. It is precisely the same when a union negotiates with a company. The company is represented by a handful of negotiators and, to stand any chance of getting an advantageous result, the union rank and file have to put their trust in a similar number of leaders. Normally, the deal which emerges from the negotiations will need to be ratified by the membership, but this is a largely formal procedure, involving very little democratic control and is generally more in the nature of giving assent to a *fait accompli*. In other words, built into the core function of unions is an internal logic which leads to the separation of a leading stratum from the rank and file. In the early stages of a union's existence, this gap between the leaders and the rank and file may be potential rather than real, but the historical record of all types of unions shows that the leadership tends to develop interests of its own which are distinct from those of the membership at large. While the members are interested in improving their wages and conditions, the leaders seek to enhance their influence and status. It is this wedge between the interests of the union leadership and its members which so often induces the former to collaborate with the employers, with whom they have much in common, in manipulating the union's rank and file.

What has been described here can be called the universal fate of unions because it flows from the ultimate function which any union has to carry out, irrespective of its organizational structure. Rengō and its constituent unions may offer particularly vivid examples of collaboration with capital, but when compared to other unions in Japan or elsewhere, there will be at most a difference of degree, not a difference of kind. What Rengō provides for other unions is a mirror in which a particularly bright image of their own collaboration is reflected. If there are unionists who feel uncomfortable with this image, they should recognize that unions and their practice of collaboration only exist because capitalism of any type divides humankind into those who buy labour power and those who sell it. It follows that collaboration could be avoided only by removing capitalism, not by unions adopting one organizational structure in preference to another.

The problem: class or capitalism?

After the Second World War, employers started to call themselves 'managers' (*keieisha*), claiming that Japan had entered an era of 'reformed capitalism' in which management was separate from ownership (Chapter 3). Over the years that followed, Nikkeiren embroidered these claims into a full-blown ideology, asserting that there were no rigid social classes in Japan (Chapter 6) and that income differentials were unusually narrow (Chapter 7). It further maintained that 'the economic leaders in our country today . . . are not "the capitalist class" that Marx talked about' (Nikkeiren 1978: 4). While it is possible to pick holes in each of these assertions, the main criticism that was directed in Chapter 6 at Nikkeiren's contention that Japan operates essentially as a classless society was that the functions which company executives fulfil are more important than their social background or their level of consumption. It was argued that, irrespective of the way in which they reproduce themselves as a social group or the manner in which they obtain their privileges, if company executives undertake the functions of the capitalist class, they *are* the capitalist class for all practical purposes. These functions, which are vital for the survival of any form of capitalism, are to restrict the use of the means of production to producing for profit and to ensure that the accumulation of capital takes precedence over the satisfaction of human needs. One could call those whom Nikkeiren represented any name under the sun, including 'managers', but it would make no difference to their having to perform these functions, on pain of their own extinction as a privileged stratum and the collapse of capitalism as a viable system.

By conceptualizing social classes in these essentially functional terms, it was possible to reject Nikkeiren's ideology that Japan only has managers and not capitalists. Nevertheless, to engage in this argument is to run the risk of solving one problem only to create another. Nikkeiren was at pains to deny the existence in Japan of classes in general and the capitalist class in particular, because it thought that by so doing it could eliminate the basis on which capitalism would be open to criticism. To respond that the capitalist class does exist, in the shape of the very people who constituted the membership of Nikkeiren, is to risk being reduced to the same level of argument as Nikkeiren. While it is necessary to establish what the functions of company executives are, and thereby identify them as the personification of capital, it is equally important to avoid the mirror image of Nikkeiren's argument. A capitalist class exists within Japanese capitalism, but its exercise of coercive class power, manipulation and mystification represents at most only half of the problem confronting working men and women. If the current capitalist class was somehow done away with and the functions it fulfils were taken over by some other social group, it would make not a scrap of difference to the fundamental nature of capitalist society or the human and environmental damage it inflicts. The relative unimportance of those who currently constitute the capitalist class is illustrated by their inability to control the system they administer or even to anticipate its erratic fluctuations. Despite the wealth and power at their disposal, Japan's employers are marionettes dancing at the end of strings which are jerked by economic forces that are infinitely more powerful than they are. However skilful they might be at coercion, manipulation and mystification, ultimately they are only intermediaries, transferring to working men and women pressures which originate from the world markets and which they themselves are powerless to resist.

This is the reason why this study does not come to the conclusion that what labour requires in Japan are powerful organizations of its own, able to beat Nikkeiren and its successor, Nippon Keidanren, at their own game. However well that game was played, labour would remain coerced, manipulated and mystified, albeit by its 'own' organizations rather than by the existing wielders of power. This is a lesson which working men and women in Japan can learn from other countries where, on occasions, Labour Parties or Communist Parties have gained power, often in association with the unions, only to administer the system of wage labour and capital accumulation in the sole way that it can be run – against the interests of the working class. Certainly, labour in Japan does need to organize afresh, so as to free itself from the coercion, manipulation and mystification it has experienced at the hands of Nikkeiren and its allies in the union movement. However, the type of organization required would need to be as different from the traditional unions and 'workers' parties' as the goal to which the struggle was directed would need to be different from any variety of capitalism, including those labourist varieties which have enthused sections of labour until now. Hence, this study concludes that, contrary to Nikkeiren's repeated claims of Japanese particularism, labour is in the same situation in Japan as elsewhere, both with regard to the way ahead organizationally and in terms of the goal worth struggling for.

Select bibliography

Abegglen, J.C. (1959) *The Japanese Factory: aspects of its social organization*, Bombay: Asia Publishing House.

—— (1973) *Management and Worker: the Japanese solution*, Tokyo: Sophia/Kōdansha.

Allen, G.C. (1972) *A Short Economic History of Modern Japan*, 3rd edn, London: George Allen and Unwin.

Asahi (2002) 'Keizai: sokuhō' ('Economy: news flash'). Online. Available HTTP: <http://www.asahi.com/business/update/0727/001.html> (accessed 26 July 2002).

Autoindustry (2003) 'World vehicle production since 1990'. Online. Available HTTP: <http://www.autoindustry.co.uk/statistics/production/world.html> (accessed 28 January 2003).

BBC (1990) 'Nippon: taking on Detroit' (broadcast on BBC 2 on 18 November).

Bookchin, M. (1977) *The Spanish Anarchists: the heroic years 1868–1936*, New York: Free Life Editions.

Buick, A. and Crump, J. (1986) *State Capitalism: the wages system under new management*, Basingstoke: Macmillan.

Burnham, J. (1945) *The Managerial Revolution*, London: Penguin.

Carlile, L.E. (1994) '*Sōhyō* versus *Dōmei*: competing labour movement strategies in the era of high growth in Japan', *Japan Forum*, 6: 145–57.

CIA (2003) *The World Factbook*. Online. Available HTTP: <http//www.cia.gov/cia/publications/factbook/geos/ja.html> (accessed 28 January 2003).

Cohen, J.B. (1973) *Japan's Economy in War and Reconstruction*, Westport: Greenwood.

Cohen, T. (1987) (H. Passin ed.) *Remaking Japan: the American occupation as new deal*, New York: Free Press.

Cook, A.H. (1966) *An Introduction to Japanese Trade Unionism*, Ithaca: Cornell University Press.

Crump, J. (1983) *The Origins of Socialist Thought in Japan*, London: Croom Helm.

—— (1996) 'Environmental politics in Japan', *Environmental Politics*, 5: 115–21.

—— (2000) 'Japanese employers' perceptions of European labour relations', in B. Edström (ed.) *The Japanese and Europe: images and perceptions*, Richmond: Curzon.

Cusumano, M.A. (1985) *The Japanese Automobile Industry: technology and management at Nissan and Toyota*, Cambridge, MA: Council on East Asian Studies, Harvard University.

Dale, P.N. (1986) *The Myth of Japanese Uniqueness*, London: Croom Helm.

Dore, R. (1987) *Taking Japan Seriously: a Confucian perspective on leading economic issues*, London: Athlone.

—— (1988) *Flexible Rigidities*, London: Athlone.

Dower, J.W. (1988) *Empire and Aftermath: Yoshida Shigeru and the Japanese experience, 1878–1954*, Cambridge, MA: Harvard University Press.

Endō, K. (1989) *Nihon Senryō to Rōshi Kankei Seisaku no Seiritsu* (The Occupation of Japan and the Establishment of Labour Relations Policy), Tokyo: Tokyo Daigaku Shuppankai.

Financial Times

Fujita, W. and Shiota, S. (1963) *Sengo Nihon no Rōdō Sōgi* (Labour Disputes in Postwar Japan), Tokyo: Ochanomizu Shobō.

Fukuda, H. (1992) *Kagekiha ni Jūrin sareru JR* (Japan Railways Overrun by Extremist Groups), Tokyo: Nisshin Hōdō.

Garon, S.M. (1984) 'Imperial bureaucracy and labor policy in postwar Japan', *Journal of Asian Studies*, 43: 441–57.

—— (1997) *Molding Japanese Minds: the state in everyday life*, Princeton: Princeton University Press.

—— and Mochizuki, M. (1993) 'Negotiating social contracts', in A. Gordon (ed.) *Postwar Japan as History*, Berkeley: University of California Press.

Genseki, T. (1990) 'Getting organized', *Look Japan*, 36 (413): 4–7.

Gordon, A. (1991) *Labor and Imperial Democracy*, Berkeley: University of California Press.

—— (1993) (ed.) *Postwar Japan as History*, Berkeley: University of California Press.

—— (1998) *The Wages of Affluence: labor and management in postwar Japan*, Cambridge, MA: Harvard University Press.

Halberstam, D. (1987) *The Reckoning*, London: Bloomsbury.

Hasegawa, H. (1993) 'Japanese employment practices and industrial relations: the road to union "compliance"', *Japan Forum*, 5: 21–35.

Hook, G.D. (1996) *Militarization and Demilitarization in Contemporary Japan*, London: Routledge.

Iwanami Shoten (1991) *Kindai Nihon Sōgō Nenpyō* (Comprehensive Chronological Table of Modern Japan), Tokyo: Iwanami Shoten.

Johnson, C. (1982) *MITI and the Japanese Miracle: the growth of industrial policy, 1925–1975*, Stanford: Stanford University Press.

Kamada (2002) 'Jinkō to rōdōryoku no suii oyobi kanzen shitsugyōritsu no suii' (Changes in population and labour power and changes in the completely unemployed rate). Online. Available HTTP: <http://www.hct.zaq.ne.jp/kamada/roudouryoku_suii.htm> (accessed 14 November 2002).

Kato, T. and Steven, R. (eds) (1993) *Is Japanese Management Post-Fordism?*, Tokyo: Madosha.

Kawamoto, K. (2001) Interview conducted in Tokyo on 23 May.

Kawanishi, H. (1992) *Enterprise Unionism in Japan*, London: Kegan Paul International.

Keidanren (1978) *Keizai Dantai Rengōkai Sanjūnen Shi* (The Federation of Economic Organizations' 30 Years' History), Tokyo: Keidanren.

Keizai Dōyūkai (1956) *Keizai Dōyūkai Jūnen Shi* (The Economic Comrades' Association's 10 Years' History), Tokyo: Keizai Dōyūkai.

—— (1976) *Keizai Dōyūkai Sanjūnen Shi* (The Economic Comrades' Association's 30 Years' History), Tokyo: Keizai Dōyūkai.

Kenney, M. and Florida, R. (1988) 'Beyond mass production: production and the labor process in Japan', *Politics and Society*, 16: 121–58.

—— (1993) *Beyond Mass Production: the Japanese system and its transfer to the US*, New York: Oxford University Press.

Kikuchi, N. (2000) 'Sengoshi no tenkanten ni okeru zaikai saihen' (*Zaikai* reorganization at turning points in postwar history), *Rōdō Hōritsu Junpō*, 1491: 34–49.

Kitagawa, T. (1968) *Nikkeiren: Nihon no shihai kikō* (Nikkeiren: Japan's ruling mechanisms), Tokyo: Rōdō Junpōsha.

Knoke, D., Pappi, F.U., Broadbent, J. and Tsujinaka, Y. (1996) *Comparing Policy Networks: labor politics in the US, Germany, and Japan*, Cambridge: Cambridge University Press.

Kōshiro, K. (1983) 'Development of collective bargaining in postwar Japan', in T. Shirai (ed.) *Contemporary Industrial Relations in Japan*, Madison: University of Wisconsin Press.

Kumazawa, M. (1996) *Portraits of the Japanese Workplace: labor movements, workers, and managers*, Boulder: Westview.

Kume, I. (1988) 'Changing relations among the government, labor, and business in Japan after the Oil Crisis', *International Organization*, 42: 659–87.

Kuribara, K. and Matsuyama, J. (1961) *Nihon Zaikai Nyūmon* (Introduction to the Japanese *Zaikai*), Tokyo: Gakufūsha.

Kurokawa, T. (1989) 'Problems of the working class', in T. Morris-Suzuki and T. Seiyama (eds) *Japanese Capitalism since 1945: critical perspectives*, Armonk: M.E. Sharpe.

Langdon, F. (1967) *Politics in Japan*, Boston: Little, Brown and Co.

Large, S.S. (1981) *Organized Workers and Socialist Parties in Interwar Japan*, Cambridge: Cambridge University Press.

Lincoln, E.J. (1990) *Japan's Unequal Trade*, Washington: The Brookings Institution.

Mainichi Shinbun (1989) *Shōwa Shi Zen Kiroku* (Complete Record of the History of the Showa Era), Tokyo: Mainichi Shinbun.

Marshall, B.K. (1967) *Capitalism and Nationalism in Prewar Japan: the ideology of the business elite, 1868–1941*, Stanford: Stanford University Press.

Marx, K. (1919) *Capital: a critique of political economy*, Chicago: Kerr.

Mochizuki, M. (1993) 'Public sector labor and the privatization challenge: the railway and telecommunications unions', in G.D. Allinson and Y. Sone (eds) *Political Dynamics in Contemporary Japan*, Ithaca: Cornell University Press.

Morishima, M. (1982) *Why Has Japan 'Succeeded'?*, Cambridge: Cambridge University Press.

Morita, Y. (1958) *Nihon Keieisha Dantai Hatten Shi* (History of the Development of Japanese Managers' Organizations), Tokyo: Nikkan Rōdō Tsūshinsha.

Naikakufu (1999) *Kokumin Seikatsu ni kansuru Yoron Chōsa* (Public Opinion Survey on National Life). Online. Available HTTP: <http://www8/cao.go.jp/survey/kokumin/2-1/html> (accessed 30 August 2001).

Nakamura, T. (1981) *The Postwar Japanese Economy*, Tokyo: University of Tokyo.

—— (1985) *Economic Development of Modern Japan*, Tokyo: Ministry of Foreign Affairs.

Naruse, T. (1993) *Nihon Keizai Tokuhon* (Reader on the Japanese Economy), Tokyo: Nikkeiren.

Nihon Kōgyō Kurabu (1972) *Nihon Kōgyō Kurabu Gojūnen Shi* (The Japan Industry Club's 50 Years' History), Tokyo: Nihon Kōgyō Kurabu.

Nikkei (2002) 'Nikkei Net: keiki uocchi' ('Nihon Keizai Newspaper net: business watch'). Online. Available HTTP: <http://rank.nikkei.co.jp/keiki/gdp.cfm> (accessed 14 November 2002).

Nikkeiren (1950) *Sangyō Rōdō Gensei Hōkoku 3* (Third Report on the Current Situation of Industrial Labour), Tokyo: Nikkeiren.

—— (1958) *Nikkeiren Jūnen no Ayumi* (Nikkeiren's 10 Years' Journey), Tokyo: Nikkeiren.

—— (1962) *Keiki Chōseika no Nihon Keizai to Chingin Mondai: bōeki jiyūka o haikei to shite* (The Japanese Economy at a Time of Economic Adjustment and Wages Problems: with trade liberalization as the background), Tokyo: Nikkeiren.

—— (1963) *Nikkeiren no Ayumi* (Nikkeiren's Journey), Tokyo: Nikkeiren.

—— (1966) *Fukyōka no Shuntō to Chingin Mondai* (*Shuntō* under Conditions of Depression and Wages Problems), Tokyo: Nikkeiren.

—— (1968a) *Nijūnen no Ayumi* (20 Years' Journey), Tokyo: Nikkeiren.

—— (1968b) *Gekidō suru Kokusai Kankyō to Nihon Keizai: sangyō heiwa to chingin gōrika* (The Convulsive International Environment and the Japanese Economy: industrial peace and wage rationalization), Tokyo: Nikkeiren.

—— (1971) *Tenki o Mukaeta Chingin Mondai to Nihon Keizai: seisansei kijun genri no shin tenkai o megutte* (Wages Problems and the Japanese Economy Faced with a Turning Point: concerning the new development of the productivity standard principle), Tokyo: Nikkeiren.

—— (1972) *Henkakuki ni Tatsu Nihon Keizai to Chingin Mondai* (The Japanese Economy in a Period of Change and Wages Problems), Tokyo: Nikkeiren.

—— (1974a) *Keiei Rōmu no Shishin* (Guide to Personnel Management), Tokyo: Nikkeiren.

—— (1974b) *Ōhaba Chin'age no Yukue Kenkyū Iinkai Hōkoku: rōshi to mo kokumin keizai no tachiba de kangaenaosō* (Report of the Committee to Study where Wholesale Wage Increases Are Leading: let both labour and management reconsider from the standpoint of the national economy), Tokyo: Nikkeiren.

—— (1974c) *Chingin Kōshō no Kiso Shiryō* (Basic Materials for Wage Negotiations), Tokyo: Nikkeiren.

—— (1976a) *Chingin Mondai Kenkyū Iinkai Hōkoku: jisshitsu chingin to koyō no iji kōjō no tame rōshi kyōryoku o* (Report of the Committee for Studying Wages Problems: labour–management cooperation for maintaining and improving real wages and employment), Tokyo: Nikkeiren.

—— (1976b) *Chingin Kōshō no Kiso Shiryō* (Basic Materials for Wage Negotiations), Tokyo: Nikkeiren.

—— (1976c) *Chingin Mondai Kenkyū Iinkai Hōkoku: infure bōshi to koyō kakudai ni rōshi no kyōryoku o* (Report of the Committee for Studying Wages Problems: for labour–management cooperation to prevent inflation and expand employment), Tokyo: Nikkeiren.

—— (1978) *Chingin Mondai Kenkyū Iinkai Hōkoku: sōryoku o agete koyō mondai no kaiketsu to infure bōshi e* (Report of the Committee for Studying Wages Problems: mustering all our strength to go forward and solve the employment problem and prevent inflation), Tokyo: Nikkeiren.

—— (1980) *Rōdō Mondai Kenkyū Iinkai Hōkoku: seisansei kijun genri no tettei to kankō bumon no kōritsuka o* (Report of the Committee for Studying Labour Problems: driving home the productivity standard principle and raising the efficiency of the public sector), Tokyo: Nikkeiren.

—— (1981) *Nikkeiren Sanjūnen Shi* (Nikkeiren's 30 Years' History), Tokyo: Nikkeiren.

—— (1982) *Rōdō Mondai Kenkyū Iinkai Hōkoku: senshinkokubyō ni ochiiranai tame ni* (Report of the Committee for Studying Labour Problems: so as not to sink into the advanced countries' disease), Tokyo: Nikkeiren.

—— (1983) *Rōdō Mondai Kenkyū Iinkai Hōkoku: sanseki suru nanmondai no kaiketsu no tame ni* (Report of the Committee for Studying Labour Problems: in order to solve the difficult problems which are piling up), Tokyo: Nikkeiren.

—— (1984) *Rōdō Mondai Kenkyū Iinkai Hōkoku: koyō no kakuho to infure bōshi ni rōshi no kōhan na kyōryoku o* (Report of the Committee for Studying Labour Problems: for wide-ranging labour–management cooperation to maintain employment and prevent inflation), Tokyo: Nikkeiren.

—— (1985) *Rōdō Mondai Kenkyū Iinkai Hōkoku: katsuryoku aru shakai o tsukuru tame ni* (Report of the Committee for Studying Labour Problems: in order to build a society full of vitality), Tokyo: Nikkeiren.

—— (1986) *Rōdō Mondai Kenkyū Iinkai Hōkoku: seisansei kijun genri o jiku ni katsuryoku to antei no kakuho o* (Report of the Committee for Studying Labour Problems: maintain vitality and stability by using the productivity standard principle as our pivot), Tokyo: Nikkeiren.

—— (1988a) *Rōdō Mondai Kenkyū Iinkai Hōkoku: shin no senshinkoku e no dappi o mezashite* (Report of the Committee for Studying Labour Problems: aiming to turn ourselves into a genuinely advanced country), Tokyo: Nikkeiren.

—— (1988b) *Shunki Rōshi Kōshō no Tebiki* (Handbook for the Spring Season Labour–Management Negotiations), Tokyo: Nikkeiren.

—— (1989) *Rōdō Mondai Kenkyū Iinkai Hōkoku: shin no yutakasa no jitsugen no tame ni* (Report of the Committee for Studying Labour Problems: for the realization of true affluence), Tokyo: Nikkeiren.

—— (1991) *Nikkeiren Kōenshū* 14 (Nikkeiren's Collected Lectures 14), Tokyo: Nikkeiren.

—— (1992) *Rōdō Mondai Kenkyū Iinkai Hōkoku: shin jidai no keizai/shakai to rōshi kankei o motomete* (Report of the Committee for Studying Labour Problems: searching for an economy/society and labour–management relations that will suit a new era), Tokyo: Nikkeiren.

—— (1993) *Rōdō Mondai Kenkyū Iinkai Hōkoku: atarashii kokusaika jidai ni okeru Nihon to rōshi no sentaku* (Report of the Committee for Studying Labour Problems: Japan in a new era of internationalization and the choices facing labour and management), Tokyo: Nikkeiren.

—— (1994) *Rōdō Mondai Kenkyū Iinkai Hōkoku: shinkokuka suru chōki fukyō to koyō iji ni mukete no rōshi no taiō* (Report of the Committee for Studying Labour Problems: long-term depression which is getting more severe and a labour–management response aimed at maintaining employment), Tokyo: Nikkeiren.

—— (1995) *Shin Jidai no 'Nihonteki Keiei': chōsen subeki hōkō to sono gutai saku* ('Japanese-style Management' for a New Era: the direction we should strive for and the concrete measures entailed), Tokyo: Nikkeiren.

—— (1996a) *Rōdō Mondai Kenkyū Iinkai Hōkoku: kōzō kaikaku ni yoru dainamikku na Nihon keizai no jitsugen ni mukete* (Report of the Committee for Studying Labour Problems: towards the realization of a dynamic Japanese economy by means of structural reform), Tokyo: Nikkeiren.

—— (1996b) *Shunki Rōshi Kōshō no Tebiki* (Handbook for the Spring Season Labour–Management Negotiations), Tokyo: Nikkeiren.

—— (1998) *Nikkeiren Gojūnen Shi* (Nikkeiren's 50 Years' History), Tokyo: Nikkeiren.

—— (1999) *Rōdō Mondai Kenkyū Iinkai Hōkoku: dainamikku de toku no aru kuni o mezashite* (Report of the Committee for Studying Labour Problems: aiming at a dynamic and virtuous country), Tokyo: Nikkeiren.

—— (2001) *Shunki Rōshi Kōshō no Tebiki* (Handbook for the Spring Season Labour–Management Negotiations), Tokyo: Nikkeiren.

Nikkeiren Times (1948–2002) (weekly in Japanese).

Nippon Keidanren (2002) 'What's Nippon Keidanren?'. Online. Available HTTP: <http://www.keidanren.or.jp/english/profile/pro001.html> (accessed 21 November 2002).

OECD (1973) *Manpower Policy in Japan*, Paris: OECD.

—— (1977) *The Development of Industrial Relations Systems: some implications of Japanese experience*, Paris: OECD.

Okimoto, D.I. (1989) *Between MITI and the Market*, Stanford: Stanford University Press.

Ōtake, H. (1987) 'The *Zaikai* under the Occupation: the formation and transformation of managerial councils', in R.E. Ward and Y. Sakamoto (eds) *Democratizing Japan: the Allied Occupation*, Honolulu: University of Hawaii Press.

Porter, M.E., Takeuchi, H. and Sakakibara, M. (2000) *Can Japan Compete?*, Basingstoke: Macmillan.

Prestowitz, C.V. (1988) *Trading Places: how we are giving our future to Japan and how to reclaim it*, New York: Basic Books.

Rōdōshō Rōseikyoku (1979) *Nenpyō: sengo rōdō undō shi* (Chronological Table: history of the postwar labour movement), Tokyo: Nikkan Rōdō Tsūshinsha.

Rothacher, A. (1993) *The Japanese Power Elite*, Basingstoke: Macmillan.

Sako, M. and Sato, H. (1997) *Japanese Labour and Management in Transition*, London: Routledge.

Samuels, R.J. (1987) *The Business of the Japanese State: energy markets in comparative and historical perspective*, Ithaca: Cornell University Press.

Satō, K. (1983) *Bulletin of the Socialist Research Centre No. 2: the labour movement in Japan since 1945*, Tokyo: Socialist Research Centre.

Schoppa, L.J. (1991) *Education Reform in Japan: a case of immobilist politics*, London: Routledge.

Shiota, S., Hasegawa, M. and Fujiwara, A. (1984) *Sengo Shi Shiryōshū* (Collected Materials on Postwar History), Tokyo: Shin Nihon Shuppansha.

Smith, A. (1880) *An Inquiry into the Nature and Causes of the Wealth of Nations*, London: Ward, Lock and Co.

Sōhyō (1964) *Sōhyō Jūnen Shi* (Sohyo's 10 Years' History), Tokyo: Rōdō Junpōsha.

Steven, R. (1983) *Classes in Contemporary Japan*, Cambridge: Cambridge University Press.

The Times

Totsuka, H. (1984) *Bulletin of the Socialist Research Centre No. 7: 'rationalization' and the Japanese trade unions*, Tokyo: Socialist Research Centre.

Tsujinaka, Y. (1993) 'Rengō and its osmotic networks', in G.D. Allinson and Y. Sone (eds) *Political Dynamics in Contemporary Japan*, Ithaca: Cornell University Press.

Tyson, L. D. and Zysman, J. (1989) 'Preface: the argument outlined', in C. Johnson, L.D. Tyson and J. Zysman (eds) *Politics and Productivity: how Japan's development strategy works*, Cambridge, MA: Ballinger.

Watanabe, O. (1990) *Yutaka na Shakai Nihon no Kōzō* (The Structure of Japan as an Affluent Society) Tokyo: Rōdō Junpōsha.

Weber, M. (1968) *The Religion of China*, New York: Free Press.

Womack, J.P., Jones, D.T. and Roos, D. (1990) *The Machine that Changed the World*, New York: Rawson.

Young, A.M. (1921) *The Socialist and Labour Movement in Japan*, Kōbe: The Japan Chronicle.

Index

For Product Safety Concerns and Information please contact our EU
representative GPSR@taylorandfrancis.com
Taylor & Francis Verlag GmbH, Kaufingerstraße 24, 80331 München, Germany